AWS Certified Solutions Architect – Associate
"Lab Manual Guide"

Step By Step Lab Exercises and Best Practices

Contents

About this Book 9
About the Author 9
    Other Helpful IT Books for You 9
Disclaimer 10
Copyright 10
1. Sign Up for AWS Free Tier Account 11
2. Getting Familiarized with the AWS Console 14
3. Creating an AWS IAM User 15
    Recommended links: 15
        Enabling MFA for IAM User 18
4. Managing Virtual Private Cloud (VPC) 22
    Recommended links: 22
        Creating VPC in AWS Cloud 22
        Creating and Adding Private Subnet in the Existing VPC 25
        Deleting VPC 26
5. Creating and Configuring Internet Gateways 28
    Recommended links: 28
    Quick facts about Internet Gateways 29
6. Creating and Configuring NAT Gateways 30
    Recommended links: 30
    Quick facts about NAT Gateways 30
7. Configuring Routing Tables 31
    Recommended links: 31
    Quick facts about Routing Tables 31
        Creating Custom Routing Table 31
8. VPC Peering Between Two VPCs 33
        Creating VPCs and Subnets 34
        Creating Subnets 34
        Creating VPC Peering Connection 35
    Quick facts about VPC Peering 35
        Updating Routing Tables and Routes 37
9. Working with Amazon Elastic Cloud Compute (EC2) 39

  Creating Amazon EC2 Linux Instance..39

  Selecting Instance Type 40

  Specify the Instance Configuration Options 41

  Adding Storage Volumes 42

  Selecting Security Group 42

  Creating/Selecting Key Pair 43

10. Creating and Configuring Security Groups...45

 Recommended links: 45

 Quick facts about AWS Security Groups 45

  Creating a Security Group..45

  Security Group Rules 45

  Modifying Security Group..46

11. Managing Elastic IP Addresses...48

 Recommended links: 48

  Elastic IP Pricing 48

  Assigning Elastic IPs to EC2 Instances 48

12. Connecting EC2 Linux Instance Using PuTTy, GitBash, and Console 50

  Connecting EC2 Instance Using Web Browser..50

  Connecting EC2 Linux Instance Using PuTTY 52

 Default EC2 Instance Users 53

  Connecting EC2 Instance Using GitBash 54

13. Connecting Private Instance using SSH Agent Forwarding 57

  Allow SSH connection from one security group to another security group 57

  Access SSH using SSH Agent Forwarding 57

14. Accessing EC2 Linux Instance Using RDP with GUI Interface 59

  Installing MATE Desktop Environment in EC2 Ubuntu Instance...59

  Allow RDP Rule in the Security Group 60

  Connecting EC2 Ubuntu using MSTSC (RDP) 60

15. Recovering and connecting EC2 instances if the SSH key is lost...61

 Recommended links: 61

  Stopping Original EC2 Linux Instance 61

  Launching New Temporary Instance 62

  Detaching Root Volume from Original Instance 62

        Attaching Root Volume to Temporary Instance 63

        Mounting Attached Volume 64

        Modifying the authorized_keys File and Updating the New Private Key 65

        Detaching Volume from Temporary Instance and Re-attaching With the Original Instance 66

        Connect your EC2 Linux Instance (Original Instance) With the New Private Key 67

        Alternative and Simple Way to Recover your EC2 Instance of which Key Pair is Lost 67

16. Changing Instance Type, Security Groups, Volumes & Other Settings 68

        Changing instance type 68

        Accidental Termination Protection 69

        Specifying Auto Start Script with EC2 Instance 70

        Changing/Adding Security Groups to EC2 Instance 71

17. Start, Stop, Reboot, and Terminate EC2 Instance 72

18. Creating and configuring Elastic Load Balancer 74

    Recommended links: 74

        Load Balancer Modes 74

        AWS Load Balancer Types 74

        Create an Application Load Balancer 75

        Domain Registration for ELB 80

19. Scheduling Auto Snapshot of Volumes 81

    Quick facts about EBS Snapshots 81

        Auto-Snapshot Schedule 81

        Creating Rule 81

        Defining Event Source 82

        Cron Expressions Syntax and Examples 82

        Specifying Target 83

        Configure Rule and Details 84

20. Creating AMI and Recovering EC2 Instance using AMI 85

    Recommended link: 85

        Creating some users and files in the source Instance 85

        Creating Image of an EC2 instance 85

        Specifying AMI settings 86

        Launching an EC2 Instance using AMI 87

        Configuring Instance Details 88

    Configuring Security Group 88

    Reviewing and launching Instance 88

    Login in to the New Instance 89

21. Configuring CloudWatch Monitoring 91

    Quick facts about AWS CloudWatch 91

    Recommended links: 91

        Amazon CloudWatch Pricing 91

        Selecting an Instance 91

        Creating a CloudWatch Alarm 92

22. Configuring Amazon Simple Notification Service (SNS) 94

    Quick facts about Amazon SNS 94

    Recommended links: 94

        Amazon SNS Free Tier vs Paid Pricing 94

        Creating a Topic 94

        Subscribing to the topic 95

23. Configuring Centralized Log Management Using CloudWatch Log Group 97

    Creating a CloudWatch Log Group 97

    Granting Permission to EC2 Instance to Use CloudWatch Logs 98

    Attaching a Policy to an IAM Role 100

    Assigning Role to an EC2 Instance 101

    Installing AWS CloudWatch Log Agent 102

    Verifying Logs in CloudWatch Log Group 104

25. Schedule Auto, Start, Stop, and Reboot EC2 Instances 106

    Create an Auto Start EC2 Instance Lambda Function 106

    Recommended Link: 106

        Creating an Auto Start-Stop Event Schedule Rule 110

        Test and Validate Auto Start-Stop EC2 Schedule 111

26. Creating and Recovering EC2 Instance Using Snapshots 113

    Creating Snapshot of Attached Volume 113

    Creating Volume of EC2 Snapshot 114

    Attaching Volume to an Instance 115

    Mounting the Attached Volume 116

27. Working with IAM User Properties 118

- Permissions 118
- Groups 118
- Security Credentials 118
- Access Advisor 119

28. Creating and Using an IAM Role 120
    - Attaching IAM role to an EC2 Instance 122

29. Configuring Password Policies for IAM Users 124
    - Changing IAM Password Policy Settings 124

30. Installing and configuring AWS CLI 125
    - Download AWS CLI for Windows System 125
    - Installing AWS CLI on Windows System 125
    - Installing AWS CLI on Linux system 126
    - Setup Credentials for AWS CLI 126

31. Configuring OpenVPN Server to Securely Access Instances 127
    - Why to Use VPN? 127
    - Launching Pre-configured AMI from AWS Market Place 127
    - Assigning Elastic IP 129
    - Configuring OpenVPN Initial Settings 129
    - Activating License. 130
    - Creating OpenVPN user accounts. 130
    - Configuring VPN Settings 131
    - Enabling Google Authenticator for VPN Clients 132

32. Connecting OpenVPN Server 134
    - Two-Factor Authentication 134
    - Setting up Two Factor Configuration 134
    - Connecting Using OpenVPN Client Tool 135
    - For Linux Platform 135
    - For Windows OS 135

33. Configuring Linux Bastion Server for Securely Access SSH of Private Instances 137
    - Launching a New Bastion Server 138
    - Configuring Security Groups 138
    - Connecting SSH using Bastion Server 139

34. Working with S3 Buckets 140

  Recommended links: 140
    Creating an S3 Bucket Using the AWS Console 140
    Creating Folders under S3 Bucket 141
    Upload Content/Files/Data in S3 Bucket 142
    Deleting S3 Bucket 144
35. Configuring Permissions and Policy for S3 Buckets 146
  Recommended links: 146
    Customizing S3 Bucket Policies 146
  Access Control List Tab 146
  Bucket Policy Tab 147
36. Configuring S3 Bucket Policies for Specific IAM Users 148
    Creating Custom S3 Policy for a Specific IAM User 148
    Attaching Policy to IAM Role, Group, or User 149
    Verifying Custom S3 Bucket Policies 149
    Verifying S3 Bucket Policy Using AWS CLI Tool 149
37. Configuring S3 Bucket Versioning and Logging 152
    Configuring S3 Bucket Versioning 152
  Recommended links: 152
    Configuring Logging for S3 Buckets 153
38. Configuring S3 Bucket Alerting and Notifications 154
  Recommended links: 154
39. Configuring S3 Bucket Lifecycle Rule 156
40. Implementing Cross-Region S3 Replication 160
    Configuring cross-replication of S3 bucket 160
    Creating Replication Rule 160
    Verifying Cross-region S3 Bucket Replication 162
    Troubleshooting S3 Cross-region Replication 162
41. Enabling and Configuring AWS CloudTrail 163
  Recommended links: 163
    Enabling CloudTrail 163
    Creating a CloudTrail 163
42. Working with Auto Scaling Group 166
  Recommended links: 166

- Creating a Launch Configuration Group 166
- Creating Auto Scaling Group 167
- Verifying Auto Scaling Group Configuration 169
- Modifying Auto Scaling Group Settings 170

43. Configuring Amazon Route 53 172
    - Recommended links: 172
        - Registering a domain name 172

44. Working with Amazon WorkDocs 174
    - Creating an AWS WorkDocs Site 174
    - Deleting WorkDocs Site 177

45. Working with AWS Trusted advisor 179
    - Recommended links: 179

Questions and Answers 181

Thank You 182
- Other Helpful IT Books 183

About this Book

This book has been written for the candidates who want to learn and use the AWS cloud platform, candidates who have just started his career with AWS Cloud services, and candidates who are already working with AWS cloud services. This is also dedicated to those candidates who are preparing themselves for one of the most popular cloud certifications AWS Certified Solutions Architect – Associate Exam (AWS SAA).

This book is mainly focused on the hands-on lab exercises and the real-world best practices rather than deep theoretical and conceptual lectures. So, please keep in mid this factor before leaving your review about this guide.

There are hundreds of theoretical documentations are available on the AWS official documentation site and a few other sites on the Internet community. But, there are very few articles on the step by step how to guide such as - how to implement, use, and configure AWS Cloud services. This guide will help you to become a handy and expert on most of the AWS Cloud services that come under the syllabus of AWS Certified Solutions Architect certification. However, this guide also contains various real-world, enterprise-level, best practices to implement and use for the production services.

These step by step lab exercises will help you to design highly-secure, scalable, and well-architecture enterprise-level Cloud solutions and designs.

We assume that you know the basic terminology and knowledge about the various AWS Cloud services. This book is not focused on the deep theory and concepts about the AWS Cloud services. However, sufficient official documentation links are given before each of the lab exercises. So, you can use those links to get familiar with the respective AWS Cloud service that is described and implemented in that particular lab exercise.

This guide also contains a few questions about the different topics. These questions are added to test your understanding and enforcing you to do some googling to find the solutions by yourself. This way, we want to make you a self-learner candidate, because eventually your passion towards learning also matter. No books, instructors, and/or videos can teach you everything. You have to start learning and exploring few things by yourself as well. However, the answers of the questions are given in the last section for your comfort.

About the Author

This book is written by an Author who has over 9+ years of experience in various IT domains such as Microsoft, Red Hat, Cisco, AWS, OpenStack, and CompTIA. He has worked with many reputed organizations with various profiles such as Content Designer, Subject Matter Expert, Technical Expert, and Solution Architect. He currently holds 15+ IT Global certifications from a wide range of IT technologies. Some of the major Global certifications hold by him includes MCP, MCTP, MCITP, MCSA, MS Hyper-V, MS Azure Cloud, CCNA, RHCSA, OpenStack, and AWS Certified Solutions Architect – Associate.

Other Helpful IT Books for You

You may also be interested in the following eBooks:

1. AWS Solutions Architect Associate - Exam Practice Questions
2. Step By Step Windows Server 2016 Lab Manual/Practical Guide
3. Step By Step Azure Cloud Lab Manual/Practical Guide for Ultimate Beginners
4. Step By Step CCNA Lab Manual/Practical Guide for Ultimate Beginners
5. Step By Step Windows Server 2012 R2 Lab Manual/Practical Guide
6. Step By Step VMware Workstation Player Lab Manual/Practical Guide
7. Docker Container: Concepts and Hands-on Exercises for Ultimate Beginners

For more step by step tutorials, please visit our blog tutorials (www.protechgurus.com).

Disclaimer

While writing the content of this book, we have tried our best to keep the content as up-to-date and accurate as possible. However, being a human, there might be some typo or grammatical errors. It might also be possible that due to the rapid changes of IT technologies and services, some of the features, limitations, and terms might get changed or updated by the respective IT vendors. Author or publisher is not liable for any such changes. The lab exercises mentioned in this book should be performed in the testing environment, not on the productions servers or environment. Author or publisher will not be liable for any loss of data, service interruptions caused while performing lab exercises either intentionally or unintentionally.

Copyright

All the content of this entire book is completely copyrighted by the author. No content of this book can be republished, copied, and reproduced in any format, including paper, e-paper, electronic media, PDF, word, and/or any in other digital media without the prior written permissions of the author.

Note: Since few of the information (such as account number, email ID, public IP address, instance ID, etc.) in the mentioned screenshots is private and confidential, so those might be greyed out or blurred. However, obviously this will not impact your learning experience at anyhow.

1. Sign Up for AWS Free Tier Account

The best thing about getting started with any cloud platform is that almost every cloud provider provides the free tier services with the limited features, duration, and service limit. AWS provides you free tire account for 12 months with the limited features for the selected services. However, as per my personal experience for the learning purpose, this free tier account is more than enough.

If you are interested to know what you will get with the free tier account, please visit the following link and spent some time to know various free services and their limitations.

- AWS Free Tier Limitations (https://aws.amazon.com/free/)
1. To sign up for an AWS free tier account, click the below link and complete the Sign Up process.
- AWS Free Tier Sign UP Link (https://portal.aws.amazon.com/billing/signup#/account)
2. In the Sign Up screen, you need to fill the basic information as shown in the following figure.

3. On the next screen, select the **Account Type** and fill the required information.

Account type ⓘ	
○ Professional	● Personal

Full name

mydemoaccount

Phone number

Country

United States ▼

Address

Street, P.O. Box, Company Name, c/o

Apartment, suite, unit, building, floor, etc.

City

State / Province or region

---

*Note: If you are creating the AWS account for hosting your organization's production services, select the Account type as **Professional**. However, if you are creating the AWS account just for your learning purpose, select the Account type as **Personal**.*

---

4. On the next screen, you need to provide the credit card details and the billing address information. Fill the required details and proceed to the next screen.
5. On the next screen, you may need to validate your contact number and you are almost done to get started with the free tier account.

Note: Here, you have to wait for a few hours as your account and associated services will be created in the AWS data center (backend). You will get a welcome and get started mail from the AWS cloud team once your account is ready.

6. By default, the email address you used to Sign Up is also used to login to the AWS console as the root account. Please visit the following link to sign in to the AWS console.
    https://console.aws.amazon.com/console/home

2. Getting Familiarized with the AWS Console

Once signed in to your AWS console, you can start using AWS cloud services. However, AWS provides hundreds of services and features. So it might be difficult for a new user to find and use the appropriate features. Which AWS services you should use depends on what you want to get from AWS cloud or what's need of your organization.

Here are the most common and basic AWS cloud services that you may like to get familiarized as a beginner.

- Elastic Cloud Compute (EC2)
- Simple Storage Service (S3)
- Relational Database (RDS)
- Route 53
- Virtual Private Cloud (VPC)
- CloudWatch, and many more depending on your specific need and requirement.

The following figure shows the common AWS Console options.

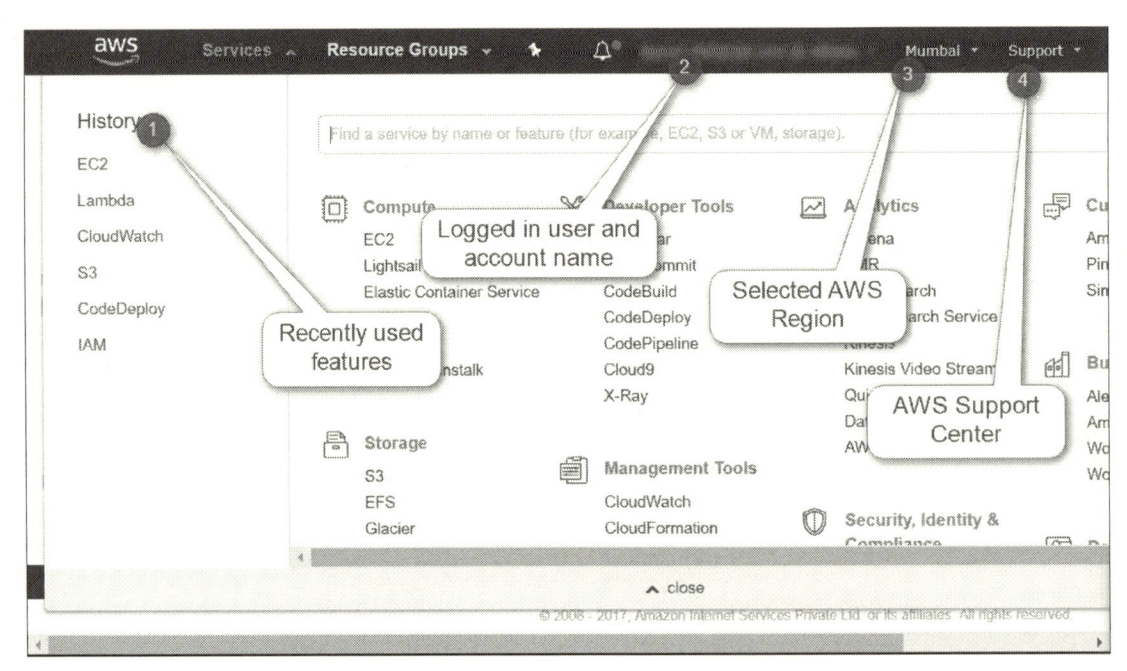

We recommend spending some time to get familiarized by navigating the AWS management console. You can always use the **Search** box to search any specific service or feature you may wish to explore.

3. Creating an AWS IAM User

Identity and Access Management (IAM) is one of the most important factors to manage and set access control for the AWS cloud resources. By default, when you sign up for the AWS account, a ROOT account (user) is already created and has super admin control. Although, the root account should not be used for every task and/or by every person in your organization. However, keep in mind, few critical tasks can only be managed by root user, such as downloading tax invoices and filling penetration testing authorization request.

For the best practices and better control, you should create separate IAM users for separate purposes and set the appropriate permissions and policies as per the requirements.

Recommended links:
- Getting started with AWS Identity and Access Management (IAM)
  http://docs.aws.amazon.com/IAM/latest/UserGuide/introduction.html

To create an IAM user, you need to perform the following steps:

1. Navigate to the **IAM** section in the AWS Console and click **Users** in the left pane.
2. In the right pane, click **Add user** to add a new user.
3. On the **Set user details** page, provide the following details:
   - **Username**: Name of the IAM user such as User1
   - **Access Type**: whether you want to give Console access or CLI access or both access.
   - **Console password**: Auto-generated password or custom password.

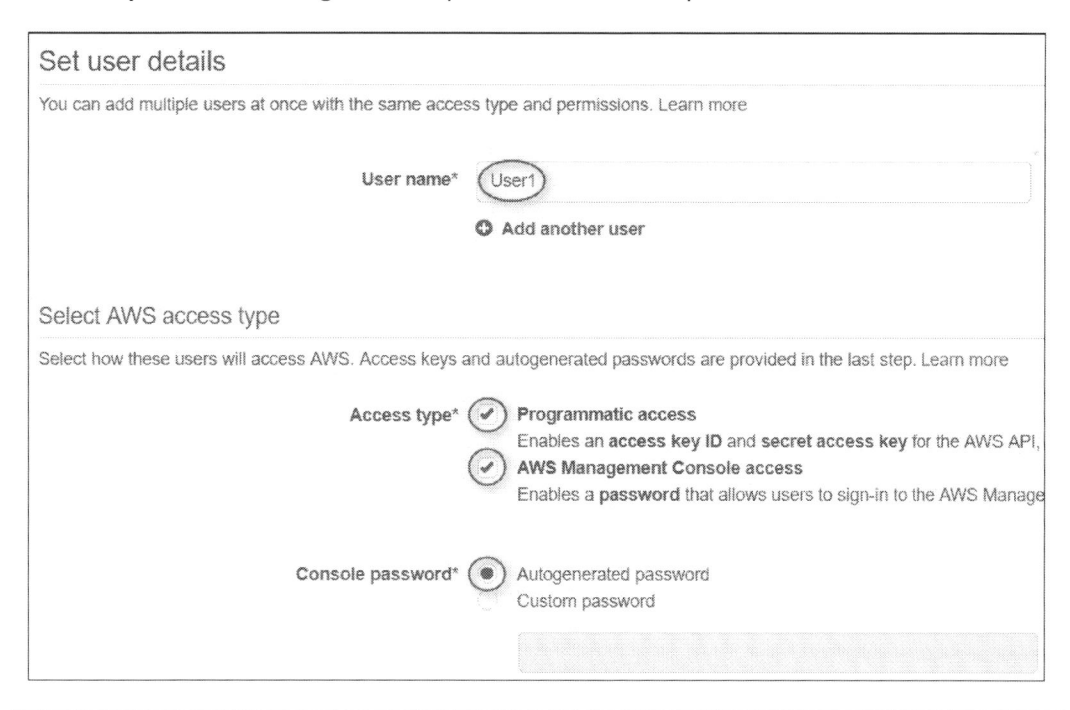

> Question 01: Which type of AWS Access type you should use while creating an IAM user?

4. Click **Next: Permissions** to proceed to the permissions page.

5. On the **Set Permissions for User1** page, you can either add a user to a group, copy existing permissions from an existing IAM user, or attach the existing policies directly to this IAM user. Since, we are creating an IAM user first time, so let's select the **Attach existing policies directly** option. Select **AmazonEC2FullAccess** as shown in the following figure and proceed to the next page.

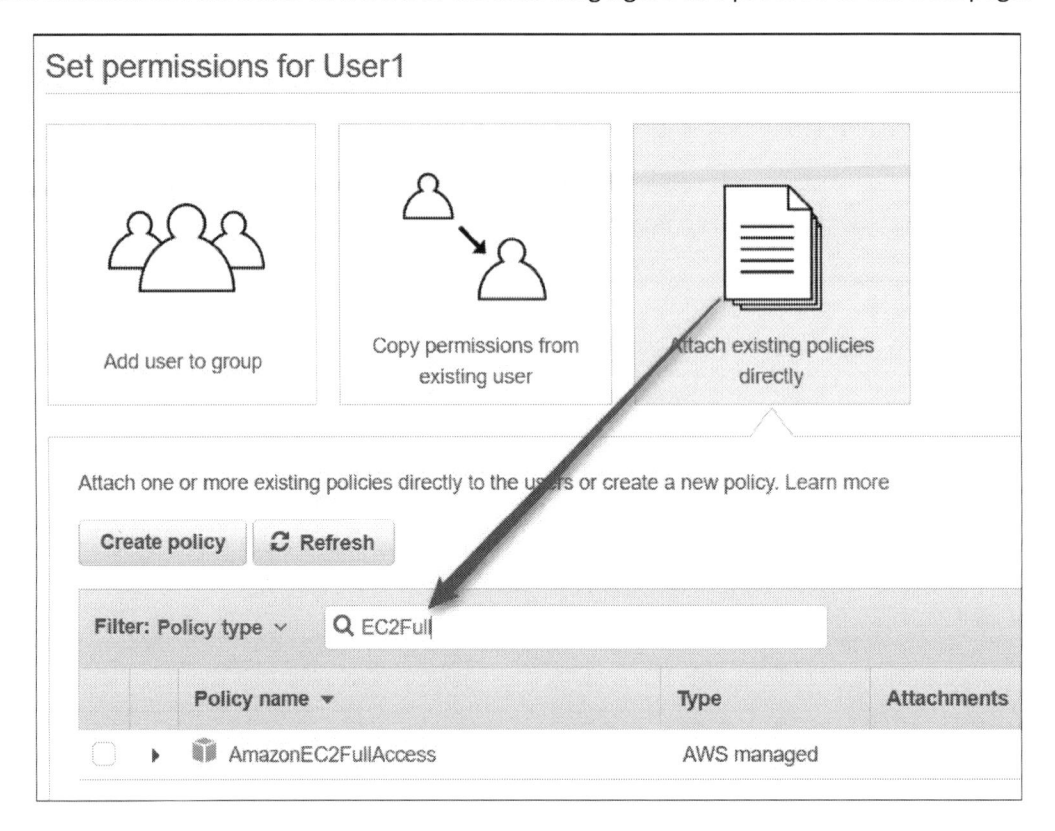

Note: There are hundreds of pre-configured IAM policies are available to use. Additionally, you can also create your custom IAM policies based on your custom requirement. We will cover the IAM policies in a later section.

6. On the **Review** page, review the options you have selected and click **Create User** to finish the wizard.
7. Once your IAM user is created, click **Download .csv** file to download it and keep it in a secret place. This file contains all the required access details such as Username, password, access key, secret key and console login link.

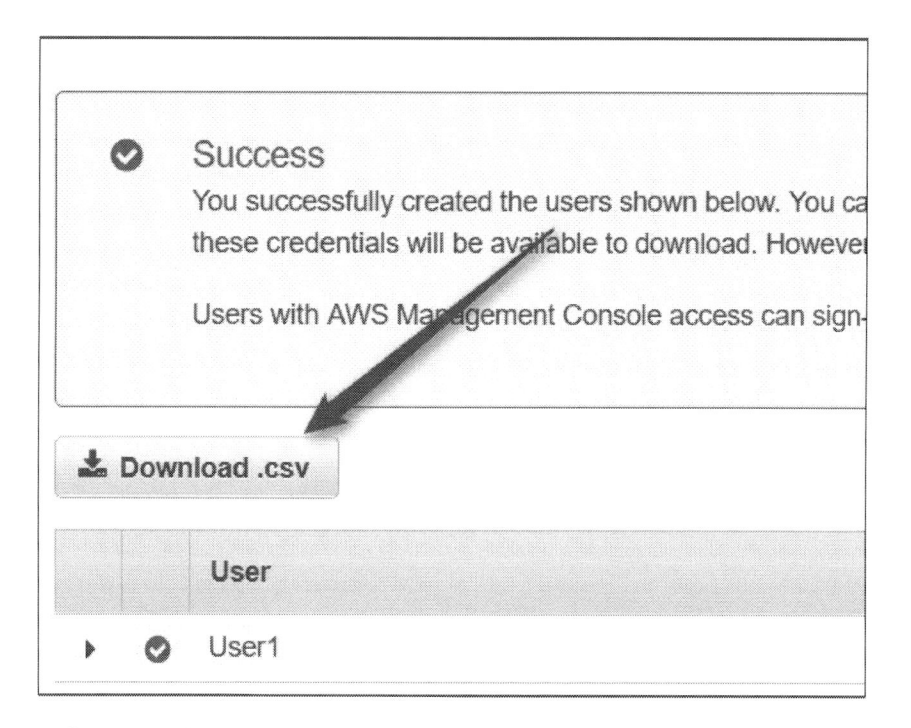

8. To login using the created IAM user, log out from the AWS console, click the AWS console link mentioned in the downloaded file.
9. Use the username and password to login to the AWS console. For the AWS CLI (covered in the later section), use the access key and secret key stored in the .csv file.

Enabling MFA for IAM User

Security for AWS console is the prime concern for the Cloud administrators. Every user, including AWS root user, should be enabled with the Multi-Factor Authentication (MFA) for secure AWS console login. The MFA feature adds an additional layer of security while login to the AWS console. You can enable MFA for an IAM user as well for the root user using either a hardware-based MFA device or a virtual MFA application.

Once you enable the MFA feature for a user, the user needs to provide the two-factor authentication code right after entering his username and password.

Please visit the following link to know more about the AWS Multi-Factor Authentication.
- Enabling MFA for AWS IAM Users
- http://docs.aws.amazon.com/IAM/latest/UserGuide/id_credentials_mfa_enable_virtual.html

Here, we are going to explain how to enable virtual MFA for the IAM users. There are various virtual MFA applications are available to use depending on the mobile platform you are using.

The following virtual MFA applications are available for mobile devices:
- Android: Google Authenticator; Authy 2-Factor Authentication
- iPhone: Google Authenticator; Authy 2-Factor Authentication
- Windows Phone: Authenticator+
- Blackberry: Google Authenticator

You can also use the hardware-based MFA devices. However, typically hardware-based MFA devices are paid and you need to purchase them. This article is focused on virtual MFA application as it is completely free to use.

Before proceeding to the next process, make sure that you have installed the appropriate virtual MFA application for your mobile device.

To enable MFA for an IAM user, you need to perform the following steps:

1. Login to the **AWS Management Console** with the admin privileges.
2. Search and open the IAM user dashboard.
3. In the left pane, click **Users** and select an **IAM user** for which you want to enable MFA.
4. In the IAM user **Summary** page, select the **Security Credentials** tab and then click **Assign MFA device** edit button as shown in the following figure.

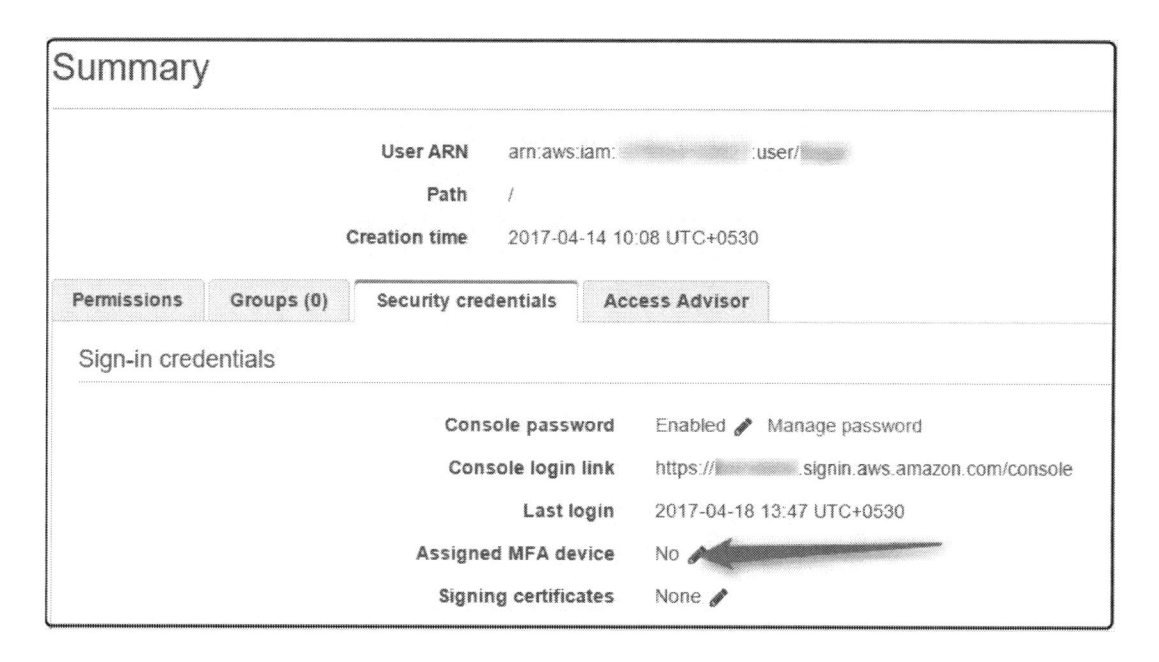

Summary

User ARN	arn:aws:iam: :user/
Path	/
Creation time	2017-04-14 10:08 UTC+0530

Permissions | **Groups (0)** | **Security credentials** | **Access Advisor**

Sign-in credentials

Console password	Enabled ✎ Manage password
Console login link	https:// .signin.aws.amazon.com/console
Last login	2017-04-18 13:47 UTC+0530
Assigned MFA device	No
Signing certificates	None ✎

5. On the **Manage MFA Device** screen, select the type of MFA device to activate. For this exercise, we will select **A virtual MFA device** option as shown in the following figure.

Manage MFA Device

Select the type of MFA device to activate:

- ⦿ A virtual MFA device
- ○ A hardware MFA device

For more information about supported MFA devices, see AWS Multi-Factor Authentication.

Cancel   **Next Step**

6. Click **Next Step** to proceed. On the warning message box, read the instructions and click the **Next Step** button to proceed.
7. On the next page, you will see a barcode that you need to scan using the Virtual MFA Application such as **Google Authenticator**.

Note: We recommend to take screenshot of your barcode and save it in a safe location. This barcode can be used to re-configure MFA on the same or another device in many use cases such as loss of your mobile device.

8. Once the code is scanned, the virtual MFA device (in our case Android mobile) should be able to detect the AWS user account.

> *Note: Alternatively, you can also enter the manual secret key in the authenticator app instead of scanning the barcode. One use case example of this is that suppose if the Camera of your mobile is not working and you are unable to scan the barcode.*

9. On the **Scan Code** page of AWS console, you also need to type two consecutive codes displayed on your Authenticator application.
10. Now, click the **Activate MFA Device** button as shown in the following figure to proceed.

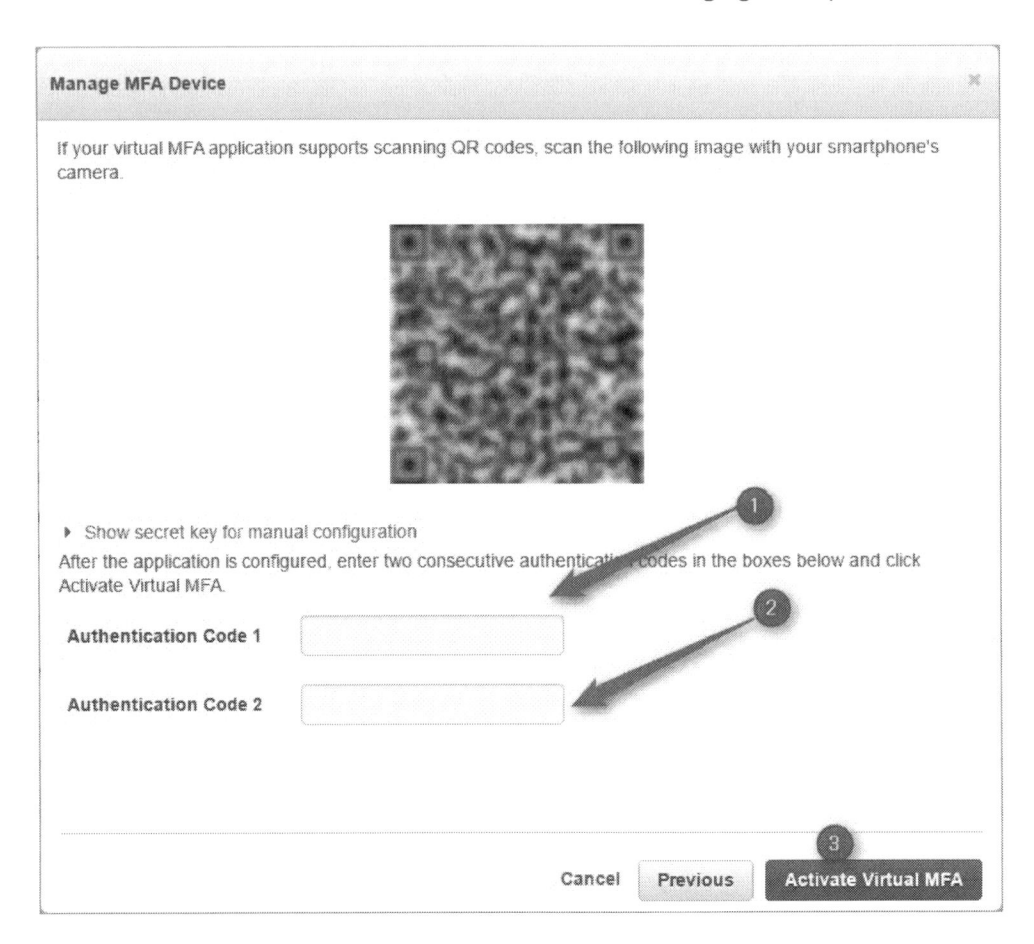

> *Note: The authentication code changes after every few seconds, so be careful while typing the authentication code.*

11. Once the process is completed "The MFA device was successfully associated" message will be displayed. Click **Finish** to complete the wizard.

12. Now, whenever the IAM user will try to login to the AWS console, he/she will need to type the dynamic security code after username and password.

> Question 02: What are the two types of methods you can use to configure the authenticator app on your mobile device?

That's all you need to enable MFA for your IAM user. The same process can be followed to enable MFA for AWS root account. However, you must be logged in with the root account to do so.

4. Managing Virtual Private Cloud (VPC)

VPC is the backbone of the AWS cloud platform. In order to become an AWS Solutions Architect, you must have a better understanding of the AWS VPC and its components. If you are from the networking background, managing VPC might be very easy for you. However, candidates from the developing background should spend a good amount of time to get familiarized with the AWS VPC and its components such as Internet Gateways, NAT Gateways, Routing tables, VPC Peering, Subnets etc. We have covered all these components in details in the separate sections.

VPC is a separate, isolated, private network in the AWS cloud. By default, the instances from one VPC to another VPC cannot communicate to each other. For some reasons, we may need to have multiple VPCs in the AWS cloud. One use case of having multiple VPCs is that suppose we want to keep our development and production instances logically isolate to each other. Here, we will see how to create, manage, and delete VPCs.

Note: The allowed block size for an AWS VPC can vary between /16 to /28 netmask. It means, you cannot create a VPC with netmask as /15 or as /29.

Recommended links:
- Getting started with AWS VPC.
- http://docs.aws.amazon.com/AmazonVPC/latest/GettingStartedGuide/getting-started-ipv4.html

Note: When you sign up for the free tier AWS account, a default VPC is created for your in each region with default settings. You should not use the default VPC for the production servers neither you should delete it. However, you can always use the default VPC for the testing purposes.

Creating VPC in AWS Cloud

In order to create a VPC, you need to perform the following steps:

1. In the AWS console, search and open the **VPC** dashboard.

   Note: There are two methods to create VPCs: using the Start VPC Wizard and Manual VPC creation. Beginners should use the Start VPC Wizard as it's an easy method to create VPC. Once you become familiar with the VPC components you can directly create and manage VPCs without using the Start VPC Wizard. So, let's get started with the Start VPC Wizard.

2. Click the **Start VPC Wizard** option as shown in the following figure.

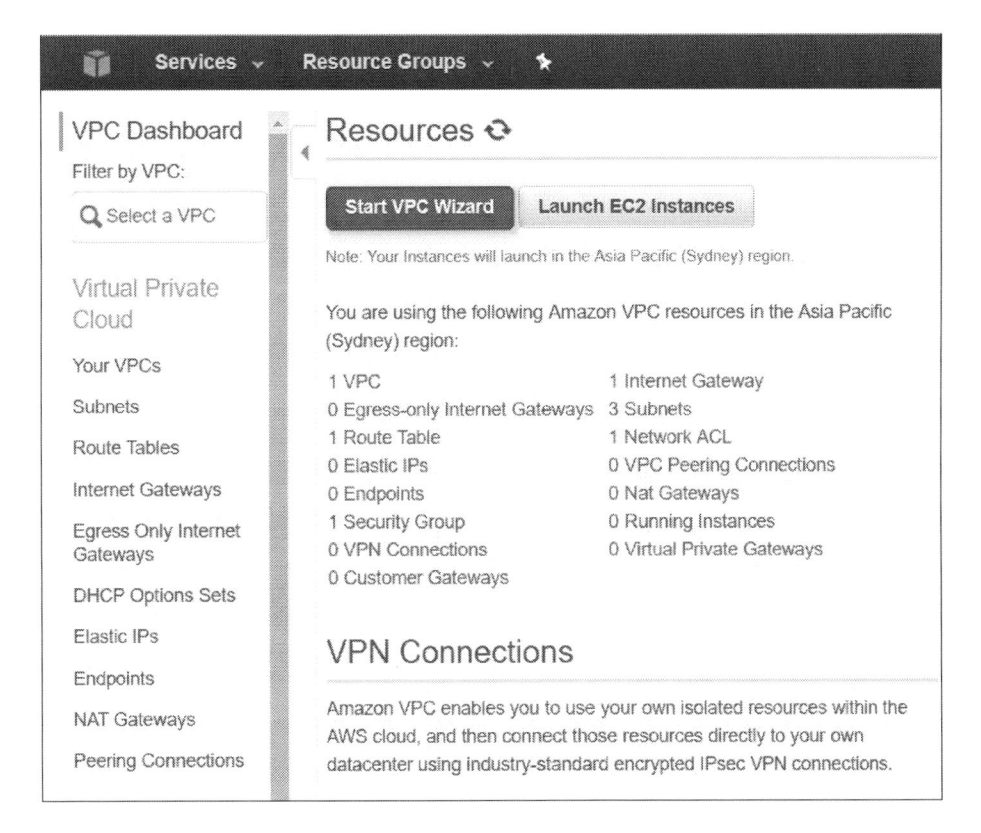

[Screenshot of AWS VPC Dashboard showing Resources panel with Start VPC Wizard button, listing VPC resources in the Asia Pacific (Sydney) region including 1 VPC, 1 Internet Gateway, 3 Subnets, 1 Route Table, 1 Network ACL, 1 Security Group, and other resource counts. Left sidebar shows Virtual Private Cloud navigation items: Your VPCs, Subnets, Route Tables, Internet Gateways, Egress Only Internet Gateways, DHCP Options Sets, Elastic IPs, Endpoints, NAT Gateways, Peering Connections.]

3. On the **Select a VPN Configuration** page, click each of the VPC Configuration options and review the description of the features provided by them.
4. Depending on your requirement, select the appropriate VPC configuration. Here, we will select the VPC with a Public Subnet option as shown in the following figure.

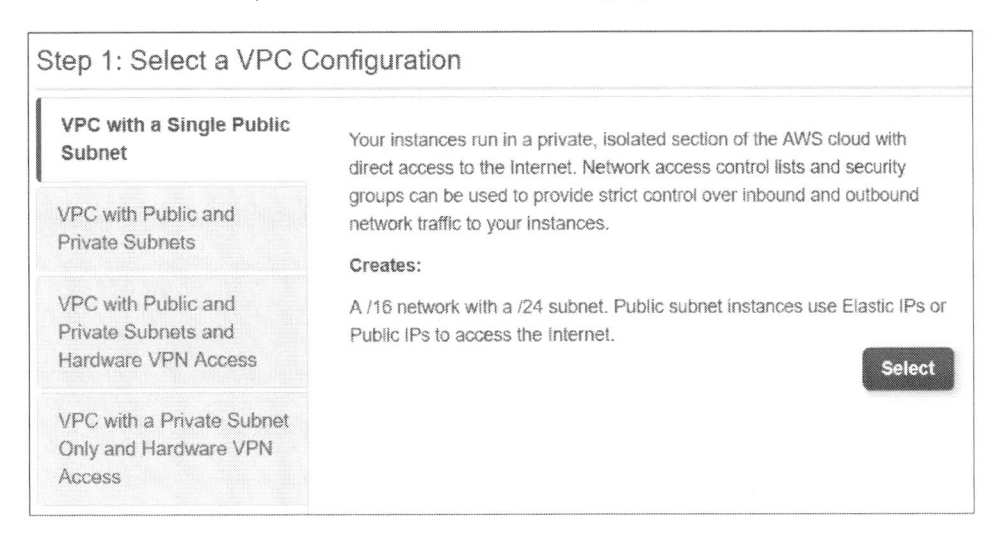

[Screenshot of Step 1: Select a VPC Configuration page. Options on left: VPC with a Single Public Subnet (selected), VPC with Public and Private Subnets, VPC with Public and Private Subnets and Hardware VPN Access, VPC with a Private Subnet Only and Hardware VPN Access. Description on right: "Your instances run in a private, isolated section of the AWS cloud with direct access to the Internet. Network access control lists and security groups can be used to provide strict control over inbound and outbound network traffic to your instances. Creates: A /16 network with a /24 subnet. Public subnet instances use Elastic IPs or Public IPs to access the Internet." With a Select button.]

Note: You can later add more subnets in the VPC and can customize your VPC options as per the requirements.

5. On the next page, specify the VPC name, subnet range, and Availability Zone etc. Here we are going to specify the following values:
   - IPv4 CIDR Block: **10.50.0.0/16**
   - VPC Name: **My_Test_VPC**
   - Public Subnet CIDR: **10.50.1.0/24**
   - Availability Zone: **Select the first availability zone**.
   - Subnet Name: **Public_Subnet1**

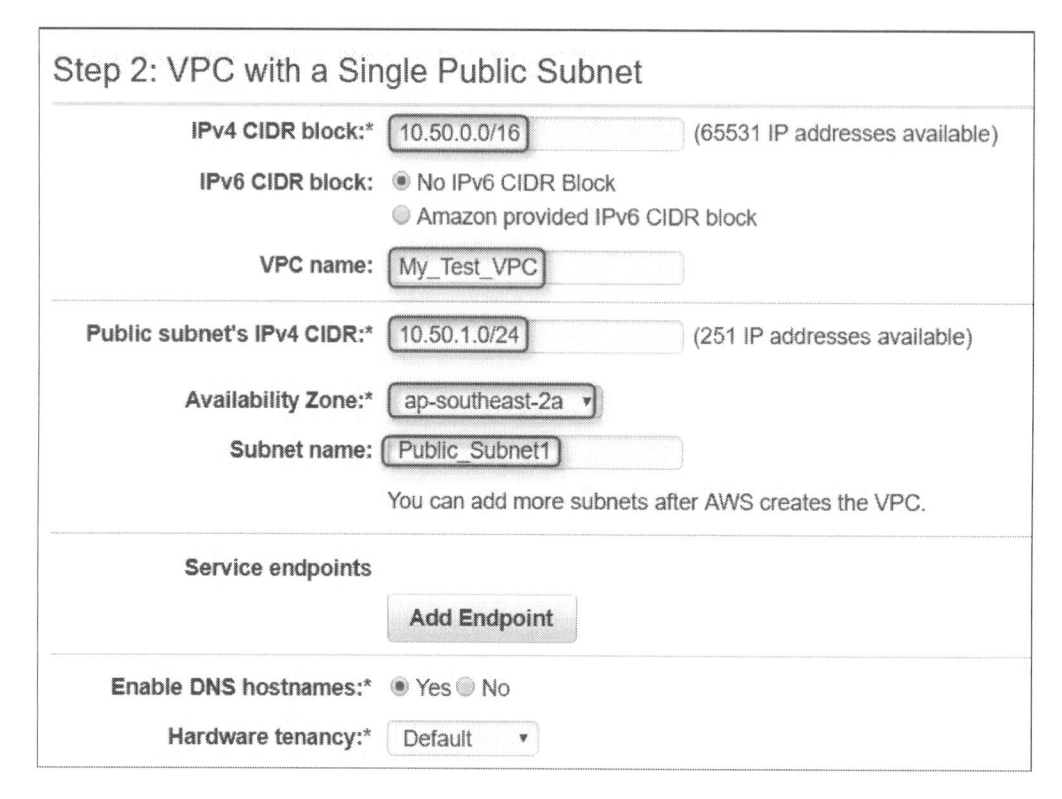

6. Click the **Create VPC** button to proceed next. The VPC will be created and available in the VPC list as shown in the following figure.

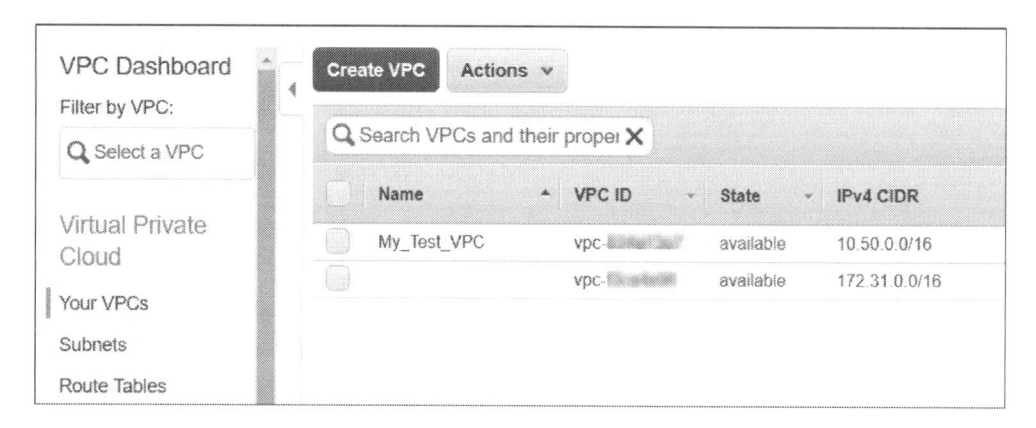

Creating and Adding Private Subnet in the Existing VPC

Since we had selected the VPC with a Public Subnet option, so we need to create Private subnets separately. A private subnet does not have direct access from the outside AWS network such as the

Internet. All private subnets require a NAT gateway to access the Internet. Typically, backend and database servers should always belong to the private subnets.

If you are interested, you can visit the following link to know more about the AWS VPC and subnets.

- AWS VPC and Subnets Getting Started.
- http://docs.aws.amazon.com/AmazonVPC/latest/UserGuide/VPC_Subnets.html

To create a private subnet, you need to perform the following steps:

1. Select the **Subnets** option in the navigation pane and then click **Create Subnet**.
2. On the **Create Subnet** page, specify the following values:
   - **Name tag**: Name of the subnet
   - **VPC**: Select the VPC in which you want to create the subnet
   - **Availability Zone**: Select the zone in which you want to create the subnet
   - **IPv4 CIDR block**: Specify the subnet IP range which must be within the VPC CIDR range.

   Note: You cannot specify the IP range for your subnet out of the CIDR range configured for your VPC. For example, if you have configured VPC with the CIDR range as 10.15.0.0/16, then you cannot create a subnet with 10.16.1.0/24 because it violates the IP networking rules.

3. For our lab exercise, let's create a Private subnet with the following values:
   - Name tag: **Private_Subnet1**
   - VPC: **My_Test_VPC**
   - Availability Zone: **ap-southeast-2b**
   - IPv4 CIDR block: **10.50.2.0/24**

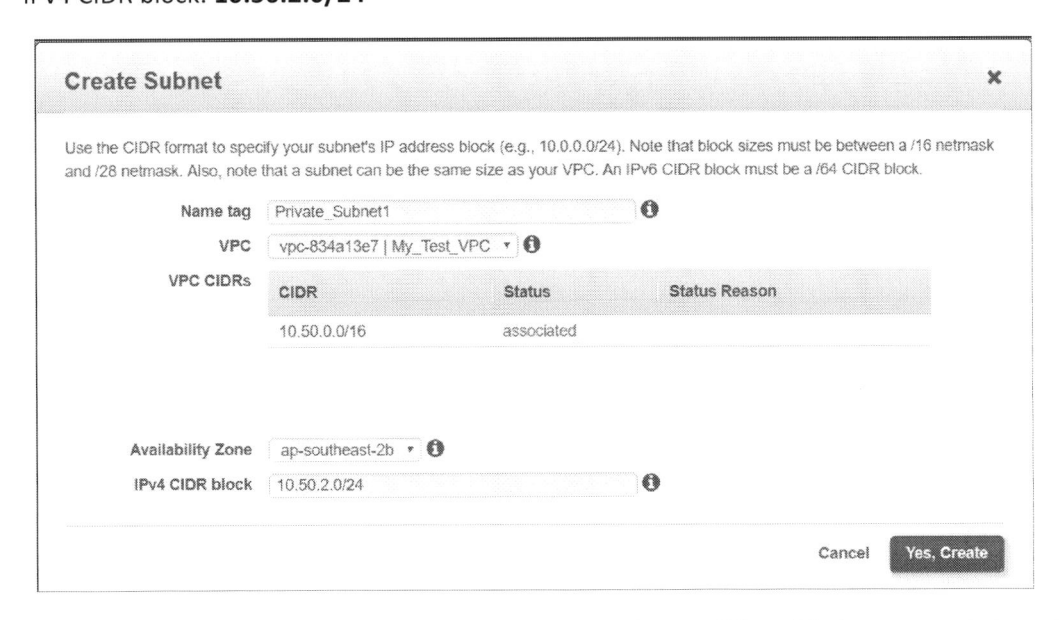

4. Click the **Yes Create** button to proceed. A new private subnet will be added to your existing VPC.

Note: In an upcoming lab, we will also explore how to configure VPC peering between two or more VPCs to allow inter-VPC communication.

Deleting VPC

If you no longer require any VPC for any reason, you can delete it anytime. For this, just select the VPC you want to delete, click **Actions** and then select **Delete VPC** to delete it as shown in the following figure.

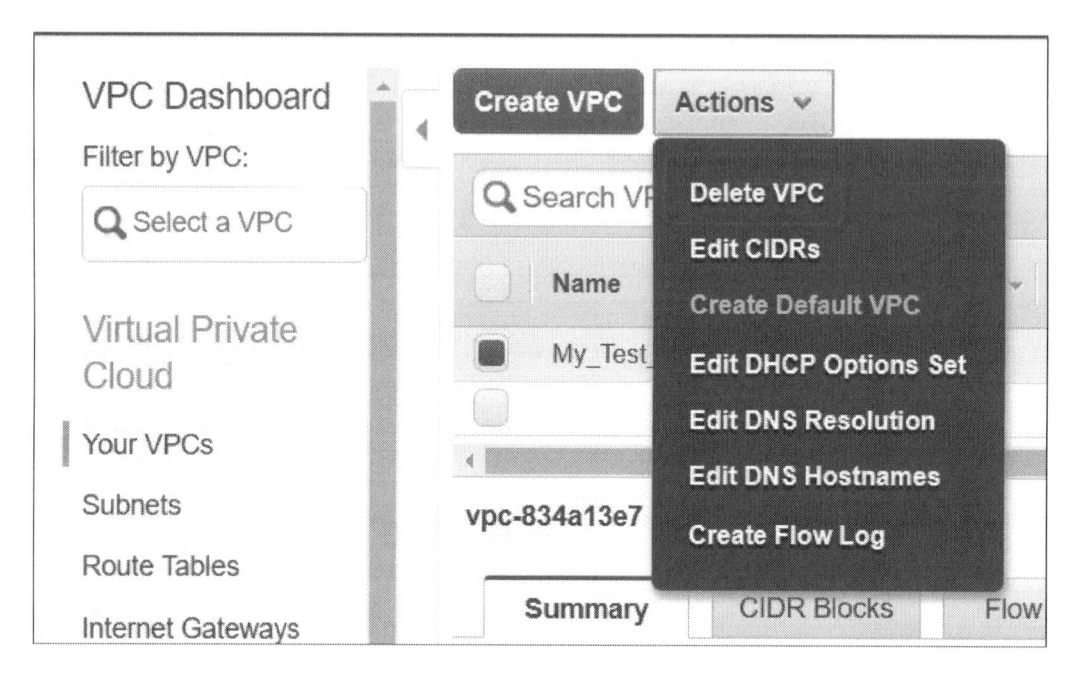

Note: Deleting VPC will also delete all its associated components such as Subnets, NAT Gateway, Routing Tables, Internet Gateways, etc. However, if your VPC has EC2 instances (running or stopped), you must first terminate your EC2 instances manually before you could delete the VPC.

Question 03: You can create a VPC with the 192.168.1.0/30 netmask?

A. True

B. False

5. Creating and Configuring Internet Gateways

An Internet gateway is an exit point for the internal EC2 instances and the entry point for the outside public users. In the AWS Cloud, you can logically consider an Internet Gateway as a Router that distinguishes the public and private networks. Each public subnet requires an Internet gateway to provide services to the public users and access the services from the Internet.

Recommended links:
- Getting Started with AWS Internet Gateways.
- http://docs.aws.amazon.com/AmazonVPC/latest/UserGuide/VPC_Internet_Gateway.html

To create an Internet gateway, you need to perform the following steps:

1. From the VPC section, select the **Internet Gateways** option in the left pane.
2. Click the **Create Internet Gateway** option and specify the name of Internet Gateway such as My_Test_IGW.
3. Click the **Yes, Create** button to complete the task.

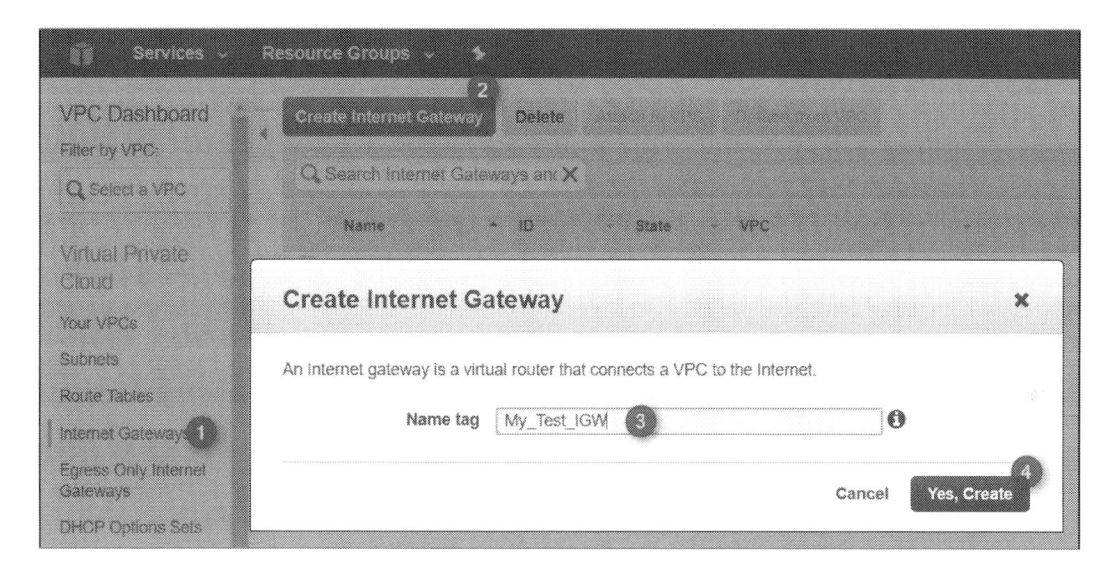

4. In the **Internet Gateways list**, select the created IGW, and click the **Attach to VPC** option.
5. In the **Attach to VPC** window, select the VPC that you want to attach with this IGW and then click **Yes, Attach** as shown in the following figure.

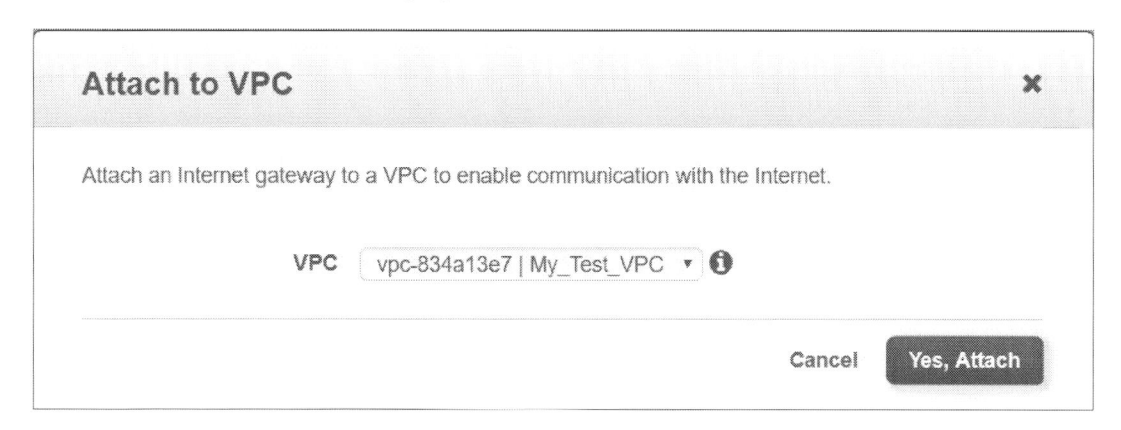

That's all you need to do to create and attach the Internet Gateways in for AWS VPC. An Internet gateway can only be attached to a single VPC. However, a single Internet Gateway can be attached to the multiple subnets (routing tables) inside a single VPC.

Quick facts about Internet Gateways
1. Internet Gateways act like as routers.
2. You can attach only single Internet Gateway to a VPC.
3. By default, you can create up to 5 Internet Gateways per VPC.
4. Internet Gateways can be attached and detached to any VPC whenever required.
5. There is no additional charge for using the Internet Gateways.

6. Creating and Configuring NAT Gateways

NAT gateways are only required when you want to provide the Internet access to your EC2 instances that are located inside the private subnets. There are two options to use with the NAT gateways: Your own EC2 instance acting as NAT gateway or an AWS NAT Gateway managed by Amazon.

A NAT instance should be used for the Dev, QA and testing infrastructures where you can stop, start, scale, and manage it as per your own requirements. However, for the enterprise production servers, it is recommended to use the NAT gateways. Because the NAT gateways are managed by AWS and auto scalable as per the need and do not require any manual interactions. Here, we will focus on NAT Gateway as a service.

Recommended links:
- Getting Started with AWS NAT Gateways.
- http://docs.aws.amazon.com/AmazonVPC/latest/UserGuide/vpc-nat-gateway.html

To create and configure a NAT gateway, you need to follow the following steps:

1. From the VPC section, select the **NAT Gateways** option in the left pane and then click **Create NAT Gateway**.
2. On the next page, you need to provide following two settings:
   - **Subnet**: Select the public subnet of your VPC to which your NAT gateway will belong.
   - **Elastic IP**: Generate a new EIP that will be attached to your NAT Gateway.

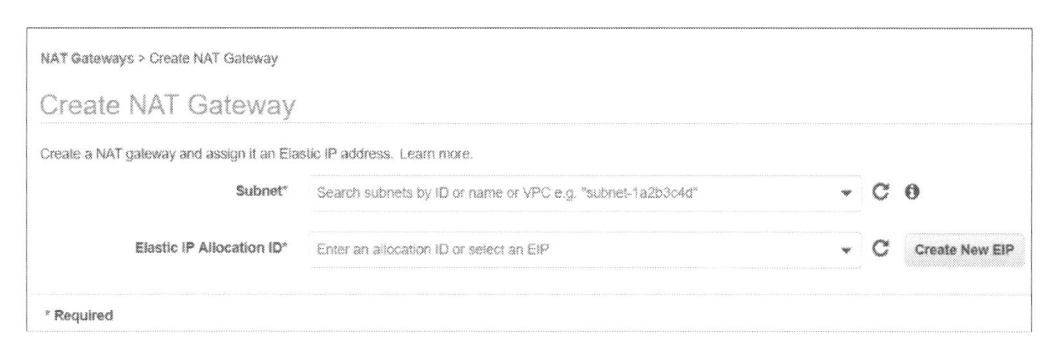

3. Click the **Create NAT Gateway** option to proceed. After few minutes, the NAT Gateway will be created.
4. On the next page, click **Close** to finish the task.

Quick facts about NAT Gateways
1. A NAT Gateway must be created in a Public subnet.
2. Security groups cannot be associated with a NAT gateway.
3. A NAT gateway supports 5 Gbps of bandwidth and can automatically scale up to 45 Gbps.
4. You must update the routing table attached to your private subnets to point internet traffic to the NAT gateway.
5. By default, you can create up to 5 NAT Gateways per VPC.
6. Unlike Internet Gateways, NAT gateways are chargeable based on the traffic passing through the NAT gateway.

7. Configuring Routing Tables

Understanding and configuring the routing tables (AWS called these as Route Tables) in the AWS Cloud is a little bit tricky and required a sound knowledge of networking fundamentals as prerequisites. Hope, you are already familiar with some routing concepts.

If you are not comfortable with the routing concepts, we recommend to visit the following link as it explained the basics of routing in a very easy way.

https://protechgurus.com/ip-routing-process-step-step-explanation

Here, we will show you how to create, edit, change, and configure routing tables in AWS Cloud.

Recommended links:
- Getting Started with AWS Routing Tables.
- http://docs.aws.amazon.com/AmazonVPC/latest/UserGuide/VPC_Route_Tables.html

Quick facts about Routing Tables

1. All VPC has a main routing table that can be modified as per your need.
2. You can have multiple routing tables in a VPC for different use cases.
3. By default, each routing table has local route information and allows all subnets of a VPC to intercommunicate to each other.
4. All subnets within a VPC must have at least one routing table attached to them.
5. By default, you can create up to 200 routing table for a single VPC.
6. Public routing tables should have an Internet Gateway as the default gateway address.
7. Private routing tables should have a NAT Gateway as the default gateway address.

Creating Custom Routing Table

By default, when you create a VPC, a default routing table called "Main Routing Table" is also created automatically. All the traffic by default is directed to this default routing table. However, you can always create additional routing tables and can attach them to the desired subnets. To design and implement a robust, secure, and scalable cloud Architecture, you must have a good understanding of VPC, Subnetting, NATing, VPC Peering, ACLs, and Routing concepts.

To create a custom Routing table, you need to perform the following steps:

1. In the VPC Dashboard, click the **Create Routing table** option.
2. In the **Create Routing Table** window, specify the name of the routing table.
3. In the VPC drop-down list, select the VPC for which you want to create the routing table and then click the **Yes, Create** button.
4. Select the created routing table. Here, you will see the various configurable tabs. Let's have a quick understanding of each of them.
   - The **Summary** tab provides the information regarding a number of attached subnets, whether it is main routing table or not, attached VPC etc.
   - The **Routes** tab provides the information regarding added routes, the attached IGW (for public routing table) or NAT gateways (for private routing table).
   - Rest of the tabs are self-explanatory. Select each of them and see what information they contain/provide.

Destination	Target	Status	Propagated
10.50.0.0/16	local	Active	No
0.0.0.0/0	igw-7b4d8f1f	Active	No

5. If you wish to modify the route information, click **Edit** and add the routes you want to add. If you need to enable intercommunication between two VPCs, you need to create a **VPC peering** connection and then you need to specify the VPC peering connection name in the Routes tab. We have covered the VPC Peering in a separate lab exercise.
6. The **Subnet Associations** tab allows you to add or remove the subnets to the selected Route table.
7. Simply click the **Edit** button and select or remove the checkbox in front of the desired subnets as shown in the following figure.

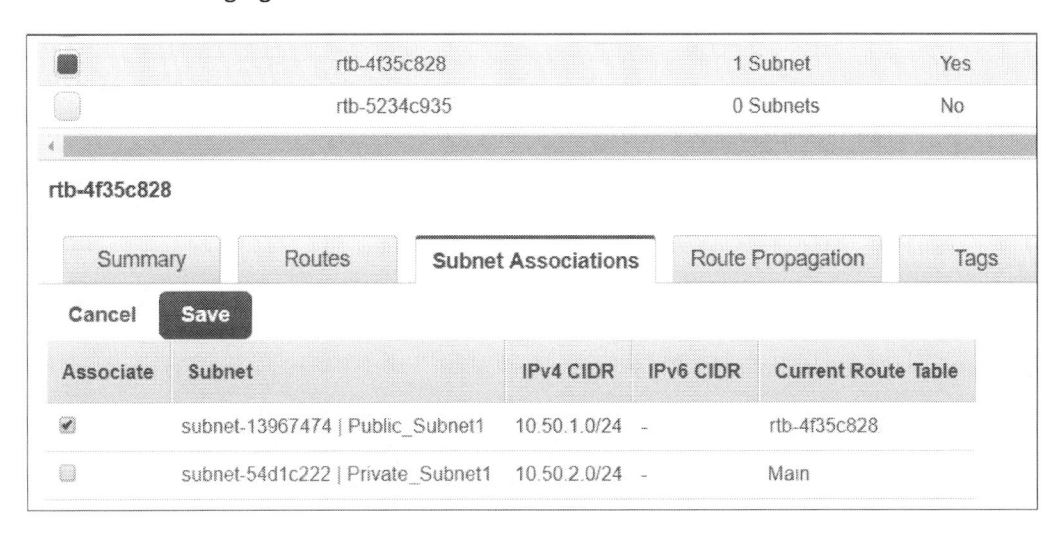

Associate	Subnet	IPv4 CIDR	IPv6 CIDR	Current Route Table
☑	subnet-13967474 | Public_Subnet1	10.50.1.0/24	-	rtb-4f35c828
☐	subnet-54d1c222 | Private_Subnet1	10.50.2.0/24	-	Main

Question 04: What is the use of Subnet Associations tab in a VPC Route Table?

8. VPC Peering Between Two VPCs

As discussed earlier, VPC is a separate, isolated virtual network in the AWS Cloud. By default, each VPC has its own Internet gateways, NAT gateways, Subnet ranges and scopes, Security groups, and associated routing tables. In addition, resources from one VPC is not accessible from another VPC until you configure VPC peering between them.

VPC peering allows one VPC to share and access resources with the other VPCs in the AWS cloud. For example, let's assume we have two VPCs named as AWS-Test-VPC1 and AWS-Test-VPC2. Each VPC has a public subnet inside which one instance is running in each subnet as shown in the following figure.

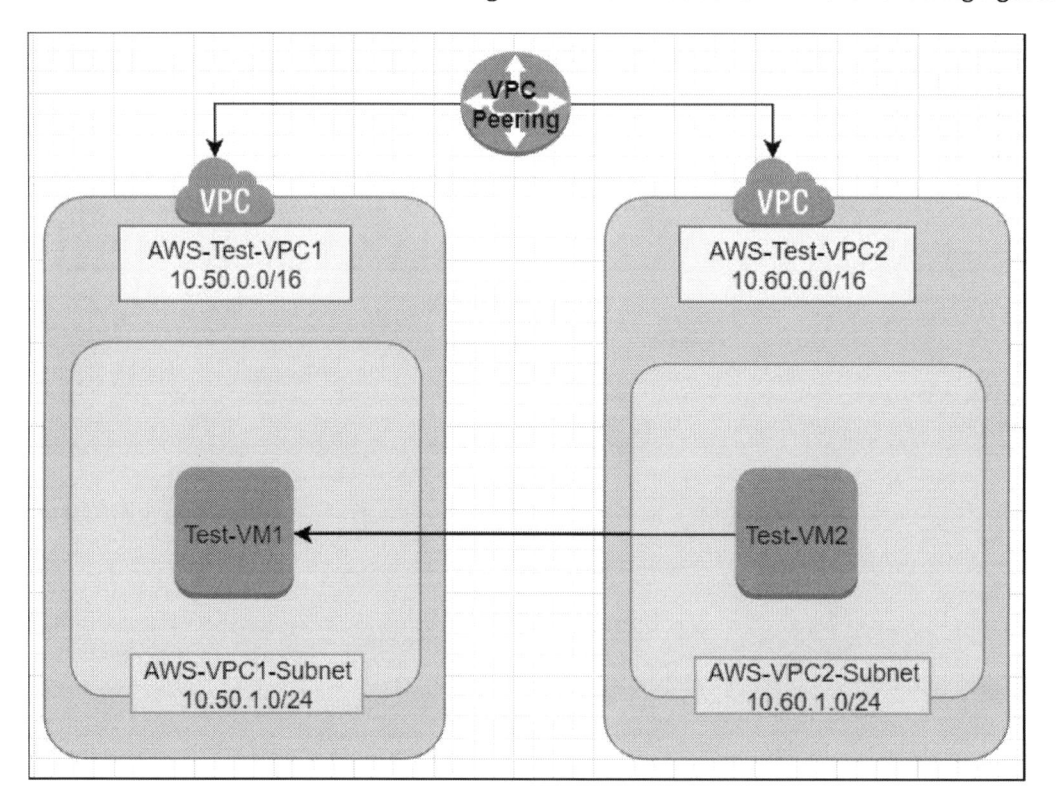

Test-VM1 cannot communicate directly to Test-VM2 because both VMs belong to the different subnets of different VPCs. However, instances from one subnet are allowed to communicate with the instances of another subnet if they (both subnets) belong to the same VPC. Please have a look at the IP scheme we have used for the above design.

Here, we will create two VPCs each having one subnet per VPC. Once VPC will have a subnet (AWS-VPC1-Subnet) range as 10.15.1.0/24 and another subnet (AWS-VPC2-Subnet) will have 10.16.1.0/24. We will create a VPC Peering connection between these VPCs. Finally, we will configure and update the routing tables of both the subnets so they can communicate to each other.

In order to allow inter-VPC communication, you need to create a VPC peering connection and update the routing tables associated with the subnets that you want to allow to communicate.

This lab exercise consists of the following tasks.

Creating VPCs and Subnets

To create a VPC and subnet, you need to perform the following steps:

1. Select your desired region where you want to perform this activity such as **us-east-1**.
2. Open the VPC home page by navigating the following link.
- https://console.aws.amazon.com/vpc
3. In the left pane, click **Your VPCs**. You will see a default VPC created already.
4. Click **Create VPC** to create a new VPC. Create AWS-Test-VPC1 with the settings shown in the following figure.

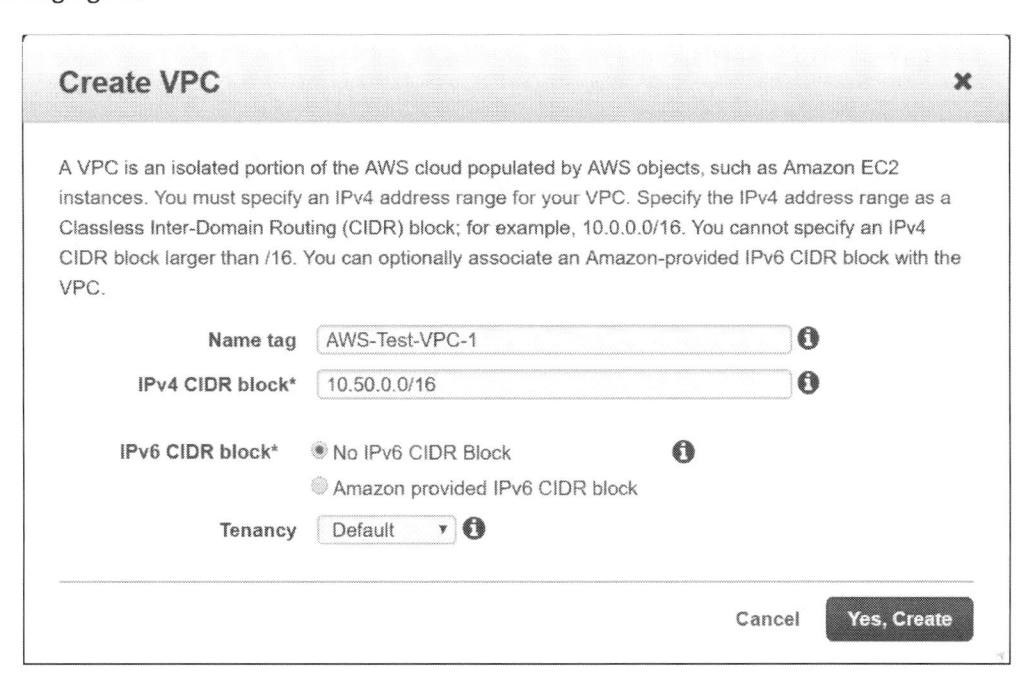

5. Click **Yes Create** to complete the wizard.
6. Similarly, create another VPC named as **AWS-Test-VPC2** with the IP scheme as 10.60.0.0/16.

Creating Subnets

To create a subnet, you need to perform the following steps.

1. In the VPC console, select **Subnets** in the left pane and then click **Create Subnet**.
2. On the **Create Subnet** window, create a subnet with the following settings:
- Name: **AWS-VPC1-Subnet**
- VPC: **AWS-Test-VPC1**
- Availability zone: **us-east-1a**
- Subnet range: **10.50.1.0/24**

Create Subnet

Use the CIDR format to specify your subnet's IP address block (e.g., 10.0.0.0/24). Note that block sizes must be between a /16 netmask and /28 netmask. Also, note that a subnet can be the same size as your VPC. An IPv6 CIDR block must be a /64 CIDR block.

Name tag: AWS-VPC1-Subnet
VPC: vpc-23da9e5b | AWS-Test-VPC-1

VPC CIDRs:

CIDR	Status	Status Reason
10.50.0.0/16	associated	

Availability Zone: us-east-1a
IPv4 CIDR block: 10.50.1.0/24

3. Now create another subnet in another VPC with the following settings:
   - Name: **AWS-VPC2-Subnet**
   - VPC: **AWS-Test-VPC2**
   - Availability zone: **us-east-1b**
   - Subnet range: **10.60.1.0/24**

Creating VPC Peering Connection

Now you have two VPCs with one subnet in each VPC. But you have still not configured the peering connection between these VPCs. Let's do it.

Quick facts about VPC Peering

1. In VPC Peering connection, one VPC acts as a requester VPC and another VPC acts as a accepter VPC.
2. Requester VPC initiates the VPC peering connection process, whereas the accepter VPC accepts the request of requester VPC.
3. VPC peering could be configured within or between regions of an AWS account.
4. VPC Peering can also be configured between same or different regions of different AWS accounts.
5. A VPC Connection peering name needs to be added to the both routing tables of both the source and destination VPCs with appropriate subnets that want to intercommunicate.

To create a VPC Peering connection between two VPCs, you need to perform the following steps:

1. Click **VPC Connection** in the left pane and then click **Create VPC Connection**.
2. On the **Create VPC Peering Connection** page, you need to specify the following settings:
   - **Peering connection name tag**: Name of the VPC peering connection such as VPC1-and-VPC2-Peer
   - **VPC Requester**: Select the source VPC such as AWS-Test-VPC1 as shown in the following figure.

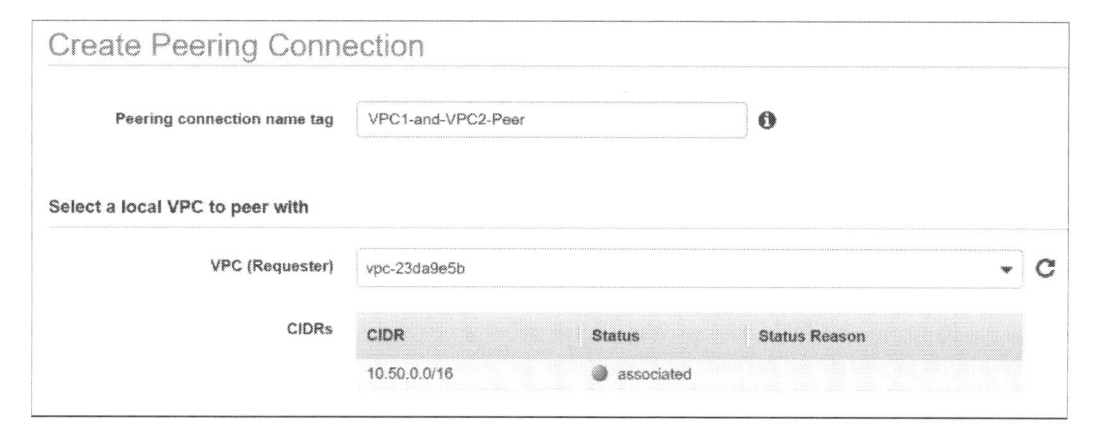

Create Peering Connection

Peering connection name tag	VPC1-and-VPC2-Peer

Select a local VPC to peer with

VPC (Requester)	vpc-23da9e5b

CIDRs

CIDR	Status	Status Reason
10.50.0.0/16	associated	

3. On the **Select another VPC to peer with** section, you need to understand the following options.
   - **Account**: It might be either your own account or another account for which you have sufficient permissions.
   - **Region**: VPC Peering can be within the same region or with a different region with a different account.
   - **VPC (Acceptor):** Select the destination VPC name to which you want to establish VPC peering such as AWS-Test-VPC2 in our case.
4. Refer the following figure for our lab exercise and complete the Peering connection wizard.

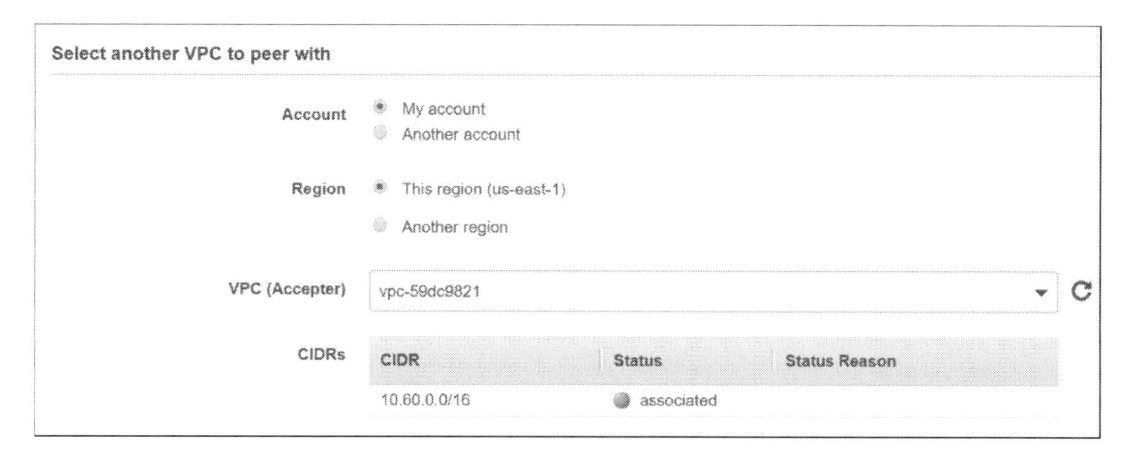

Select another VPC to peer with

Account	● My account ○ Another account
Region	● This region (us-east-1) ○ Another region
VPC (Accepter)	vpc-59dc9821

CIDRs

CIDR	Status	Status Reason
10.60.0.0/16	associated	

5. Once you created a VPC Peering connection between the desired VPCs, it will be listed as pending in the VPC Peering list. Accepter (Destination) VPC holder needs to approve the VPC Peering connection manually as shown in the following figure.

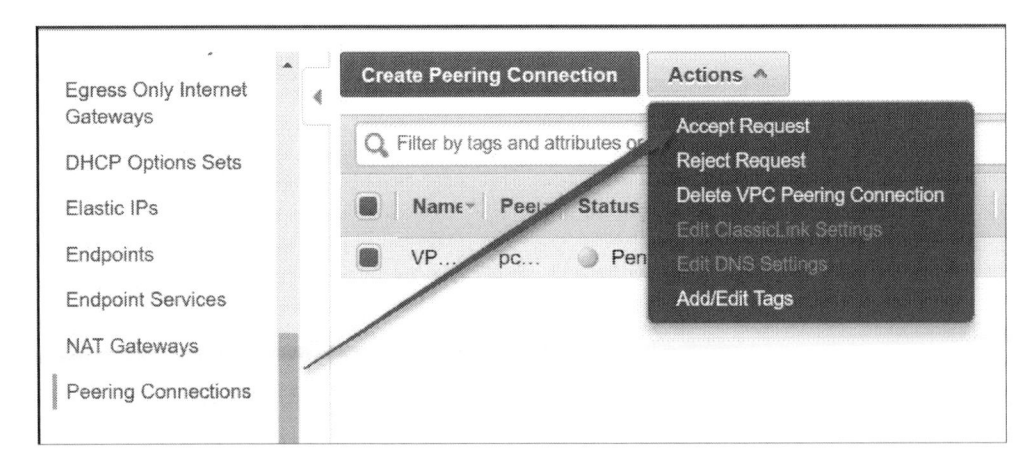

6. Now, the VPC Peering connection is done. However, instances from AWS-VPC1-Subnet would still not be able to communicate with the instances of the AWS-VPC2-Subnet. Think, why?
7. Yes, because you have not updated the routing information yet. Let's do it.

Updating Routing Tables and Routes

To update routing tables and adding routes, you need to perform the following steps:

1. Select the **Subnets** option in the left pane.
2. Select AWS-VPC1-Subnet and then select the **Route Table** tab.
3. Open the attached routing table with this subnet in a new tab as shown in the following figure.

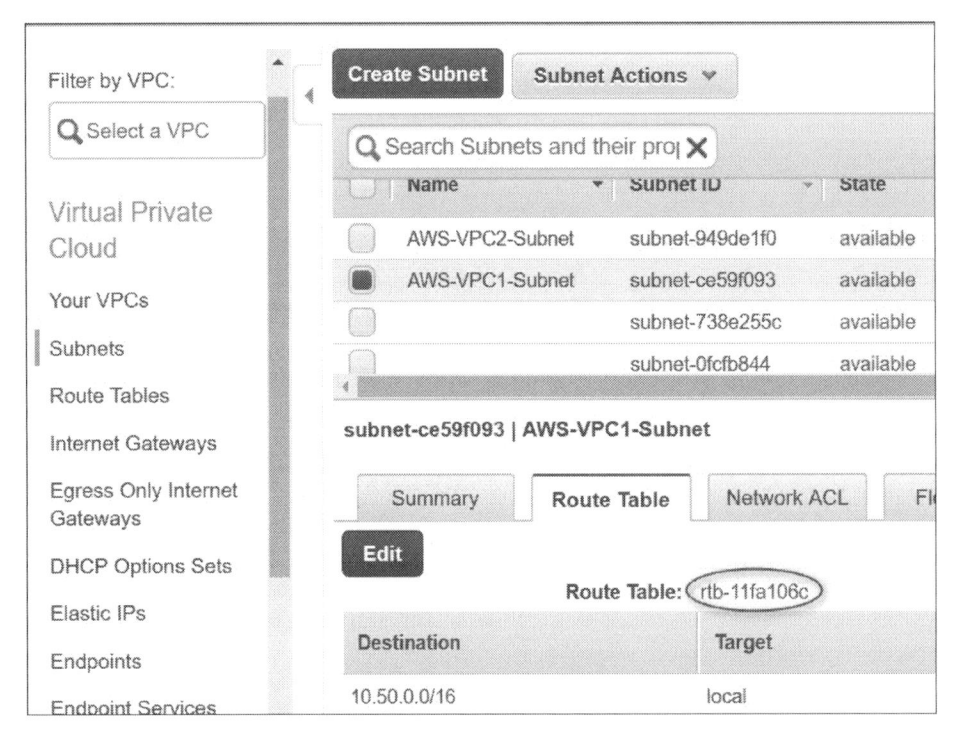

4. In this routing table, you can see that routes for the only local network are allowed. Here, you need to add routes for other subnet(s) of other VPC which is in our case 10.60.1.0/24.
5. For this, click **Edit** and then click **Add another route**.
6. In the **Destination** section, type the subnet range of remote subnet.

7. In the **Target** section, select the VPC Peering Connection name that has appropriate requestor and Acceptor VPCs as shown in the following figure.

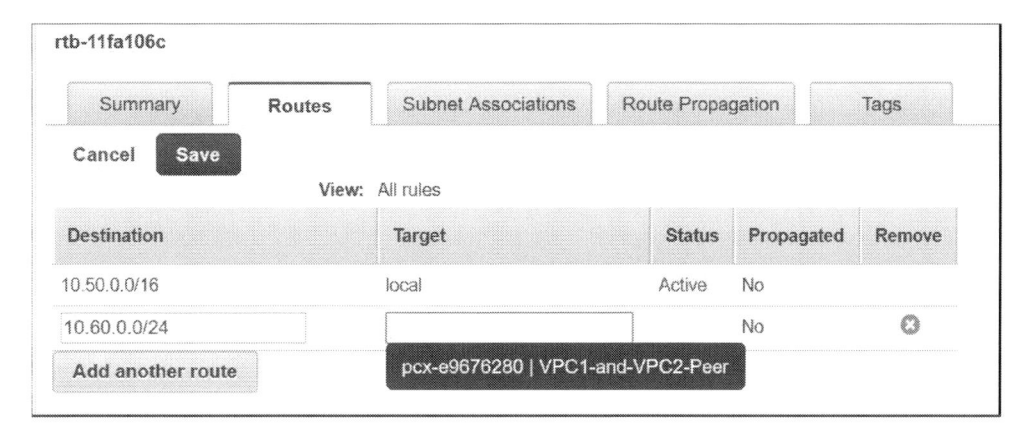

8. Finally, click **Save** to save the route information.
9. Using the same steps, go to the routing table attached to the AWS-VPC2-subnet, update the route for 10.50.0.0/24 and select the same VPC Peering connection name.

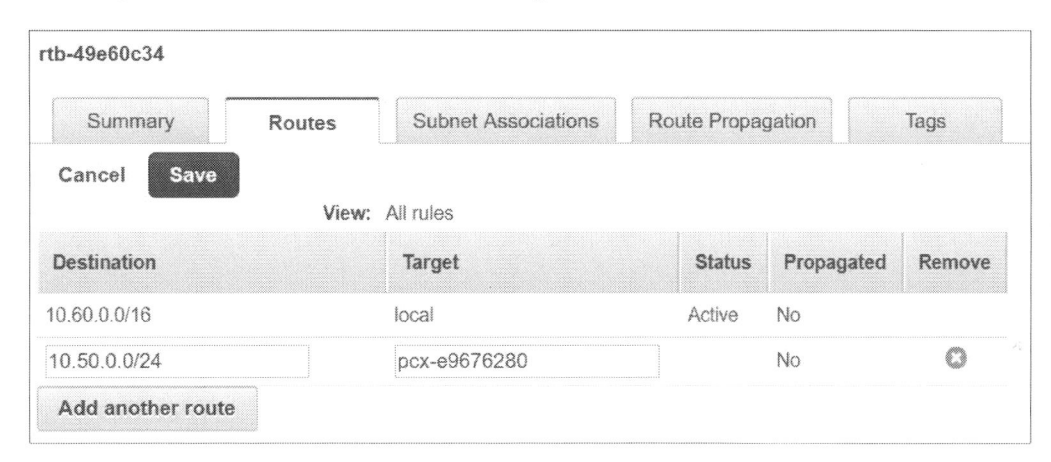

Now resources (instances) between AWS-Test-VPC1 and AWS-Test-VPC2 can communicate to each other. However, you still need to use and configure Network Access Control List (ACL) and Security Groups as per the service and/or application requirements. These topics are covered in the separate sections.

9. Working with Amazon Elastic Cloud Compute (EC2)

EC2 is one of the premier services of AWS cloud. One should have an excellent understanding and hands-on the Amazon EC2 components, features, services, and configurations. Amazon EC2 provides you almost everything that you may need for your Infrastructure as a Service (IaaS).

Managing EC2 is more than just launching or creating virtual machines (called as instances in AWS term). Once you become comfortable with Amazon EC2 services, you are almost on the track of becoming an AWS cloud expert.

Since EC2 is a broad level of topic, so we recommend you to remain focused on the basics of EC2 as a beginner. We will try to cover all the things that are necessary for an AWS Certified Solution Architect – Associate level. Since this book is focused on mainly for the hands-on lab exercises, so we will cover only the basic terms and theories for EC2.

The following are the major terms, components, features, and services you should know along with Amazon EC2.

- **EC2 instance**: Amazon EC2 instance is a term used to define a virtual machine hosted on AWS cloud.
- **Amazon Machine Image (AMI)**: AMI is a preconfigured virtual machine with all the predefined/preinstalled software and settings. It acts as a template for other instances that you would launch using this template image.
- **AWS Region**: Region is a geographical location where AWS hosts its services with the locally hosted data centers. There are various AWS regions and increasing year by years. However, each region is completely independent and have at least two or more availability zones.
- **Availability Zone (AZ)**: Each Availability Zone is isolated and can be considered as different data centers. But the Availability Zones in a region are connected through low-latency links.
- **Instance Type**: AWS instance types are covered in the later sections.
- **Security Groups**: Security groups act as a virtual firewall for the EC2 instances. Each VPC has a default security group. Security groups are covered more in detail in the coming sections.

Now, you are familiar with the most common terms of EC2, let's create and launch an Amazon Linux instance.

Creating Amazon EC2 Linux Instance

The following steps need to be followed to launch an EC2 instance.

1. In the **EC2 dashboard**, click **Launch Instance** button.
2. On the **Choose an Amazon Machine Image (AMI)** page, you can select either of the following options:
   - **Quickstart**: Select this option if you want to launch a fresh instance and want to configure it as per your wish.
   - **My AMIs**: Here you will see the list of AMIs that have been created earlier
   - **AWS Market Place**: There are thousands of pre-configured VMs are available in the AWS market. Few of them are free and few of them are chargeable. If the pre-configured AMI fulfills your requirements, you can directly launch it. We will cover this in an upcoming section.

- **Community AMIs**: There are few AMIs which are created and shared by the community people. You can search and find the desired pre-configured AMIs for your own use. But, these AMIs may not be trusted, so be careful before to use them.
3. For this demo, make sure that the **Quick Start** option is selected. Select the platform (e.g. Linux or Windows) and variant (e.g. RHEL, Ubuntu) you wish to use and proceed to the next page. For this demo, select the **Ubuntu 16.04** and proceed to the next page.

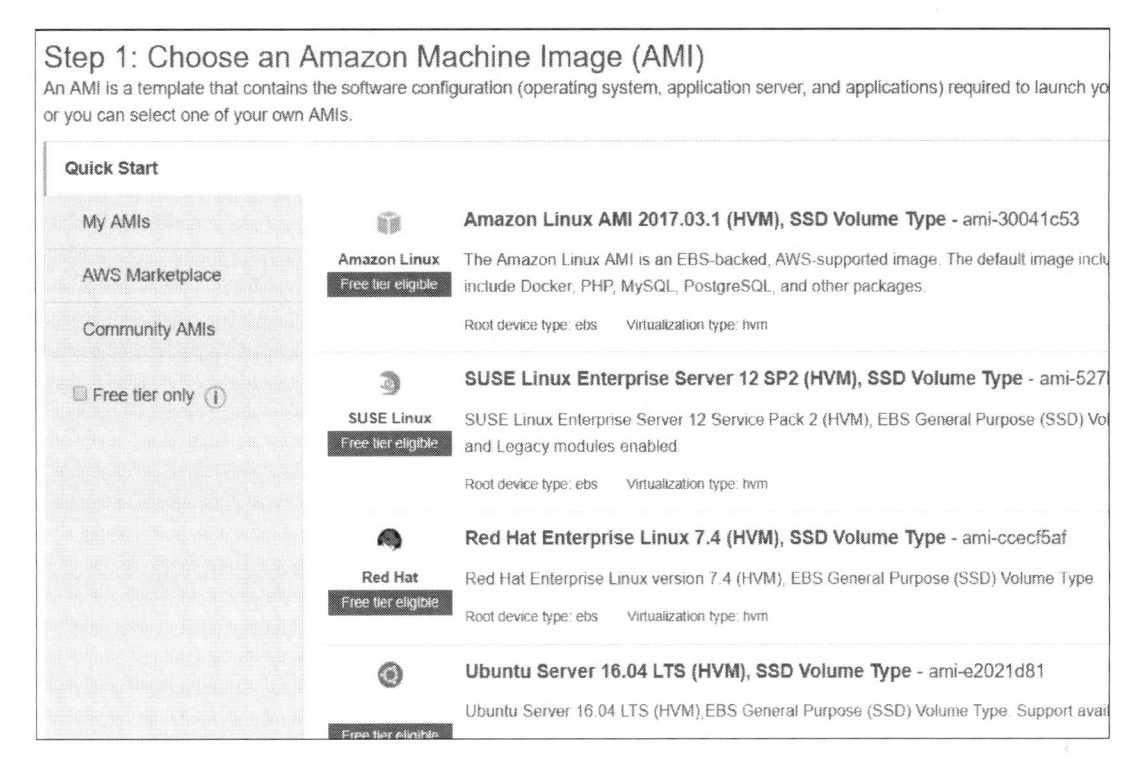

Selecting Instance Type

In the AWS Cloud, instance type defines the configuration and performance of your VMs. There are various categories and types of EC2 instances. Each type of instance has its own configuration, features, prices, and performance. For example, M4 and C4 instance categories provide greater network performance and better bandwidth than T2 instance categories such as T2 Medium and T2 Large instance. You should plan well in advance before to choose instance categories and types for your server.

We highly recommend you to visit the following link to know more about the EC2 instance types. Don't try to remember everything, just go through once at high-level and get familiar with few terms.

- EC2 Instance Categories and Types
  https://aws.amazon.com/ec2/instance-types/
- EC2 Instance Pricing
  https://calculator.s3.amazonaws.com/index.html

For this demo, we just select the free tier eligible t2.micro instance type and proceed to the next page.

Step 2: Choose an Instance Type

Amazon EC2 provides a wide selection of instance types optimized to fit different use cases. Instances are virtual se give you the flexibility to choose the appropriate mix of resources for your applications. Learn more about instance t

Filter by: All instance types ▾   Current generation ▾   Show/Hide Columns

Currently selected: t2.micro (Variable ECUs, 1 vCPUs, 2.5 GHz, Intel Xeon Family, 1 GiB memory, EBS only)

	Family	Type	vCPUs	Memory (GiB)
☐	General purpose	t2.nano	1	0.5
■	General purpose	t2.micro (Free tier eligible)	1	1
☐	General purpose	t2.small	1	2
☐	General purpose	t2.medium	2	4
☐	General purpose	t2.large	2	8
☐	General purpose	t2.xlarge	4	16

Specify the Instance Configuration Options

On the **Configure Instance** page, you need to specify the various options based on you requirements. Few of the important options are described as follow:

- **Number of instances**: Specify the no. of instances you want to launch like this. For example, 1.
- **Network**: Select the VPC in which you wish to launch the instance. For example, My_Test_VPC
- **Subnet:** Select the subnet in which you want to launch this instance. For example, Public_Subnet1
- **Auto-assign Public** IP: Keep it disabled as of now.

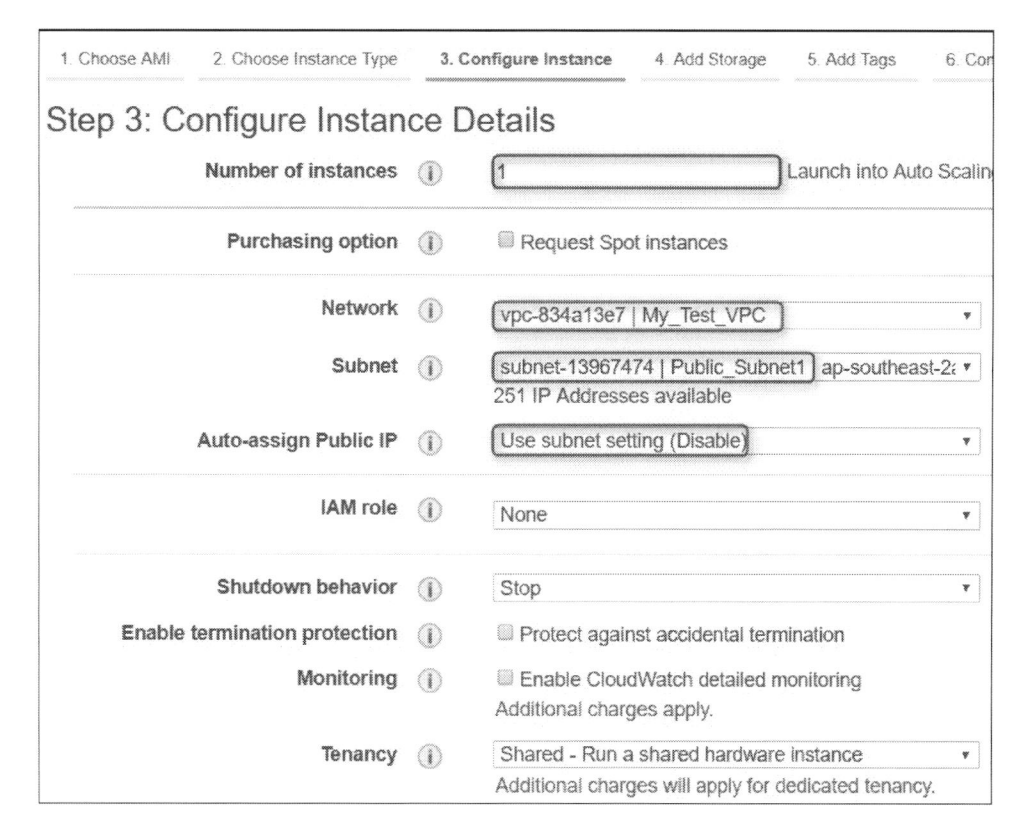

![Step 3: Configure Instance Details screenshot showing Number of instances: 1, Network: vpc-834a13e7 | My_Test_VPC, Subnet: subnet-13967474 | Public_Subnet1 ap-southeast-2, Auto-assign Public IP: Use subnet setting (Disable), IAM role: None, Shutdown behavior: Stop, Tenancy: Shared - Run a shared hardware instance]

We have covered the rest of the options of this page in the upcoming sections.

Adding Storage Volumes

On the **Add Storage** page, you can specify the size of Root volume or you can also add additional volumes to this instance as per your requirement.

> *Note: We will cover the AWS Storage Types in an upcoming section.*

Proceed to the next page and specify the tag name such as **My_Test_VM1**.

Selecting Security Group

Security Group is one of the most important features that you should understand. Although, it has been covered in a later section. Think AWS security groups as virtual firewalls. As of now, just create a descriptive security group that allows SSH to connect an EC2 instance.

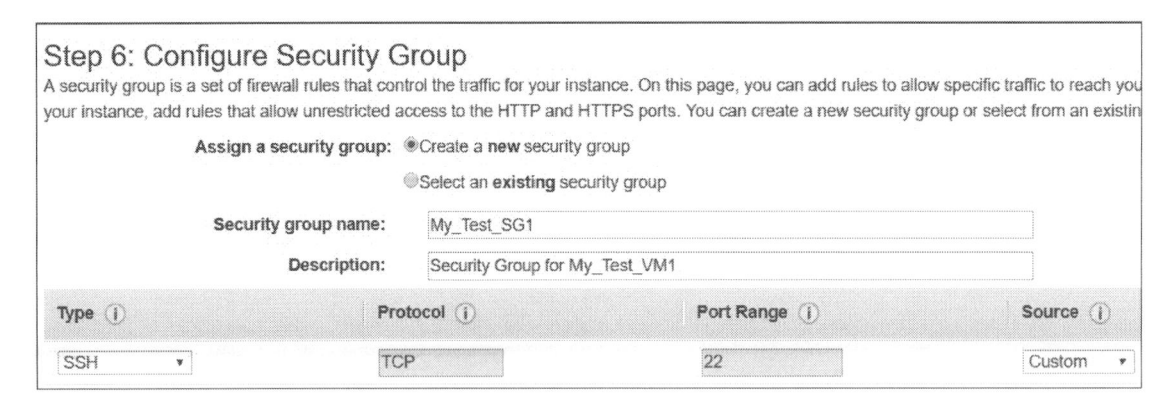

Step 6: Configure Security Group

A security group is a set of firewall rules that control the traffic for your instance. On this page, you can add rules to allow specific traffic to reach you your instance, add rules that allow unrestricted access to the HTTP and HTTPS ports. You can create a new security group or select from an existin

Assign a security group:	● Create a **new** security group
	○ Select an **existing** security group
Security group name:	My_Test_SG1
Description:	Security Group for My_Test_VM1

Type	Protocol	Port Range	Source
SSH	TCP	22	Custom

On the **Review** page, just review all the settings and options you have chosen. If you have selected anything incorrectly, you can go back and correct the settings or options you may wish. Finally, click **Launch** to launch the instance.

Creating/Selecting Key Pair

On the **Key Pair** page, you can either select an existing key pair if you have already created or you can create a new key pair. In AWS Cloud, Linux instances do not have a username and password authentication enabled for SSH access. By default, you can only access SSH of an EC2 Linux instance using the key pair.

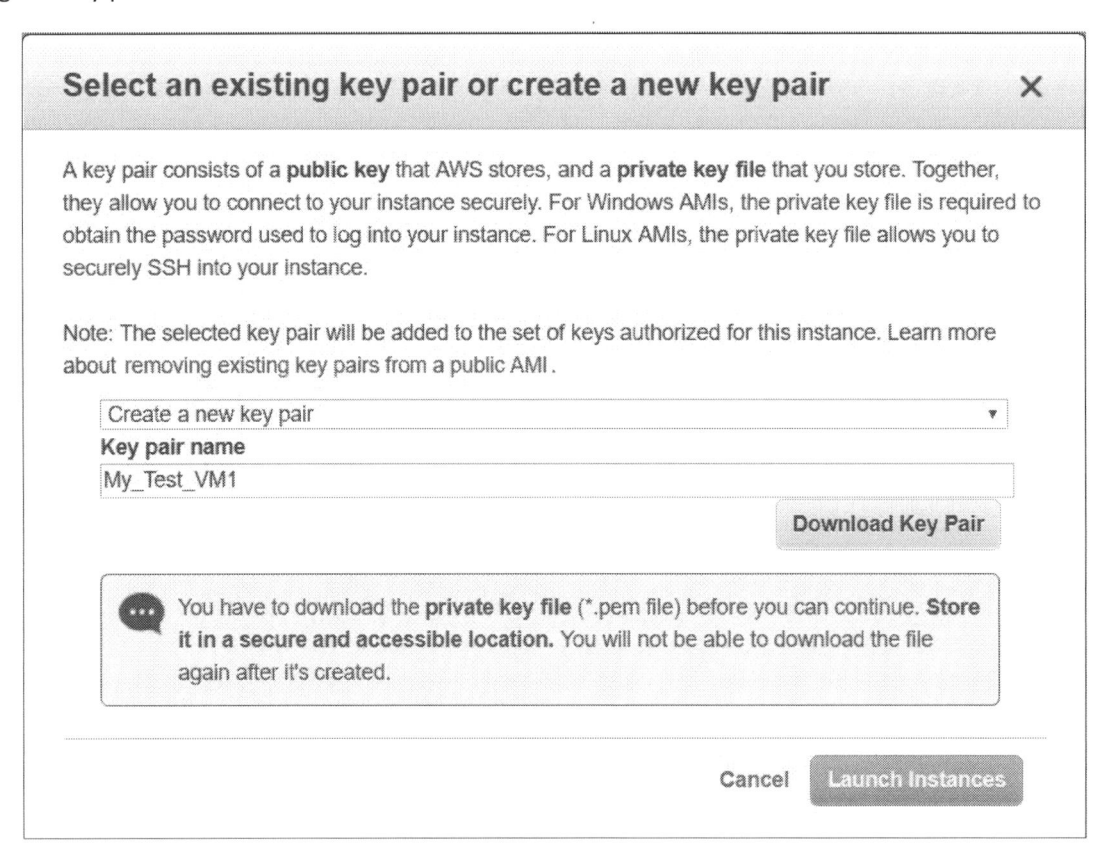

Select an existing key pair or create a new key pair ✕

A key pair consists of a **public key** that AWS stores, and a **private key file** that you store. Together, they allow you to connect to your instance securely. For Windows AMIs, the private key file is required to obtain the password used to log into your instance. For Linux AMIs, the private key file allows you to securely SSH into your instance.

Note: The selected key pair will be added to the set of keys authorized for this instance. Learn more about removing existing key pairs from a public AMI.

Create a new key pair
Key pair name
My_Test_VM1

Download Key Pair

💬 You have to download the **private key file** (*.pem file) before you can continue. **Store it in a secure and accessible location.** You will not be able to download the file again after it's created.

Cancel | **Launch Instances**

Note: If you are launching a Windows instance, then you will required the key pair to decrypt the administrator password.

Finally, click **Launch Instances** to complete the task. The instance creation process will start and your instance will be available in the EC2 instance list within a few minutes.

Practice lab exercise: Using the mentioned steps in this hands-on lab, create one more EC2 with the following settings:

- Instance type: T2 Micro/Ubuntu 16.04
- VPC name: My_Test_VPC
- Subnet name: Private_Subnet1
- Auto-assign Public IP: Disable
- Storage: Default
- Instance name: My_Test_VM2
- Security group name: My_Test_SG2
- Key pair name: My_Test_VM2

Note: We assume that you created the above-mentioned instance, as this instance will be used in few of the upcoming hands-on lab exercises.

10. Creating and Configuring Security Groups

Security groups act like virtual firewalls for the EC2 instances. A Security Group controls the incoming and outgoing traffic for the EC2 instances. You can attach multiple security groups, having different rules, to a single EC2 instance. You can modify the rules for a security group at any time as per your requirements.

Recommended links:
- Getting Started with AWS Security Groups.
  http://docs.aws.amazon.com/AWSEC2/latest/UserGuide/using-network-security.html

Quick facts about AWS Security Groups
1. By default, security groups allow all outbound traffic.
2. There are two types of AWS security groups: EC2-VPC and EC2-Classic.
3. Keep in mind that changing the outbound rules for an EC2-Classic security group is not allowed.
4. Security groups do not allow to create rules for denying access.
5. Security groups are stateful.
6. You can add and remove rules in your security groups whenever required.

Note: The scope of a security group is limited to a specific VPC in which you have created it. Means, if you have created a security group in a VPC called My_Test_VPC1, you cannot attach this security group to the instances of other VPC called My_Test_VPC2 (unless you have not configured the VPC Peering).

Creating a Security Group

To create a Security Group, you need to perform the following steps:

1. Select the **Security Groups** option in the EC2 dashboard.
2. Click the **Create Security Group** button.
3. On the **Create Security Group** window, specify the name, description, and VPC for which you want to create Security Group.
4. Select the **Inbound** tab and click **Add Rule** to add the desired rules.

Security Group Rules

A Security Group rule consists of the following options:

- **Type**: Select the protocol or service for which you want to create a rule. There are multiple major services such as HTTP, SSH, ICMP are already available to use for you. However, you can also select a Custom Protocol option if the service is not listed that you may wish to add.
- **Protocol**: Typically this either will be TCP or UDP.
- **Port range**: This option specifies the specific port or port range for the selected protocol or service.
- **Source**: There are three options in this drop-down:
    - **Custom**: Source can be either a specific IP address, specific another security group in your AWS cloud, or I can also be CIDR range.

- **Anywhere**: This allows to access the specified protocol or service worldwide.
- **My IP**: The protocol or service will only be allowed for your connected ISP's public IP. For SSH access, this is very handy and useful if you don't have further security (such as OpenVPN and Linux bastion for SSH access) in your AWS cloud.

5. Similarly, you can create, add, and customize the outbound rules. By default, all the outgoing traffic is allowed from anywhere.
6. For this demo, just create an SSH rule for your own Public IP and click **Create** to complete the task. Now, this rule can be attached to any instance available in the selected VPC.

Note: A security group can be referenced and linked with other security groups. However, if the two security groups belong to different VPCs, you will not be able to link those until you configure proper VPC peering.

Modifying Security Group

To modify a security group, just select the security group and click the **Actions** button to perform the available functions. Please refer the following figure for the available options.

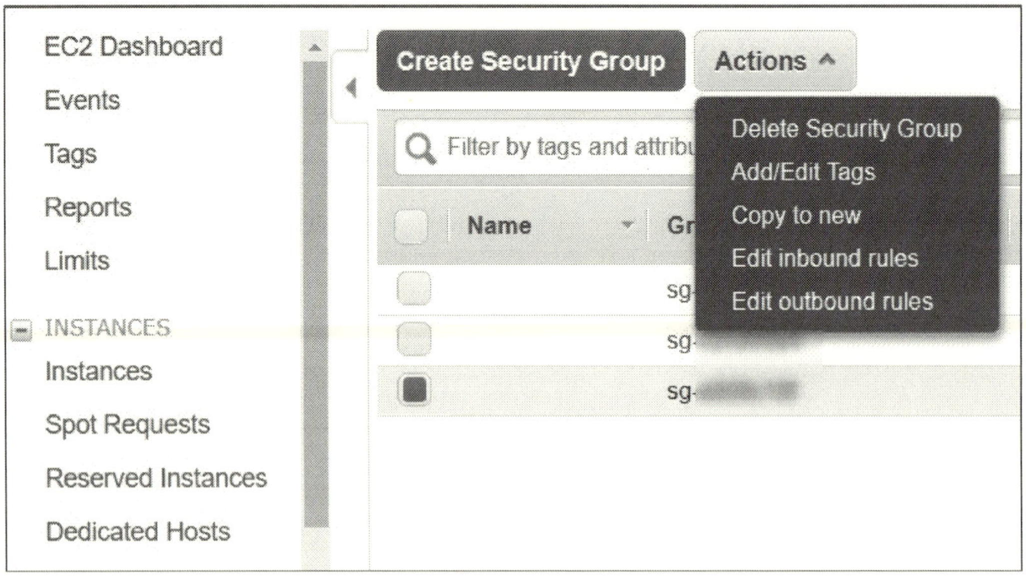
EC2 Dashboard
Events
Tags
Reports
Limits
INSTANCES
Instances
Spot Requests
Reserved Instances
Dedicated Hosts
Create Security Group
Actions
Filter by tags and attribu
Name
Gr
sg-
sg-
sg-
Delete Security Group
Add/Edit Tags
Copy to new
Edit inbound rules
Edit outbound rules

11. Managing Elastic IP Addresses

Elastic IPs are the manually assigned and fixed public IPs that you can assign to any AWS Instance. Instances running in the public subnet must have a valid public IP in order to access the internet. Depending on the public subnet's "Auto–Assign Public IP" setting, the instance may or may not get a public IP assigned automatically. Or you may need to fix a specific public IP for a specific instance – This can be done using the Elastic IPs.

Note: If you have assigned an Elastic IP to an instance and you stopped that instance, you will be charged for not using the associated Elastic IPs. As a free tier account, we recommend sticking with the dynamically provided IPs rather than associating EIPs manually.

Recommended links:

- AWS Elastic IPs Basics.
  http://docs.aws.amazon.com/AWSEC2/latest/UserGuide/elastic-ip-addresses-eip.html#eip-basics

---

Note: By default, all AWS accounts are limited to 5 Elastic IP addresses per region.

Elastic IP Pricing

Pricing for EIPs varies depending on the region you have selected. The following are the pricing for the Mumbai region. However, pricing for any AWS resource may slightly change at any time depending on the AWS policies and regulations.

- $0.00 for one Elastic IP address associated with a running instance
- $0.005 per additional Elastic IP address associated with a running instance per hour on a pro rata basis
- $0.005 per Elastic IP address not associated with a running instance per hour on a pro rata basis
- $0.00 per Elastic IP address remap for the first 100 remaps per month
- $0.10 per Elastic IP address remap for additional remaps over 100 per month

To know the pricing for other regions, please visit the EC2 official pricing page and select the appropriate region.
https://aws.amazon.com/ec2/pricing/on-demand/#Elastic_IP_Addresses

Assigning Elastic IPs to EC2 Instances

To assign an EIP, you need to perform the following steps:
1. In the EC2 Dashboard, click **Elastic IPs** in the left pane.
2. In the right pane, click **Allocate new address** option and then click **Allocate**.

3. Select and right-click the allocated EIP and then click the **Actions** menu.
4. Select the **Associate address** option as shown in the following figure.

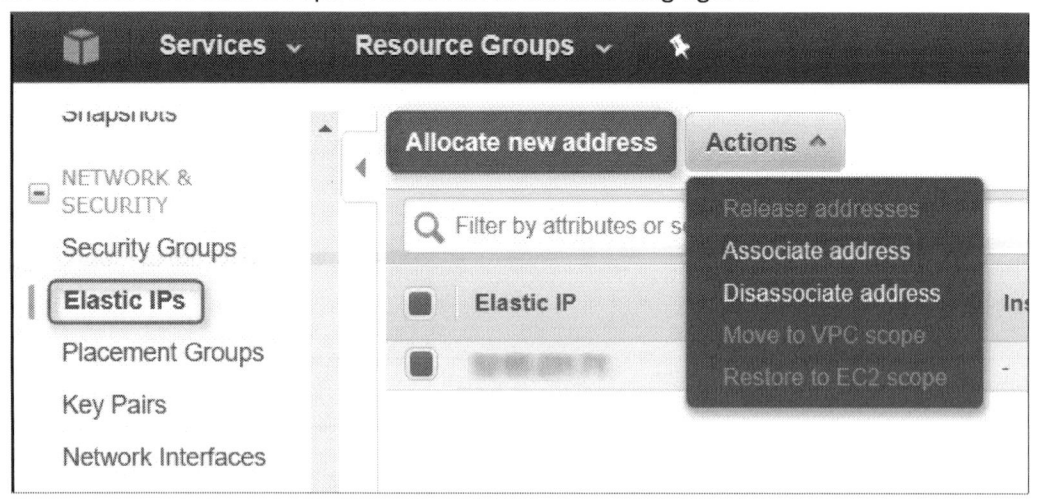

5. On the **Associate address** page, select the instance to which you want to allocate this EIP as shown in the following figure.

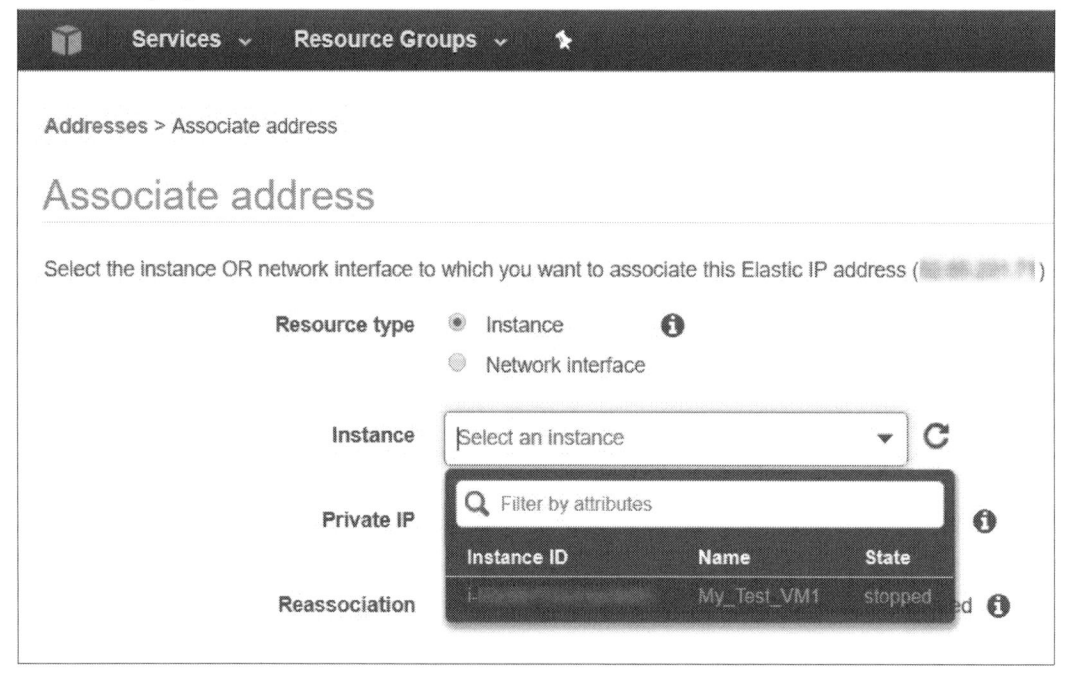

6. Finally, click the **Allocate** button to finish the task.

   Now, you have assigned an EIP to an EC2 instance. The EIP will remain same for this instance regardless whether you stop or start your EC2 instance.

   > *Question 05: Why do you need to assign an EIP when AWS allows an EC2 instance to get a dynamically assigned Public IP address?*

12. Connecting EC2 Linux Instance Using PuTTy, GitBash, and Console

In the previous sections, we have created an EC2 instance in the Public subnet and allowed SSH protocol for My IP. However, we need to attach an Elastic IP to the public instance in order to access it from outside network. There are various options and tools to access a Linux EC2 instance using SSH protocol. The most popular such tools are PuTTy and GitBash.

Here, we will just explain how to connect your EC2 Linux instances belonging to the Public subnet directly. In a later section, we will also explain how to access EC2 Linux instances more securely using OpenVPN and Linux Bastion servers.

Once you have launched the EC2 instances and assigned the Elastic IPs (if required), now you can connect your EC2 instance and perform the actions such as installing and configuring packages and services.

There are various methods that can be used to connect your EC2 Linux and Windows instances. Please visit the following link for more details, if you are interested.

- Connecting EC2 instances.
  http://docs.aws.amazon.com/AWSEC2/latest/UserGuide/AccessingInstances.html

You can connect an EC2 Linux instance using the following method:

1. Connect EC2 Linux Instance Using Web Browser
2. Connect EC2 Instance Using PuTTy
3. Connect EC2 Linux Instance Using GitBash

Connecting EC2 Instance Using Web Browser

In this method, you can use your Web Browser to connect an EC2 instance. However, you need to install the compatible version of Java for your browser. Few of the Web Browsers such as Chrome may not work properly for the EC2 Web Browser based connections. We recommend using Internet Explorer with a compatible version of Java installed. To connect your EC2 instance using a Web Browser, you need to perform the following steps:

1. First, download the compatible version of **Java** and install it properly. The process is pretty simple and should not be a challenge for a technical guy.
2. Once the Java is installed, make sure that you have also turned on the **Java Adds-on** in Internet Explorer as shown in the following figure.

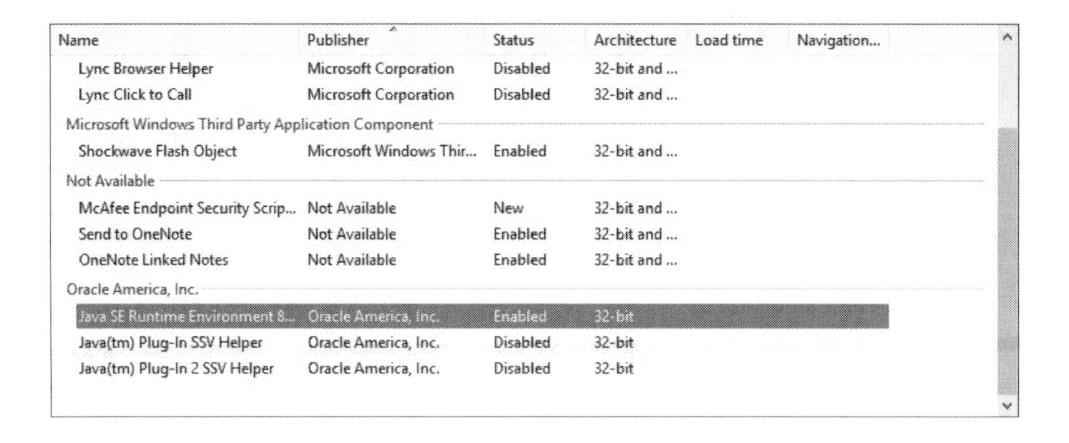

Name	Publisher	Status	Architecture	Load time	Navigation...
Lync Browser Helper	Microsoft Corporation	Disabled	32-bit and ...		
Lync Click to Call	Microsoft Corporation	Disabled	32-bit and ...		
Microsoft Windows Third Party Application Component					
Shockwave Flash Object	Microsoft Windows Thir...	Enabled	32-bit and ...		
Not Available					
McAfee Endpoint Security Scrip...	Not Available	New	32-bit and ...		
Send to OneNote	Not Available	Enabled	32-bit and ...		
OneNote Linked Notes	Not Available	Enabled	32-bit and ...		
Oracle America, Inc.					
Java SE Runtime Environment 8...	Oracle America, Inc.	Enabled	32-bit		
Java(tm) Plug-In SSV Helper	Oracle America, Inc.	Disabled	32-bit		
Java(tm) Plug-In 2 SSV Helper	Oracle America, Inc.	Disabled	32-bit		

3. Now, select and right-click your EC2 instance and then click **Connect**.
4. On the **Connect To Your Instance** window, select **A Java SSH Client Directly** option.
5. Browse and select the key pair associated with this instance, and then click **Launch SSH Client** as shown in the following figure.

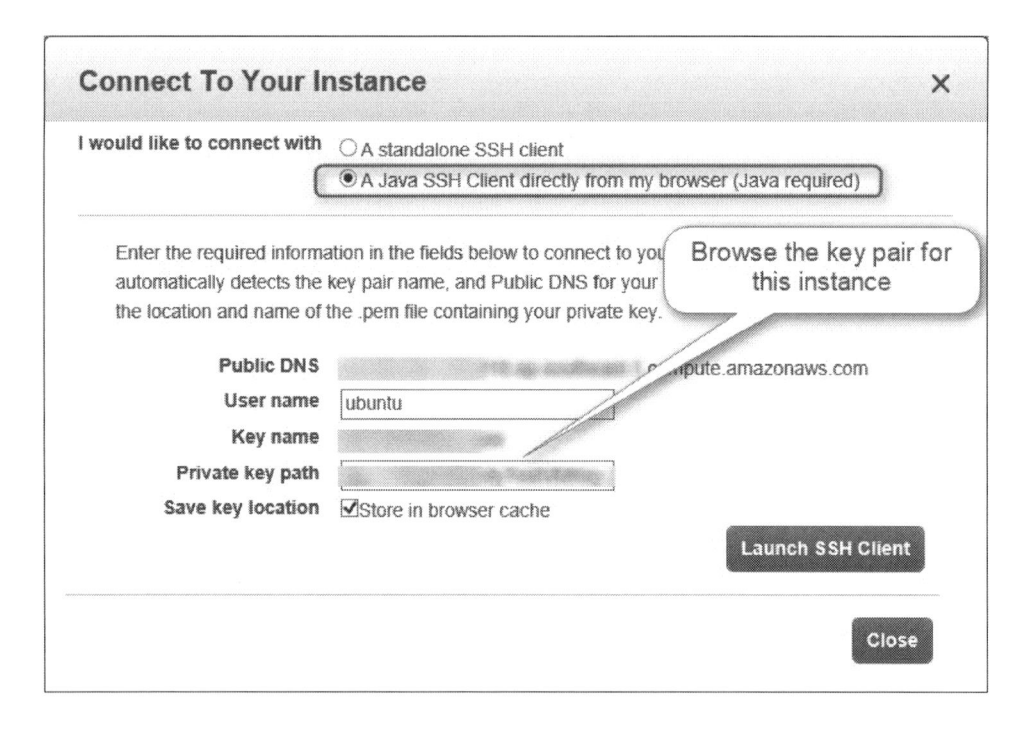

6. A new terminal console will be displayed and you will get the EC2 terminal console, where you can perform the desired tasks for your EC2 instance as shown in the following figure.

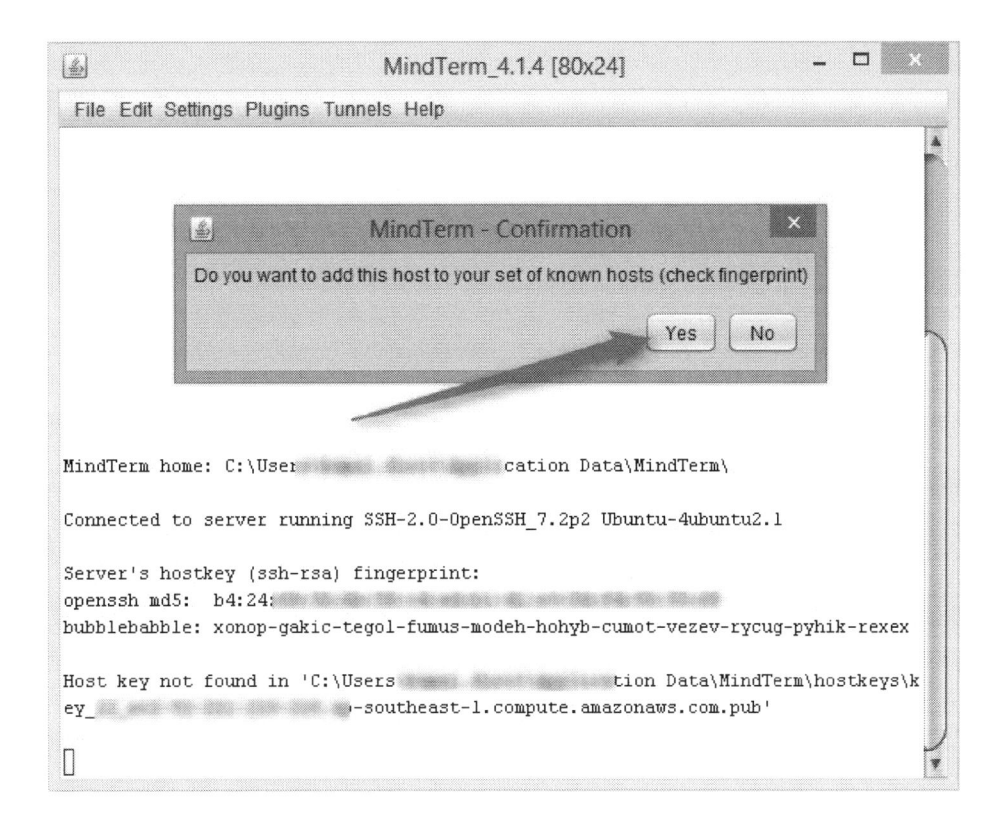

Connecting EC2 Linux Instance Using PuTTY

PuTTY is the most popular tool to access SSH and other remote connections such as Telnet. Most of the AWS Administrators use PuTTY to connect EC2 Linux instances. In this method, we are going to explain how to use PuTTY to connect your EC2 instances.

First, you need to download and install PuTTY and PuTTYgen tools on your local system. It's a pretty straightforward process and you should be able to do it very easily.

- Download PuTTY and PuTTYgen Tools.
  http://www.chiark.greenend.org.uk/~sgtatham/putty/latest.html

> *PuTTYgen allows you to convert .pem key format into .ppk key format. By default, the EC2 SSH key pair extension is .pem but PuTTY require .ppk key pair extension. So you need to convert .pem key pair to .ppk format before to use with PuTTY.*

1. Once you have downloaded and installed the above-mentioned tools, open the PuTTYgen console.
2. Click **Load** and browse the key pair, in the browse window, select the **File Types** as **All** and then select the **.pem** file.
3. Click **Load** to save the key pair file from .pem to .ppk. Optionally, you may also set the passphrase for this converting key for more security.

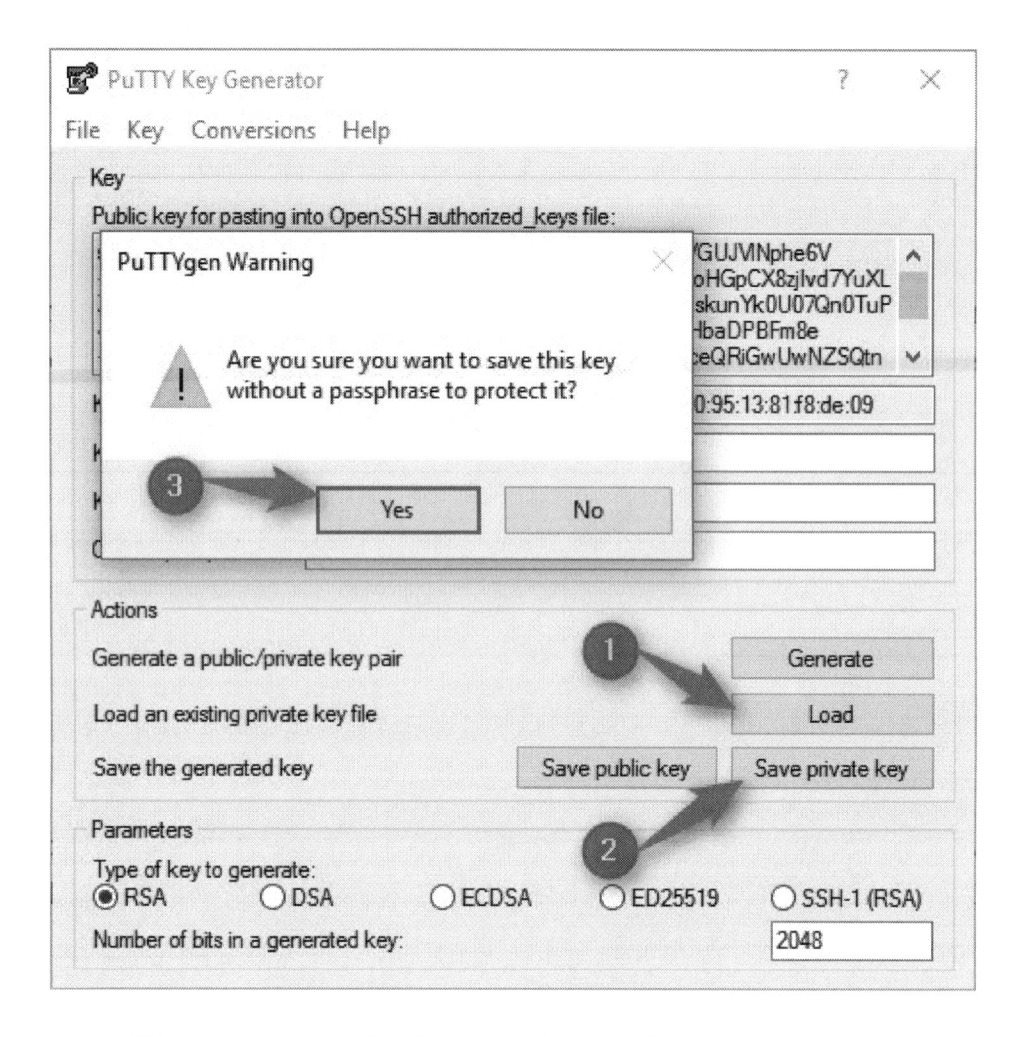

4. Now, open the PuTTY tool and type the Public IP or DNS name of your EC2 instance.

Default EC2 Instance Users

The default username for the EC2 instances may vary depending on the AMI type and OS platform you have selected.

The following table describes the default usernames for different AWS AMI types.

Sr. No.	AMI Type	Default User
1	Amazon	ec2-user
2	Ubuntu	ubuntu
3	RHEL	ec2-user or root
4	CentOS	centos
5	Suse	ec2-user or root
6	Debian	admin
7	Fedora	fedora

5. Continue from the previous step and scroll down in the left pane, expand the **SSH** section and select the **Auth** option.
6. Browse and select the converted key pair (extension .ppk) and then click **Open** to open the SSH console.

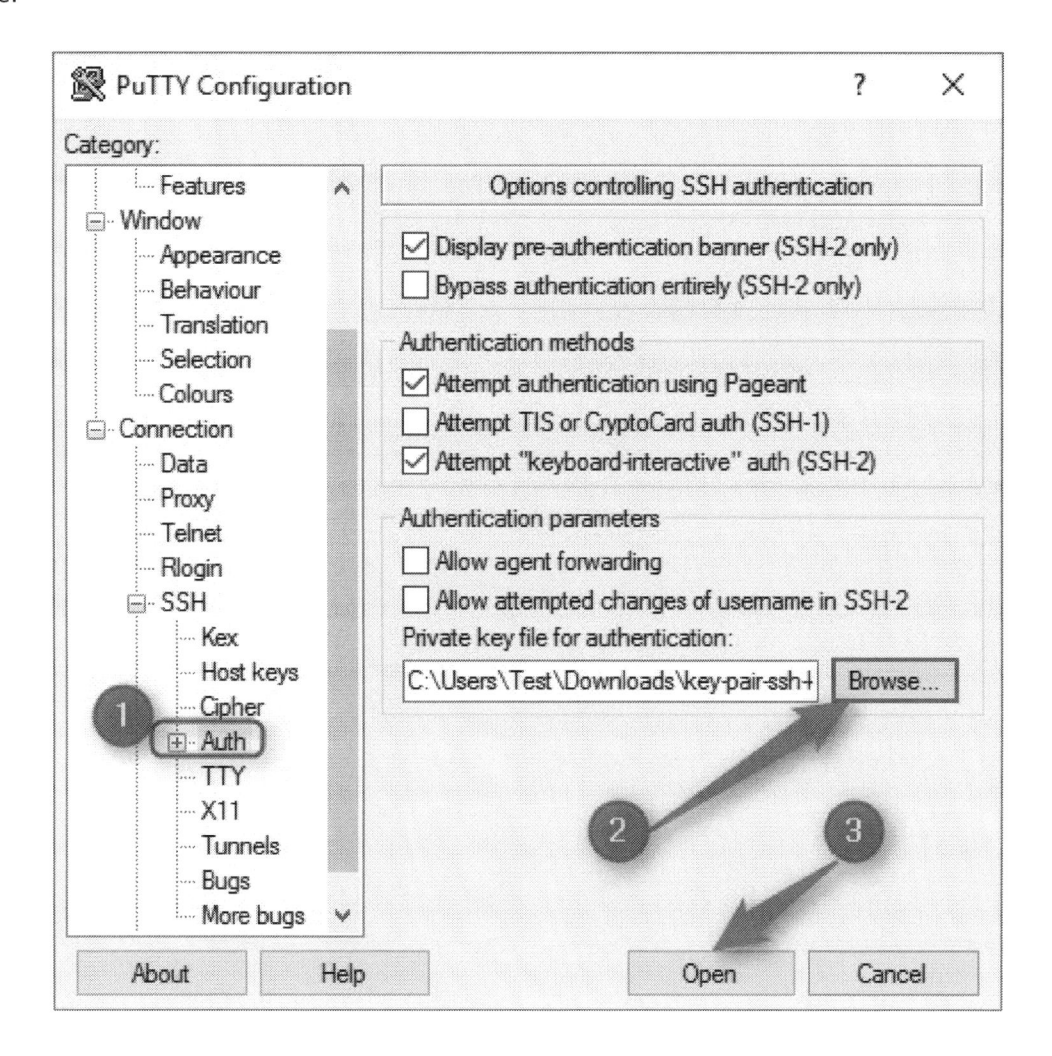

A **Security Alert** will be displayed, better to read it before clicking **Yes** to proceed. Now, you should be able to access terminal of an EC2 instance using the PuTTy tool.

Connecting EC2 Instance Using GitBash

Apart from the above-mentioned methods to connect your EC2 instances, there are few more tools such as GitBash that you can use to connect EC2 Linux instances. GitBash is my favorite tool for connecting EC2 Linux instances. You can download the GitBash for your system using the following link.

- Download Gitbash for Windows/MAC/Linux
  https://git-scm.com/downloads

You just need to download and install it, which is pretty simple. You can install GitBash for Windows as well for Mac OS.

1. For the Windows version of GitBash, double-click the setup file and just follow the on-screen installation instructions.

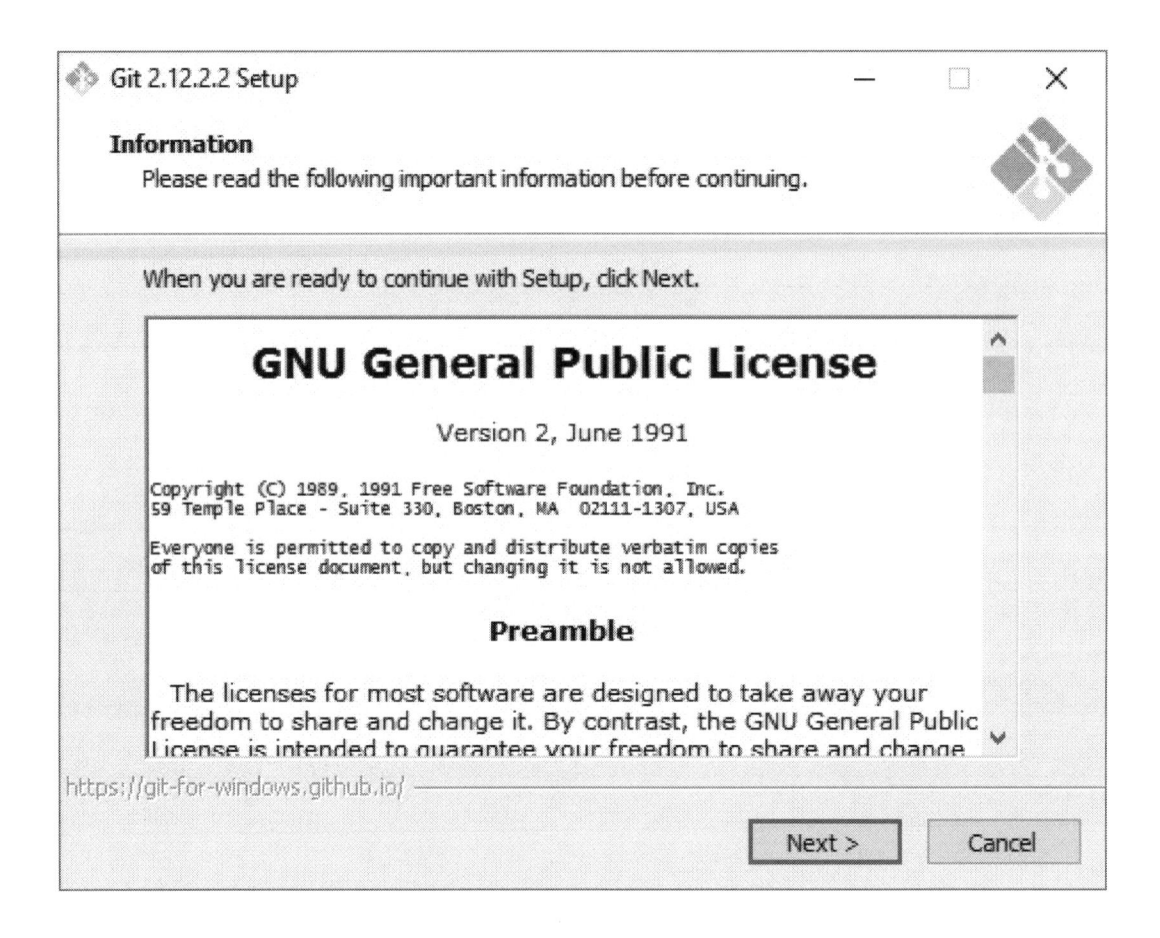

2. Once the GitBash tool is installed, open it and go the directory where you have saved the key pair file.
3. On the GitBash terminal, paste the EC2 instance's public IP address or domain name in the following format:

    $ ssh -i "ec2-key-pair-name.pem" user@ec2-public-ip-address
    $ ssh -i "ec2-key-pair-name.pem" user@ec2-domain-name

4. Here, **ssh** is the command, **-i** means importing SSH key, **ec2-key-pair-name.pem** is the key pair name. For example, to connect an Ubuntu EC2 instance using its public IP, let's have a look at the following figure.

Hope, you are now familiar with the various options that can be used to connect an EC2 Linux instance using SSH protocol.

13. Connecting Private Instance using SSH Agent Forwarding

This is an optional exercise, you should only proceed if you have created a second test VM named as My_Test_VM2 as mentioned in a previous lab exercise.

We have two instances: **My_Test_VM1** belongs to a public subnet and has a public IP and My_Test_VM2 belongs to a private subnet and does not have any public IP address associated. There are various methods to connect your private EC2 instance from your local machine such as using OpenVPN, Bastion and SSH Agent Forwarding tool.

Here, we will only explain how to access a private EC2 instance using the SSH agent forwarding service. The rest have been covered in the separate sections. The SSH agent forward service allows you to carry the key pair file of an instance to another private or public instance.

Allow SSH connection from one security group to another security group

You can allow one security group to allow or deny specific protocol or port to another security group in your VPC. If the two security groups belong to different VPCs, then first you need to establish the VPC peering. In our scenario, My_Test_VM1 is already allowed SSH incoming connection using the public IP address. But, we have not assigned any public IP for My_Test_VM2 instance, so we need to allow SSH incoming connection for My_Test_VM2 instance's security group (My_Test_SG2) for public instance's (My_Test_VM1) security group (My_Test_SG1). For this, let's follow us and perform the following steps:

1. Select the **Security Groups** in the EC2 dashboard.
2. Copy the SG ID of the **My_Test_SG1** security group.
3. Select the **My_Test_SG2** security group.
4. Select the **Inbound** tab and click **Edit** to edit the rule.
5. In the **Source** drop-down list, select **Custom** and paste the group id of the **My_Test_SG1** security group.

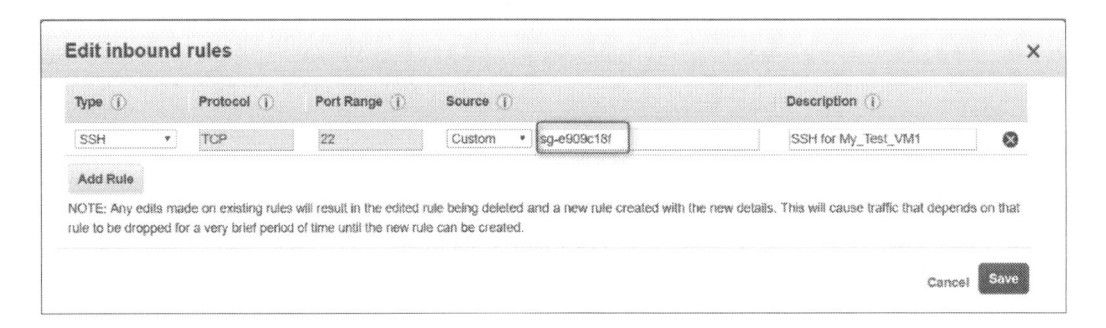

6. Finally, click the **Save** button.

Access SSH using SSH Agent Forwarding

Now, open the GitBash tool from the location where you have saved your key pairs. Or, open GitBash and navigate to the location where your SSH pem key is stored. Optionally, you can also give the absolute path with **-i <key-path>** option while connecting your EC2 instance.

1. Execute the following command to start the SSH forward agent service
- $eval (ssh-agent)
2. Add the key pairs you want to use with SSH forward agent using the following commands.
- $ssh-add -k My_Test_VM1
- $ssh-add -k My_Test_VM2
3. Connect the public instance with the agent forward option using the following command.
- $ssh -A ubuntu@<public-instance-ip-address>
4. You will be connected to your public instance that is My_Test_VM1. From this instance, just type the following command to connect your internal private instance that is My_Test_VM2.
- $ ssh ubuntu@<internal-instance-private-ip>
5. You should be able to connect your private instance as shown in the following figure.

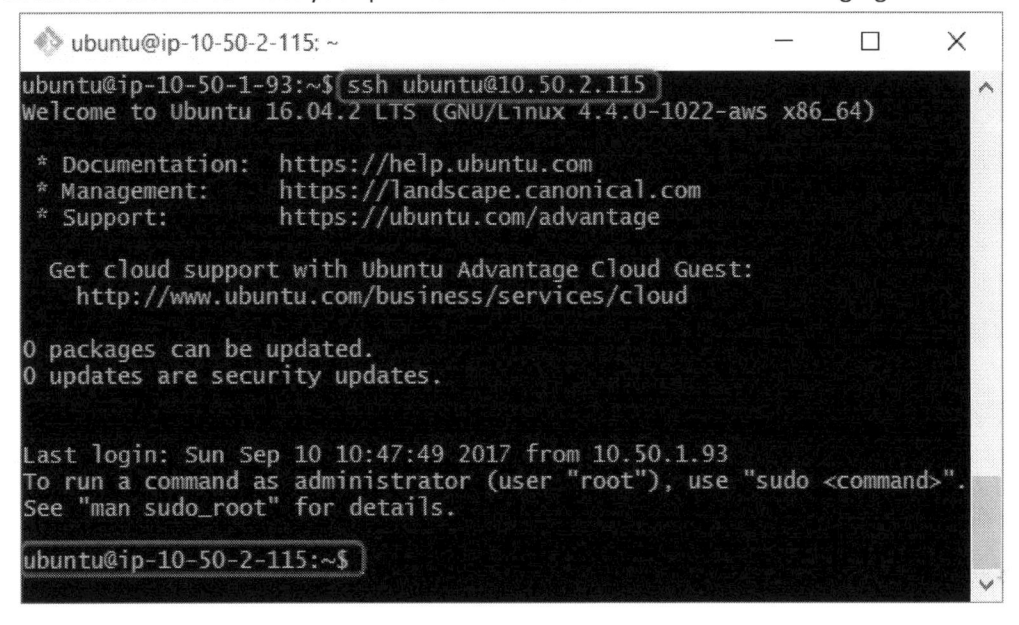

```
ubuntu@ip-10-50-1-93:~$ ssh ubuntu@10.50.2.115
Welcome to Ubuntu 16.04.2 LTS (GNU/Linux 4.4.0-1022-aws x86_64)

 * Documentation:  https://help.ubuntu.com
 * Management:     https://landscape.canonical.com
 * Support:        https://ubuntu.com/advantage

  Get cloud support with Ubuntu Advantage Cloud Guest:
    http://www.ubuntu.com/business/services/cloud

0 packages can be updated.
0 updates are security updates.


Last login: Sun Sep 10 10:47:49 2017 from 10.50.1.93
To run a command as administrator (user "root"), use "sudo <command>".
See "man sudo_root" for details.

ubuntu@ip-10-50-2-115:~$
```

Note: We highly recommend to always use OpenVPN and Bastion server as a secure channel to connect your production servers. OpenVPN server implementation is covered in a later section.

14. Accessing EC2 Linux Instance Using RDP with GUI Interface

By default, EC2 Linux instances have only the CLI interface to work with them. However, sometimes, you may need to work with GUI interface for a few reasons. But, before you could access your EC2 Linux instance with graphical interface, you need to install the graphical packages and enable the GUI remote access tool such as RDP to access it. Although, you can use various Graphical tools to work with the EC2 Linux instances. These tools include MATE, TigerVNC and many more.

Here, we will explain you how to install graphical packages on an Ubuntu EC2 Linux instance and access remotely it using the RDP.

My favorite GUI Ubuntu Desktop interface is MATE. So, we will discuss here how to access an Ubuntu-based EC2 Linux instance using the MATE graphical interface.

Installing MATE Desktop Environment in EC2 Ubuntu Instance

The following steps need to be followed to install MATE Desktop on an Ubuntu system:

1. Execute the following command to add the MATE repository
- *$ sudo apt-add-repository ppa:ubuntu-mate-dev/xenial-mate*
2. Run the following commands to update the repository and install the MATE packages
- *$ sudo apt-get update*
- *$ sudo apt-get install mate*
3. Run the following command to apply any of the available upgraded packages on your system.
- *$ sudo apt-get dist-upgrade*

> *Note: Please don't upgrade your production server with the **dist-upgrade** command. We highly recommend to test it with your testing, QA, or Staging server first and then proceed for the production servers, (if required).*

4. It will take around 10-12 minutes to complete and upgrade the package installation process.
5. If you are using a local Ubuntu system, you can reboot the system, choose the MATE desktop as your environment and start using it. Since, we are focusing on EC2 instances, we need to enable a Remote Desktop method such as VNC or RDP.
6. Once the MATE desktop environment is ready, install the XRDP packages to enable RDP for your Ubuntu instance. For this, just execute the following command.
- *$ sudo apt-get install xrdp -y*
7. Since by default, a Linux EC2 instance does not have any user password set. Here, you need to set the password for your instance user. For Ubuntu VM, the default username is Ubuntu. Execute the commands mentioned in the following figure to set the desired password for your ubuntu user.

```
ubuntu@ip-10-50-1-93:~$ sudo passwd ubuntu
Enter new UNIX password:
Retype new UNIX password:
passwd: password updated successfully
ubuntu@ip-10-50-1-93:~$
```

8. Now, your EC2 instance is ready to be accessed over the network using the GUI interface. However, you need to allow the incoming protocol and port (in security group) for the method you wish to use, in this case, RDP (port-3389).

Allow RDP Rule in the Security Group

We will not discuss security group in detail here as we have already discussed it in a previous section. To modify the security group, perform the following steps:

1. Open the security group that is attached to your Ubuntu instance.
2. Select the **Inbound** tab and then click **Edit** to edit the rules.
3. In the **Edit inbound rules** window, set the values as shown in the following figure.

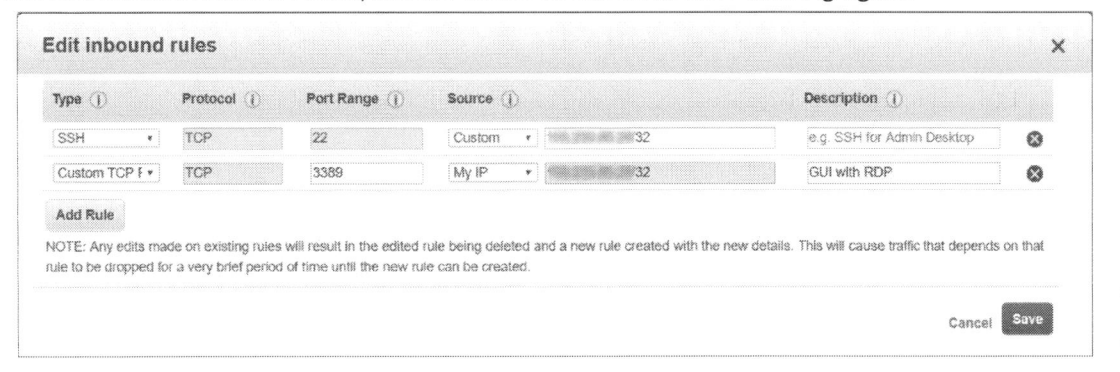

Connecting EC2 Ubuntu using MSTSC (RDP)

1. Once the security group is configured, open the **MSTSC** dialog box on a Window machine.
2. Type the public IP or public DNS name of your instance and click **Connect**.
3. On the **Login to xrdp dialog** box as shown in the following figure, type the username and password to connect it.

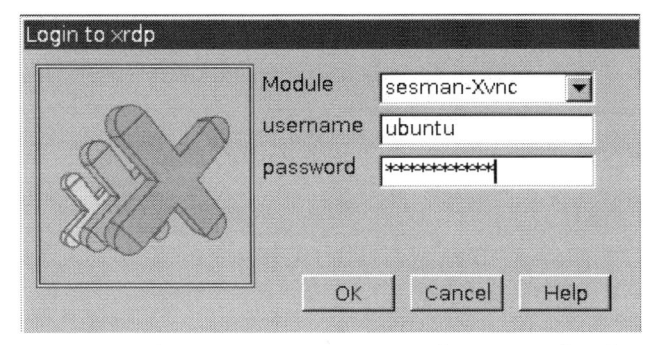

4. You should be able to access EC2 Ubuntu Linux instance with GUI graphical interface using RDP.

15. Recovering and connecting EC2 instances if the SSH key is lost

We know that EC2 Linux instances are accessible through the private SSH keys (.pem keys), by default. However, SSH is allowed but you cannot use SSH password authentication to access Linux instance as it is disabled by default. So, what would happen if you lose the private key of your EC2 Linux instance? Here are few things that you should know before to proceed to this topic:

- You cannot recover the private key for Linux instance if you have chosen **Root** Device Type as **Instance Store**.
- You can connect and access your Linux instance, in case of private key lost and you have chosen **Root** Device Type as **EBS Store**.

Recommended links:

- Instance Store vs EBS Store Volumes
- https://aws.amazon.com/premiumsupport/knowledge-center/instance-store-vs-ebs

Keeping the above guidelines in the mind, let's begin the whole process "How can we connect a Linux Instance, if we lost the private key or .pem key file?

You need to perform the following steps in order to connect an EC2 Linux instance, if the private key is lost:

1. Stop your EC2 Linux Instance.
2. Detach the Root Volume attached to your EC2 Linux instance.
3. Launch a new Temporary Linux Instance with same AMI type and configuration.
4. Attach the Root Volume (that you have just detached from your inaccessible EC2 Linux instance) to New Instance
5. Modify the authorized_keys File
6. Reattach the Root Volume to the Original Instance
7. Start and Connect the Original Instance with the New Private Key

Before starting this exercise, note down the following key information of your instance:

- Instance ID, AMI ID, and Availability Zone of original Instance
- Name of the Root Device volume such as /dev/sda1
- Volume ID of Root Volume

Stopping Original EC2 Linux Instance

Stopping an EC2 instance is pretty simple, you just need to perform the following steps:

1. Login to AWS console, navigate to the EC2 dashboard, and select the instance.
2. Right-click instance and select **Instance State** and then select **Stop** to stop it.

Launching New Temporary Instance

In this task, we need to launch a new EC2 instance with the exact same settings and **in the same availability zone**. Refer the following information which you need to provide while creating a new instance.

- **Instance Name**: Give a Temporary Name
- **AMI**: Select the same as selected for the original instance
- **Security Group**: Select the same Security Group that is attached to the original instance
- **Key pair**: Create a new key pair and named it as new-key-pair.pem as shown in the following figure, and store it in the safe location.

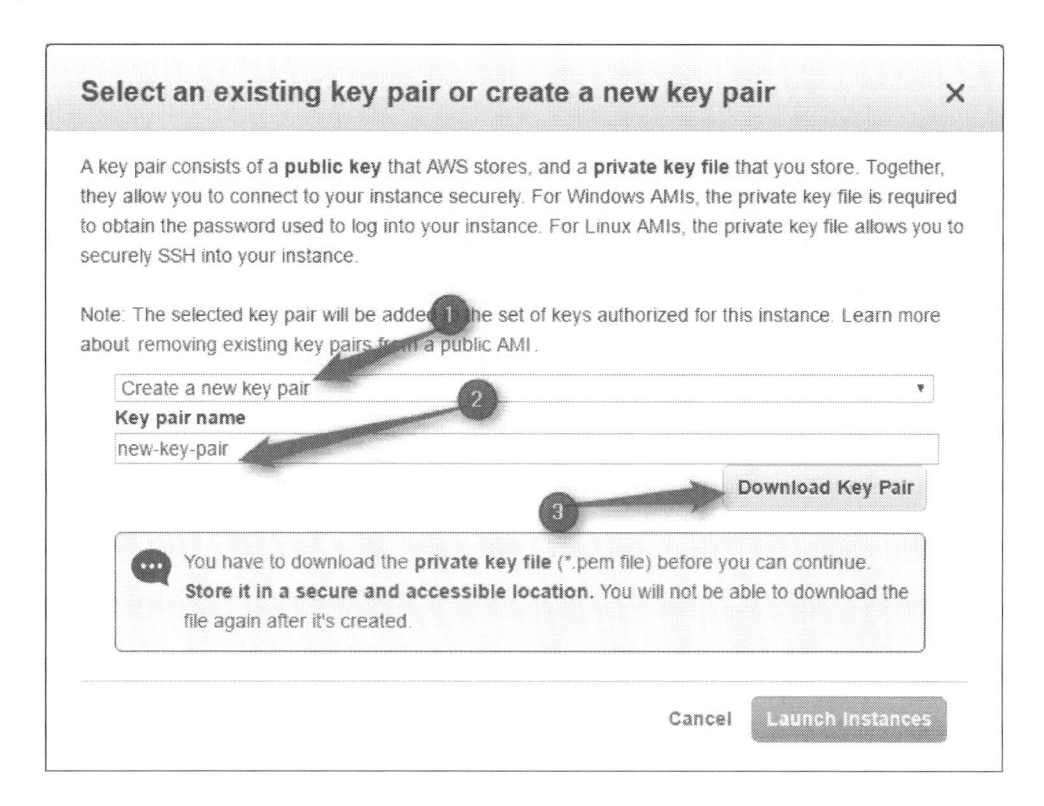

![Select an existing key pair or create a new key pair dialog showing: Create a new key pair option selected, Key pair name "new-key-pair", and a Download Key Pair button with a warning that the private key file (*.pem file) must be downloaded before continuing. Cancel and Launch Instances buttons at the bottom.]

Detaching Root Volume from Original Instance

To detach the root volume from the instance of which you lost the .pem key, you need to perform the following steps:

1. Select the **Volumes** section in the left pane, type the volume ID of root volume of the original instance in the search box.
2. Select the **Root Volume**, click **Actions** and then select **Detach Volume** to detach it as shown in the following figure.

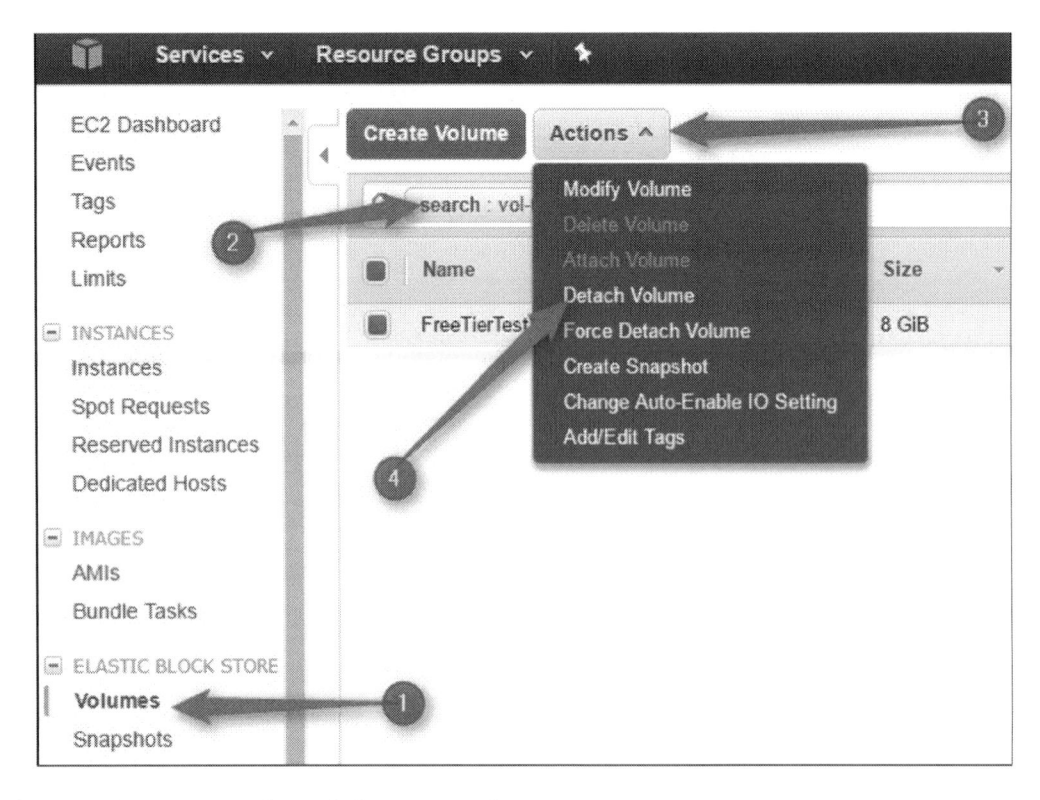

3. On the **Warning** message box, click **Yes Detach**.

Attaching Root Volume to Temporary Instance

We assume that the Root Volume is still selected that you have detached in the previous steps. To attach the Root Volume to the (newly launched) Temporary instance, you need to perform the following steps:

1. Click the **Actions** menu and then select **Attach Volume** to attach a volume.
2. In the **Attach Volume** dialog box, type new instance name "**Temporary**" in the **Instance name** box. Alternatively, you can also type instance ID (of the temporary launched instance) if you remember or noted-down it somewhere.
3. Note down the new volume device name (such as /dev/sdf) and then click **Attach** to proceed.

Note: Make sure that new (temporary) instance and attaching volume both are in the same availability zone.

Attach Volume

Volume: vol-088cf4880f919c7b0 (FreeTierTestVM) in ap-southeast-1b
Instance: i-0fb9................... in ap-southeast-1b
Device: /dev/sdf
Linux Devices: /dev/sdf through /dev/sdp

Note: Newer Linux kernels may rename your devices to /dev/xvdf through /dev/xvdp internally.

Question 06: If your EC2 instance belongs to availability zone A and your EBS volume belongs to availability zone B, then you cannot attach your EBS volume to any of the EC2 instances belonging to the availability zone A. Think why?

Mounting Attached Volume

To mount the attached volume, you need to perform the following steps:

1. Select and right-click the new instance (Temporary) and open its console. We assume that the volume name was /dev/sdf.
2. Use the **lsblk** command to view the partitions and note down the newly attached volume name such as /dev/xvdf1.
3. Use the following commands to create a mount point named as /tempvol and mount the attached volume under it.
- *$lsblk*
- *$sudo mkdir /tempvol*
- *$sudo mount /dev/xvdf1 /tempvol*

```
ubuntu@ip-172-31-26-84:~$ lsblk
NAME    MAJ:MIN RM SIZE RO TYPE MOUNTPOINT
xvda    202:0    0   8G  0 disk
└─xvda1 202:1    0   8G  0 part /
xvdf    202:80   0   8G  0 disk
└─xvdf1 202:81   0   8G  0 part
ubuntu@ip-172-31-26-84:~$ sudo mkdir /tempvol
ubuntu@ip-172-31-26-84:~$ sudo mount /dev/xvdf1 /tempvol
ubuntu@ip-172-31-26-84:~$
```

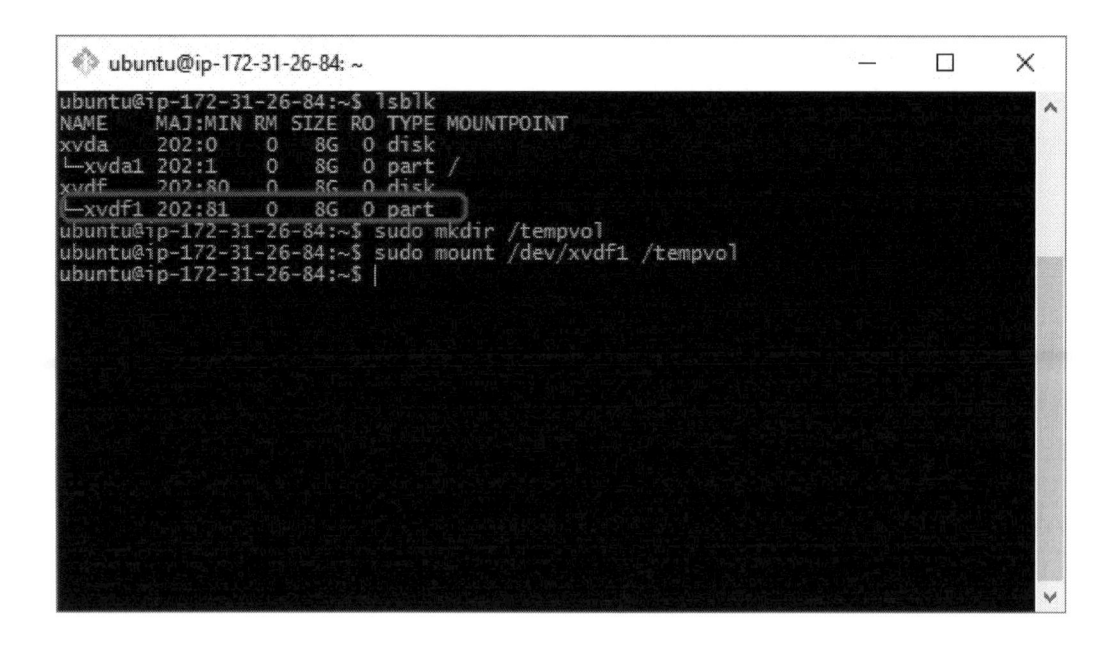

Note: The volume may appear with the different name depending on the Linux variant you use. For this demo, it shows as /dev/xvdf1.

Modifying the authorized_keys File and Updating the New Private Key

Here, we will copy the SSH key file of the connected instance (temporary) to the user's SSH authorized_keys file of the mounted volume. For this, you need to perform the following steps:

1. Use the following command to update the new key pair and to access the original instance:
   - *$cp .ssh/authorized_keys /tempvol/home/ubuntu/.ssh/authorized_keys*
2. If the above command failed to execute, you may need to change the permission of /home/user/.ssh file with write permission. For this, execute the following command:
   - *$sudo chmod 757 /tempvol/home/ubuntu/.ssh/authorized_keys*
3. Once the file is copied, you may revert back the permission as 755.

Note: The username may vary depending on your EC2 instance variant. For example, ubuntu for Ubuntu Linux and ec2-user for Amazon Linux.

4. Next, unmount the attached volume using the following command as shown in the below figure.
   - *$sudo umount /tempvol*

```
ubuntu@ip-172-31-26-84:~$ sudo cp .ssh/authorized_keys /tempvol/home/ubuntu/.ssh
/authorized_keys
ubuntu@ip-172-31-26-84:~$ sudo ls -l /tempvol/home/ubuntu/.ssh/
total 4
-rw------- 1 ubuntu ubuntu 394 Apr 24 14:51 authorized_keys
ubuntu@ip-172-31-26-84:~$ sudo umount /tempvol
ubuntu@ip-172-31-26-84:~$
```

Detaching Volume from Temporary Instance and Re-attaching With the Original Instance

Now, you are almost done the required changes. Just detach the old root volume from the temporary instance and re-attach it with the original instance. For this, perform the following steps:

1. Go to the **Volumes** section, select the root volume (of the original instance), click **Actions** and select **Detach Volume** to detach volume.
2. Once the volume is detached, click again **Actions**, and select **Attach Volume** to attach it.
3. In the **Attach Volume** window, type the original instance name or ID, change the volume name as **/dev/sda1** (mandatory) and then click **Attach** as shown in the following figure.

Attach Volume

Volume	ⓘ	vol-088cf4880f919c7b0 (FreeTierTestVM) in ap-southeast-1b
Instance	ⓘ	i-02d892f28b501d2d8 in ap-southeast-1b
Device	ⓘ	/dev/sda1
		Linux Devices: /dev/sdf through /dev/sdp

Note: Newer Linux kernels may rename your devices to /dev/xvdf through /dev/xvdp internally, even wh

Connect your EC2 Linux Instance (Original Instance) With the New Private Key

Now, you have done all the necessary tasks to recover your lost key pair. You can connect the original instance with the newly created private key. For this, start the original instance and connect it with the key pair you created for Temporary instance that is in our case: new-key-pair.pem.

You should be able to access and connect EC2 Linux instance as shown in the following figure.

```
Test@DESKTOP-32IBHJ3 MINGW64 ~/Downloads
onaws.com"new-key-pair.pem" ubuntu@ec2-              ap-southeast-1.compute.amazo
Welcome to Ubuntu 16.04.2 LTS (GNU/Linux 4.4.0-1013-aws x86_64)

 * Documentation:  https://help.ubuntu.com
 * Management:     https://landscape.canonical.com
 * Support:        https://ubuntu.com/advantage

  Get cloud support with Ubuntu Advantage Cloud Guest:
    http://www.ubuntu.com/business/services/cloud

2 packages can be updated.
0 updates are security updates.


Last login: Mon Apr 24 15:06:28 2017 from
To run a command as administrator (user "root"), use "sudo <command>".
See "man sudo_root" for details.

ubuntu@ip-172-31-27-217:~$
```

That's all you need to do to connect EC2 Linux instance if the private key is lost.

Alternative and Simple Way to Recover your EC2 Instance of which Key Pair is Lost

Note: Alternatively, you can create an AMI of your EC2 instance of which you lost the key pair. Launch a new EC2 instance with the same VPC, same Subnet, same configuration, and same Security group. Just create a new key pair while launching the new EC2 instance and you would be able to access your EC2 instance with the new key pair.

The only problem with this method is that your new EC2 instance will have a different private IP address. Some of the applications are deeply integrated with the private IP addresses during their configuration. Such applications may not work as you may need to replace the private IP address in each and every configuration file of your application, which might be a time-consuming and tedious job. Hence, above method makes more sense.

16. Changing Instance Type, Security Groups, Volumes & Other Settings

It is always recommended to plan well before to launch an instance. You should plan about the following things before to launch an EC2 instance:

- Instance type that suits your application
- VPC name in which the instance will be launched
- Subnet name and type (private or public)
- Security group name and rules
- SSH key you want to use

However, the good thing in the cloud is that you have the flexibility to upgrade and downgrade servers as per your requirement. But, you may need to stop your instance to change few settings which will finally cause the downtime for the production servers. Here, we will explain the major settings that you may wish to change for an EC2 instance.

Changing instance type

Sometimes you may wish/need to upgrade/downgrade the hardware resources (RAM and vCPU) for an instance. For example, suppose you have chosen the T2.Large instance type for your xyz application. But later, you realize that your application is not using so much resources and you are paying more than you need. Here, you can downgrade your instance form T2.Large to T2.Small instance type. For this, first make sure that your instance is stopped and then perform the following steps:

1. Select your instance, click **Actions** and navigate to the **Change Instance Type** as shown in the following figure.

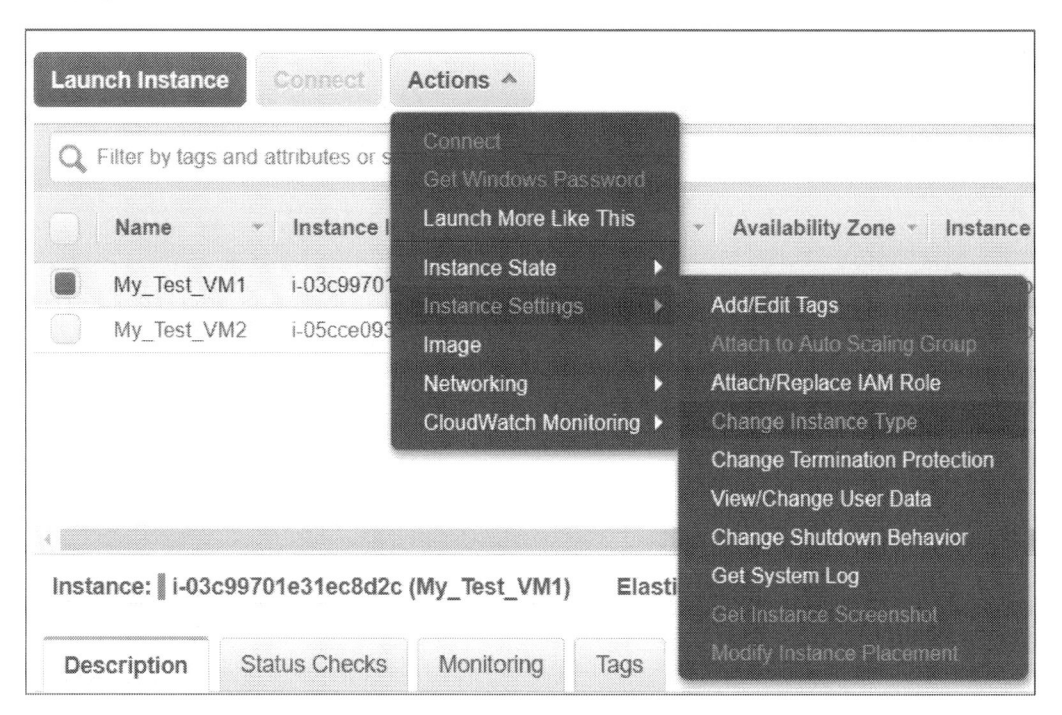

2. On the **Change Instance Type** window, as shown in the following figure, select the instance type you may wish to use, and then click **Apply**.

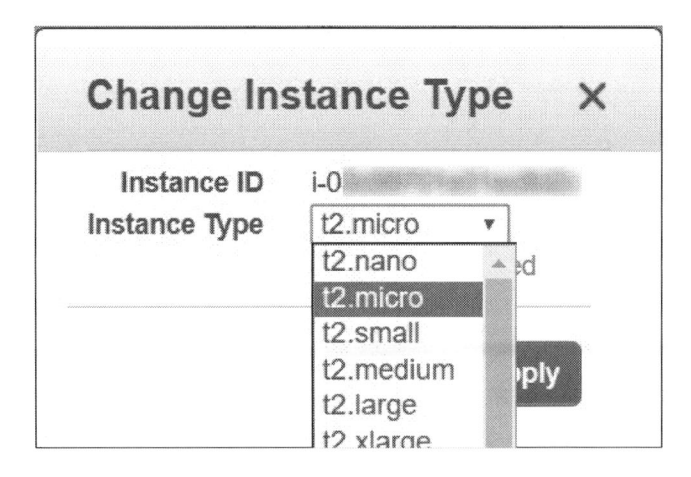

Accidental Termination Protection

A mistake can be made by anyone, anytime, we should always be ready with a mitigation plan to reduce the risk as much as possible. EC2 termination means simply destroying your EC2 instance permanently. Once you click the terminate button and confirm the Yes, you will no longer be able to recover that instance and its data. Even, AWS will not be able to help you in recovering the terminated instance. We recommend you to enable Termination Protection for all your critical instances.

For this you need to perform the following steps:

1. Select the instance for which you want to enable Termination Protection and then click **Actions**.
2. Navigate to the **Change Termination Protection** option as shown in the following figure.

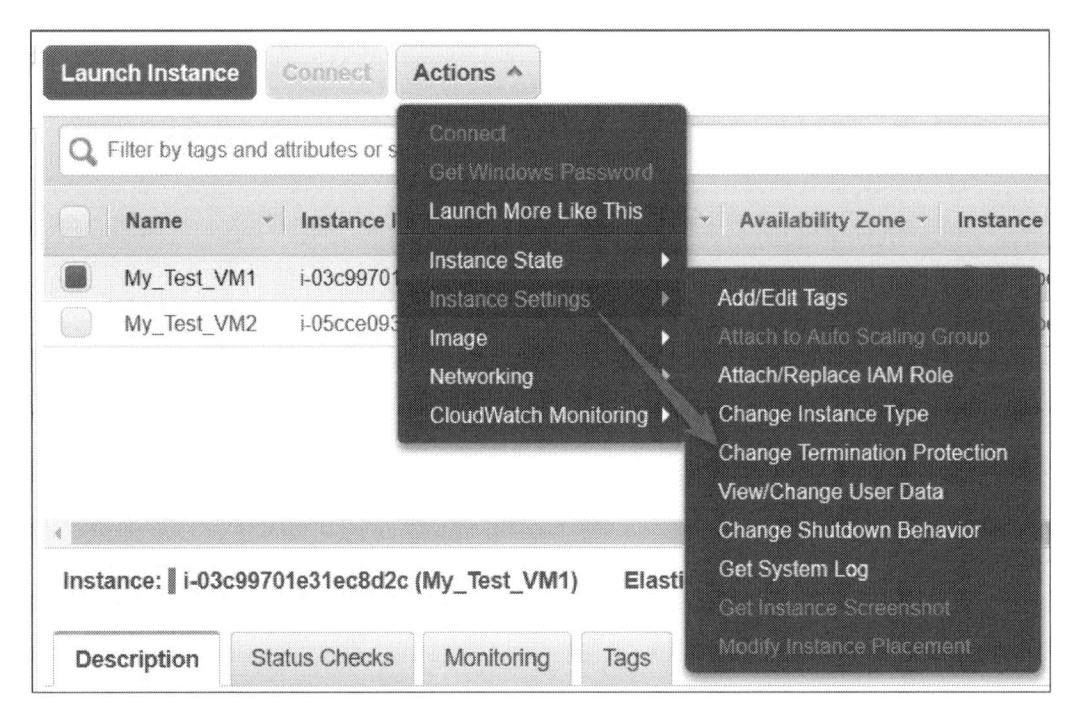

3. On the **Enable Termination Protection** window, click the **Yes, Enable**.

4. Now the termination protection for your instance is enabled. If someone will try to terminate the protected instance, the **Yes, Terminate** button will be greyed out as shown in the following figure.

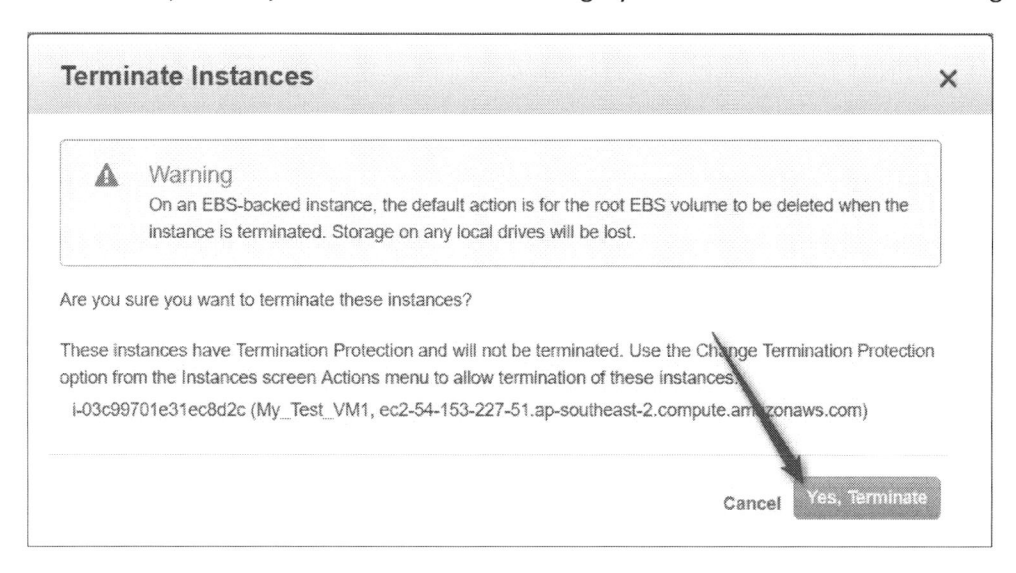

Now, first, you would need to disable the Terminate Protection feature manually before to terminate this instance.

Specifying Auto Start Script with EC2 Instance

Sometimes, you may need to run a series of commands (or script) that should be executed when the instance starts. This works in the similar way as we set the login scripts or startup scripts in Windows machines. This can be done by using a setting called **View/Change User Data**.

1. Just navigate to the **View/Change User Data** option and type the commands or script you want to execute when the instance starts.
2. For example, the following command will set the instance's hostname automatically as My_Test_VM1, as shown in the following figure, when the instance starts.

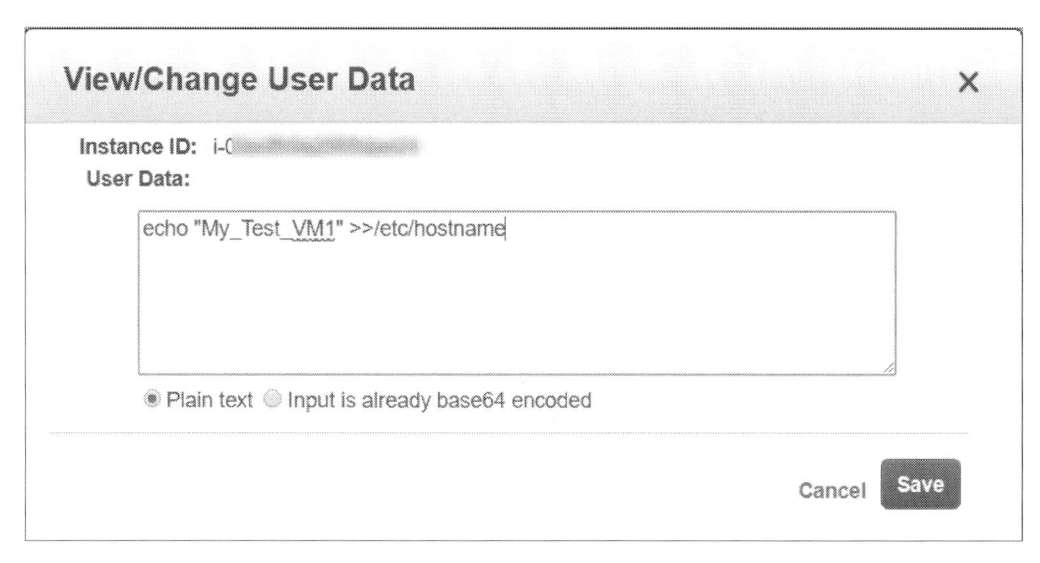

The View/Change user data option is very handy and useful in Auto Scaling that we will cover in the later sections.

Changing/Adding Security Groups to EC2 Instance

As discussed earlier, security groups control the incoming and outgoing traffic for the EC2 instances. You can always add or remove the security groups to and from your EC2 instance without rebooting.

1. For this, just select the instance, click **Actions**, and navigate to **Change Security Groups** option as shown in the following figure

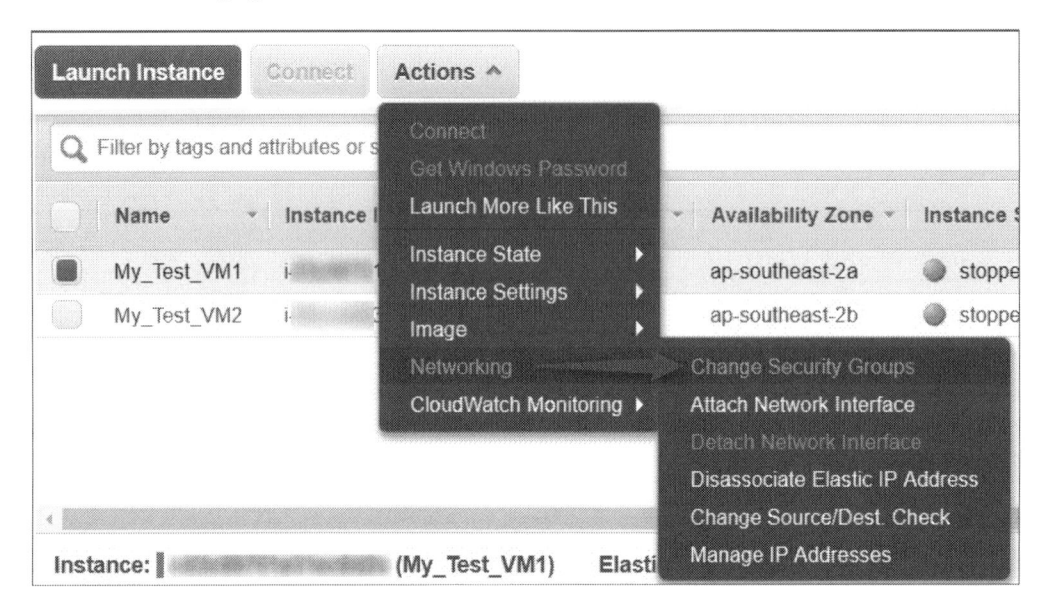

2. In the **Change Security Groups** window, select or remove the checkbox in front of the security group that you want to add or remove and then click **Assign Security Groups** to apply the changes.

17. Start, Stop, Reboot, and Terminate EC2 Instance

Starting, stopping, rebooting, and terminating an EC2 instance is pretty simple and straightforward. Just select an instance that you want to terminate, click **Actions** and navigate to the **Instance state** option as shown in the following figure.

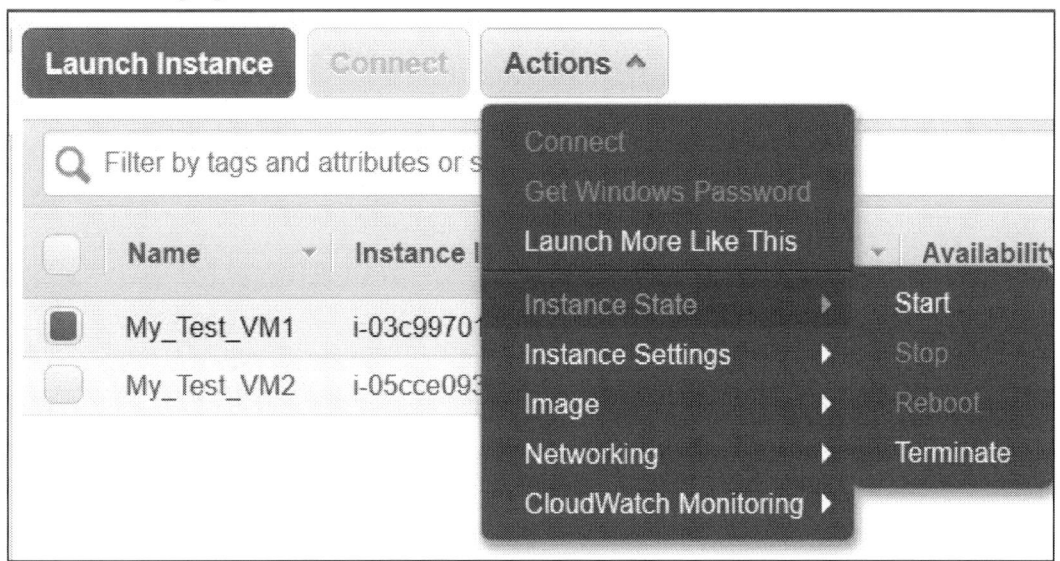

Here you can see the four options. Start, stop, and reboot options are self-explanatory and do not require to be explored further.

Terminating an instance means removing or deleting the instance along with its entire data. However, the attached volume will also be removed or not, it depends on the setting you configured on the volume properties.

By default, root volume is marked as **delete on termination,** but the additional volumes are not marked as delete on termination by default. So if you want to keep the attached volume, just remove the Delete on terminate option before to terminate the instance.

If there is an EIP also attached to that instance, you have the option to keep this EIP or release this EIP while terminating the instance.

![Terminate Instances dialog screenshot]

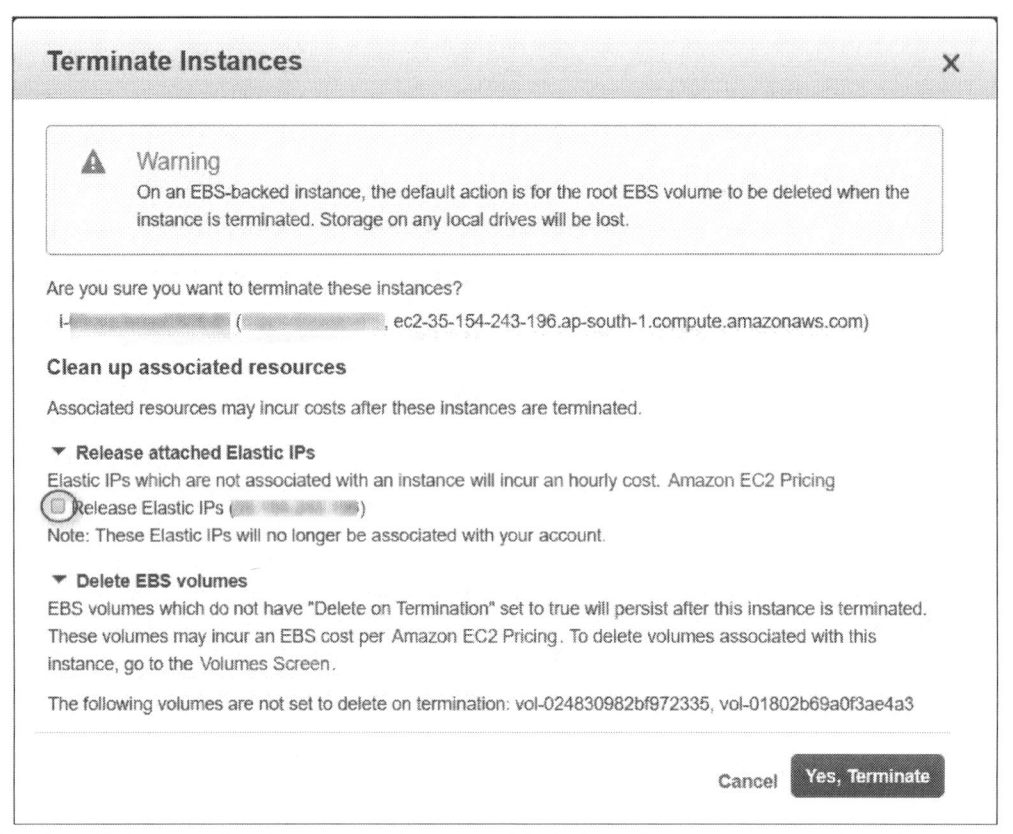

As discussed earlier, if the **Termination protection** is enabled, then first you need to disable it before you could terminate an instance. Once the termination process is started, it may take around half and an hour to disappear from the instance list in the console, but you will have no option to do anything with the terminated instance. So be very careful before to terminate any instance.

18. Creating and configuring Elastic Load Balancer

A Load Balancer is a service that distributes and balances the load into different servers that are grouped together to serve a specific service. For example, you can configure a load balancer for a web server. You can then have multiple servers behind this ELB with the same settings.

Recommended links:
- Getting Started with AWS Load Balancers
  http://docs.aws.amazon.com/elasticloadbalancing/latest/userguide/load-balancer-getting-started.html
- AWS Load Balancing Pricing
  https://aws.amazon.com/elasticloadbalancing/pricing/

Load Balancer Modes

The ELB can act in either of the following modes:
1. **Active-Active**: In this mode, multiple servers can share a load of users' traffic simultaneously.
2. **Active-Passive**: In this mode, one server waits until the primary server fails to respond for a specific time duration.

AWS Load Balancer Types

If we talk about the AWS load balancer concept, at the time of writing this guide there are three types of load balancers:
1. **Application load balancer**: Choose an Application Load Balancer when you need a flexible feature set for your web applications with HTTP and HTTPS traffic.
2. **Classic load balancer**: Choose this Load Balancer when you have an existing application running on the EC2-Classic network
3. **Network load balancer**: Choose a Network Load Balancer when you need ultra-high performance and static IP addresses for your application.
   - https://www.sumologic.com/aws/elb/aws-elastic-load-balancers-classic-vs-application/
   - https://aws.amazon.com/elasticloadbalancing/details/

> *Note: It may also be possible that a few of the Load Balancer type not available or supported in a specific AWS region.*

Here, we are going to show you how to configure and use an Elastic Load Balancer using the below network design.

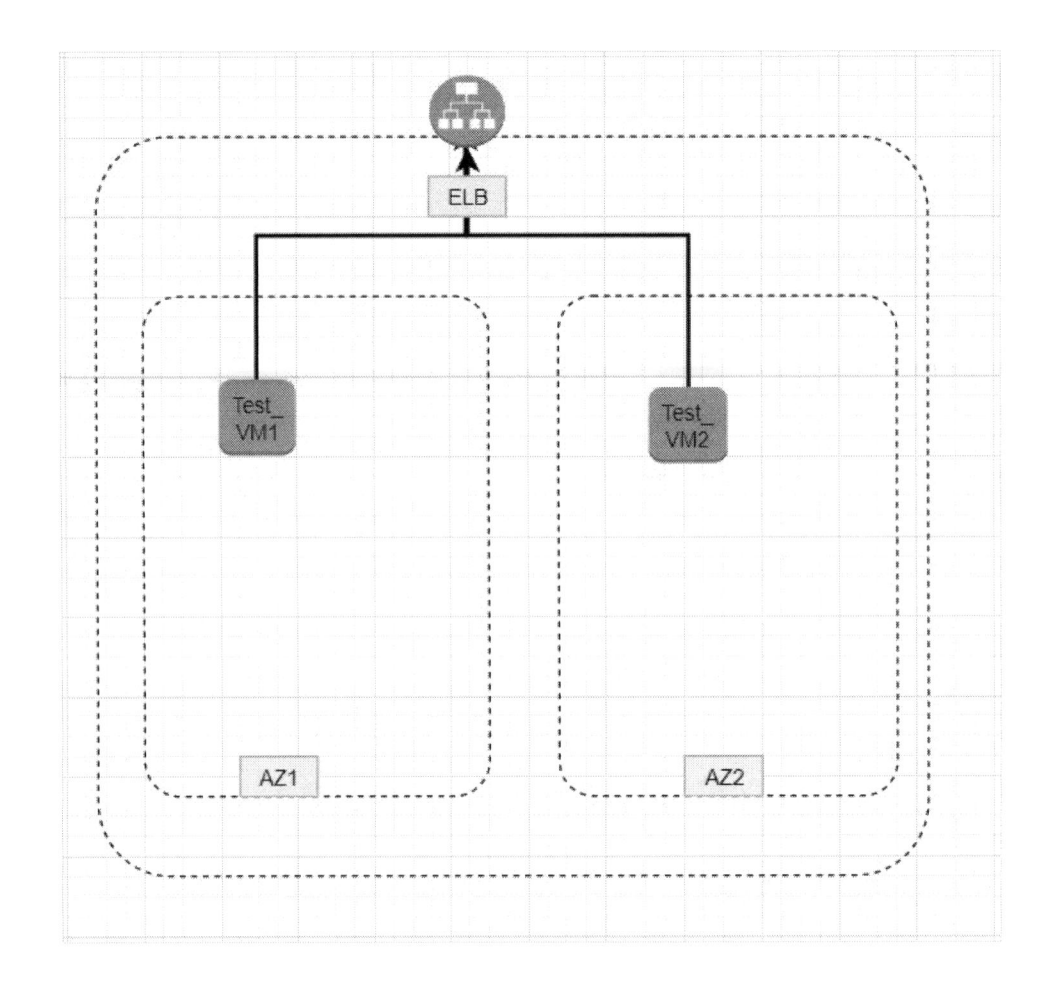

Before to proceed with the ELB creation, make sure that you meet the following prerequisites:
1. Make sure you have two subnets and two availability zones, at least one subnet in each availability zone.
2. Make sure you have an application running on at least a single instance of any availability zone. For the demo purpose, having multiple instances is not mandatory.

Once you are ready, let's begin with the hands-on practice.

Create an Application Load Balancer

To create and configure an ELB, you need to perform the following steps:
1. In the **EC2 dashboard**, click **Load Balancers** in the left pane, and then click **Create Load Balancer** as shown in the following figure

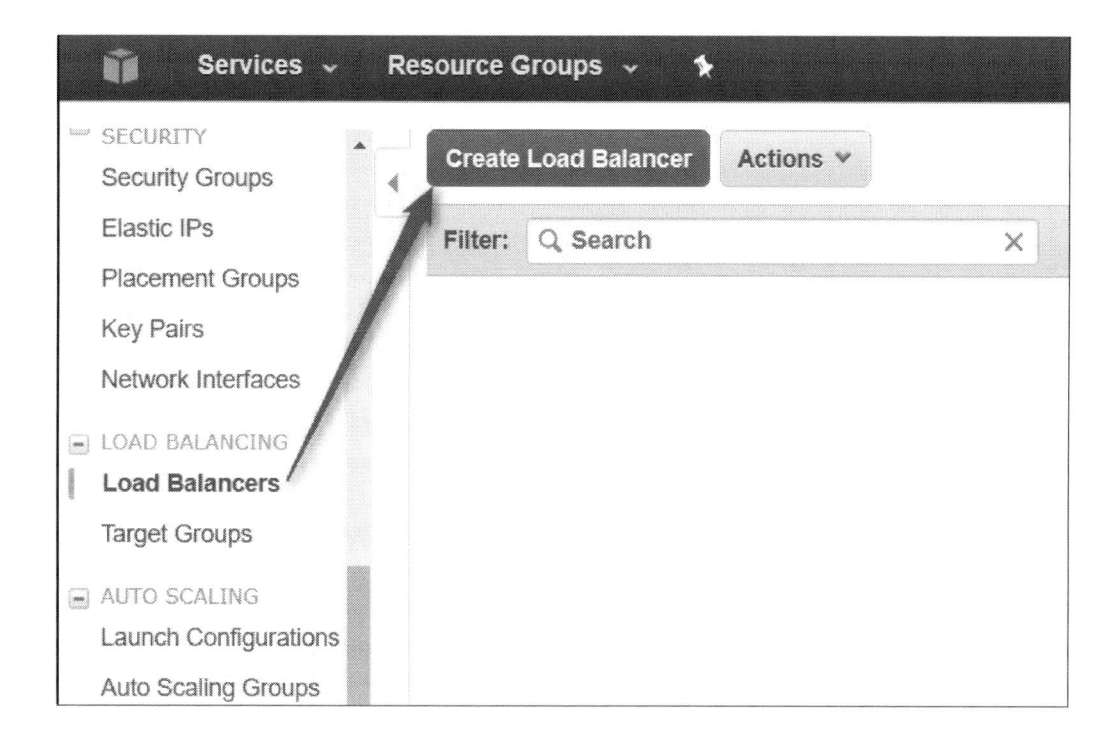

2. On the **Select load balancer types** page, select the type of load balancer that suits most with your application, for example, application load balancer and proceed to the next page.
3. In the **Basic Configuration** section, you need to set the following values:
   - **Name**: Name of the ELB
   - **Scheme**: Internet-facing or internal facing
   - **IP address type**: IPv4 or dual stack
4. For the demo purpose, select the setting as given in the following figure.

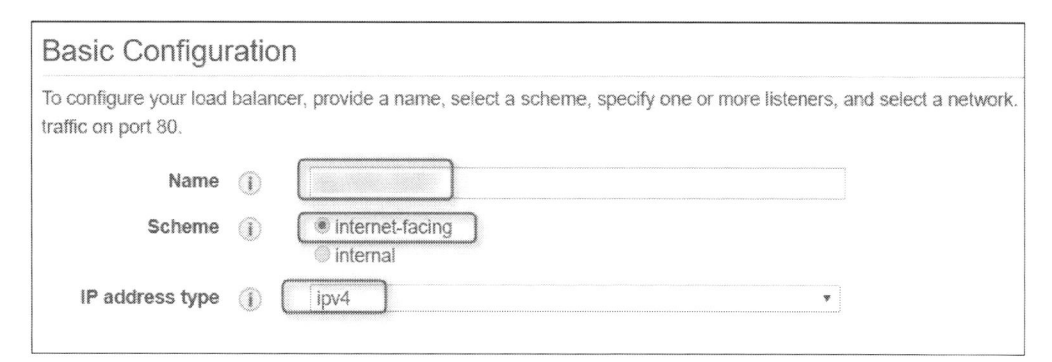

5. In ELB, you also need to specify the listener settings. A listener checks the health status of your instances that hosting the application. Since application load balancer only supports the HTTP or HTTPS protocol, so you can host only web services with the Application load balancers. For example, if your web server is running on 8080 port, you have to set the listener as given in the following.

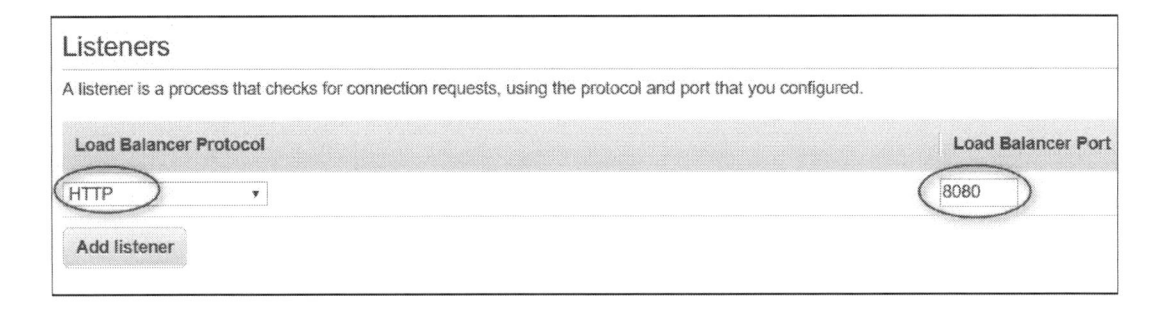

[screenshot: Listeners section showing Load Balancer Protocol HTTP and Load Balancer Port 8080, with Add listener button]

6. In the **Availability Zone** section, select the VPC in which your application is hosted. Select at least one subnet per availability zone and proceed to the **Configure Security Groups** page.

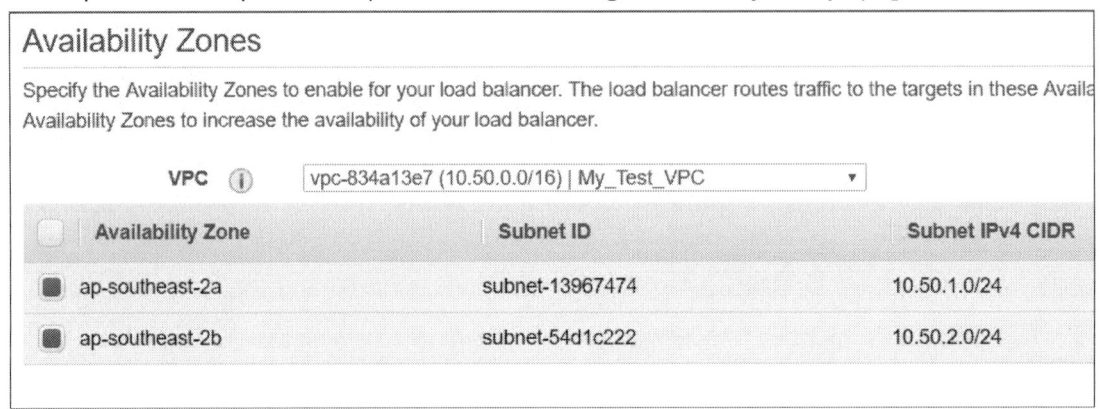

[screenshot: Availability Zones section showing VPC vpc-834a13e7 (10.50.0.0/16) | My_Test_VPC, with subnets ap-southeast-2a (subnet-13967474, 10.50.1.0/24) and ap-southeast-2b (subnet-54d1c222, 10.50.2.0/24)]

7. Select **Create a new security group** option and specify the name and description
8. In the **Rule** section, enable the port on which the application is running, in our case TCP/8080 as shown in the following figure.

[screenshot: Assign a security group: Create a new security group selected; Security group name: My_Test_ALB_SG; Description: My_Test_ALB_SG; Rule with Type Custom TCP, Protocol TCP, Port Range 8080]

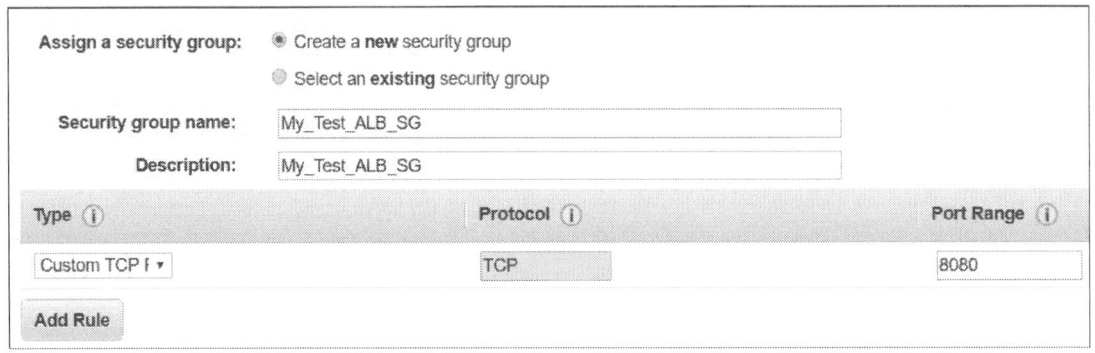

9. On the next page, specify the **Target name**, **Protocol**, **Port**, and **Health check path** as per your application settings as shown in the following figure.

Step 4: Configure Routing

Your load balancer routes requests to the targets in this target group using the protocol and port that only one load balancer.

Target group

Target group	ⓘ	New target group ▼
Name	ⓘ	MyTestTG1
Protocol	ⓘ	HTTP ▼
Port	ⓘ	80
Target type	ⓘ	instance ▼

Health checks

Protocol	ⓘ	HTTP ▼
Path	ⓘ	/

▶ Advanced health check settings

---

*Note: In the Path section, you need to specify the accessible home page of your web application that ELB will keep checking at the regular intervals to verify whether your instance is healthy or not. For example, if your web server's default home page is configured with **index.html** under **/var/www/html** directory, then type **/index.html** in the path section.*

---

10. On the **Register Targets** page, select the instance, application port and add them to the registered target group as shown in the following figure.

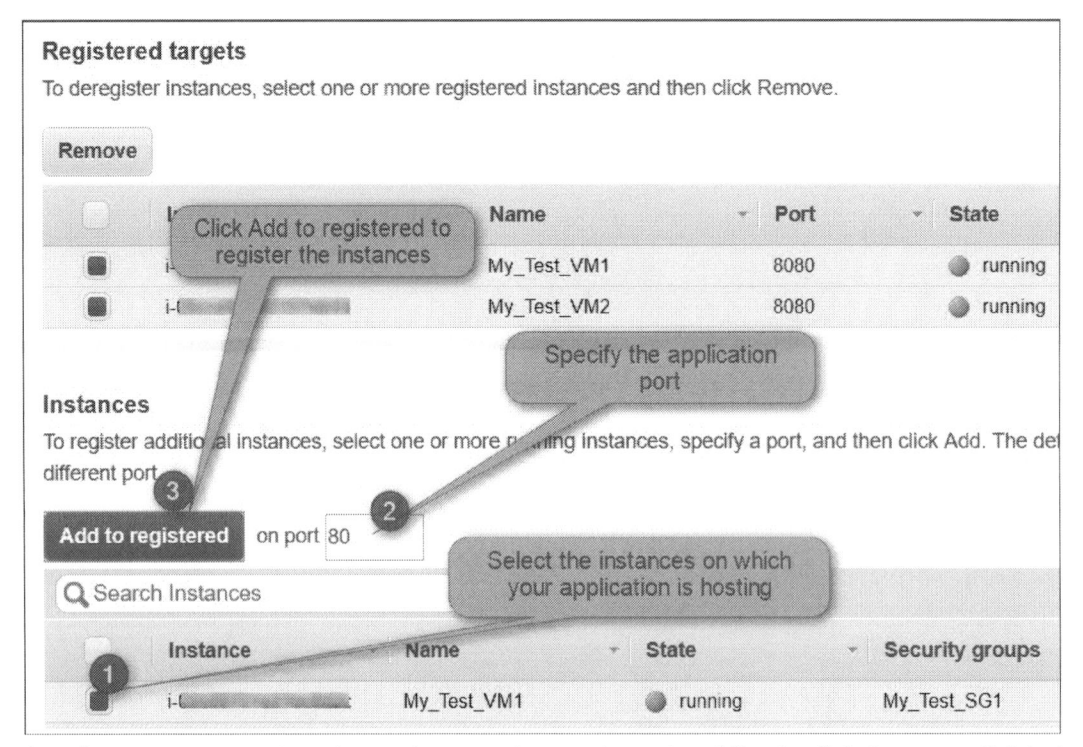

[Figure: Registered targets screen with annotations showing "Click Add to registered to register the instances", "Specify the application port", and "Select the instances on which your application is hosting"]

11. Proceed to the next page, review the settings you have selected and finally click **Create** to finish the wizard.
12. After a few minutes, your Application load balancer will be active. Now, allow your ELB's security group to communicate with the application hosting instances. For this, you need to modify the instance's security groups as shown in the following figure.

[Figure: Edit inbound rules screen with annotation "Type the security group ID of your ELB here"]

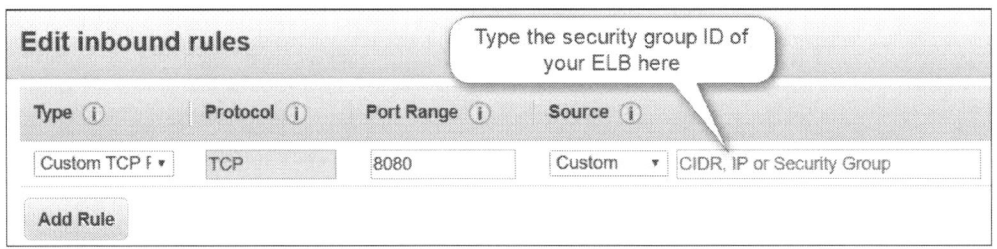

13. Navigate to the **Load balancers** page in the EC2 Dashboard and copy the load balancers **A record** as shown in the following figure.

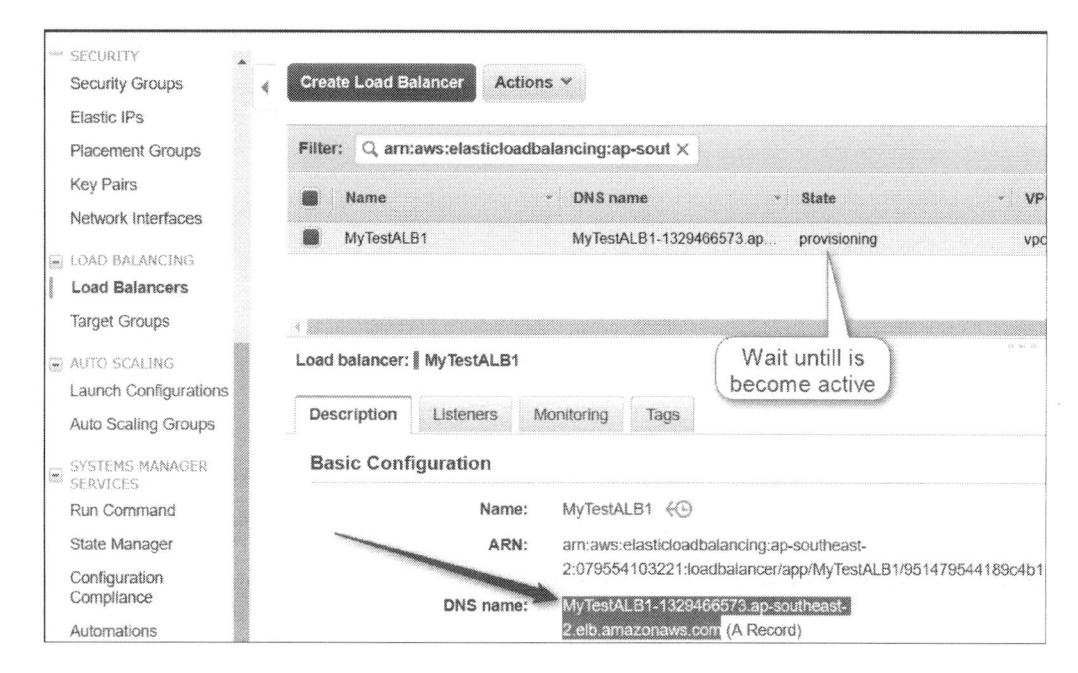

Domain Registration for ELB

If you also own the DNS registration account, you can register this ELB's A record with the respective DNS record such as **www.myapp.com** or you can use this A record directly in the browser to check the application functionalities with the Application Load Balancer.

Similarly, you can also create and configure Network load balancer and Classic load balancer. However, few steps and options will different obviously.

19. Scheduling Auto Snapshot of Volumes

Snapshots are good and cheaper solution for the EC2 instance's backup. You can take a snapshot of any attached volume either manually or schedule it for a specific recurring time interval.

Quick facts about EBS Snapshots
1. Snapshots are incremental by nature.
2. With snapshots, only data changed after your most recent snapshot are saved.
3. Snapshots can be shared with other AWS accounts.
4. The scope of an EBS snapshot is limited to a specific region in which you create it.
5. Snapshot can also be encrypted for the security purposes.

Auto-Snapshot Schedule

For the auto snapshot scheduling, you need to create a rule that will specify the following values:

1. **Event source**: The source can be either an event pattern or a fixed schedule.
2. **Rule name and description**: Name of the rule and description.
3. **Rule permission**: An IAM role that grants the permission to take a snapshot.
4. **Targets**: Target can be a lambda function, API call, SNS alert etc.

Creating Rule

For now, you can just follow the CloudWatch rule steps and not to go deeper inside it here. We will cover CloudWatch in detail in an upcoming section.

1. To create a CloudWatch rule for auto snapshot backup, open the CloudWatch console and select **Rules** in the left pane.
2. On the **Rule** page, click **Create rule** to create a new rule as shown in the following figure.

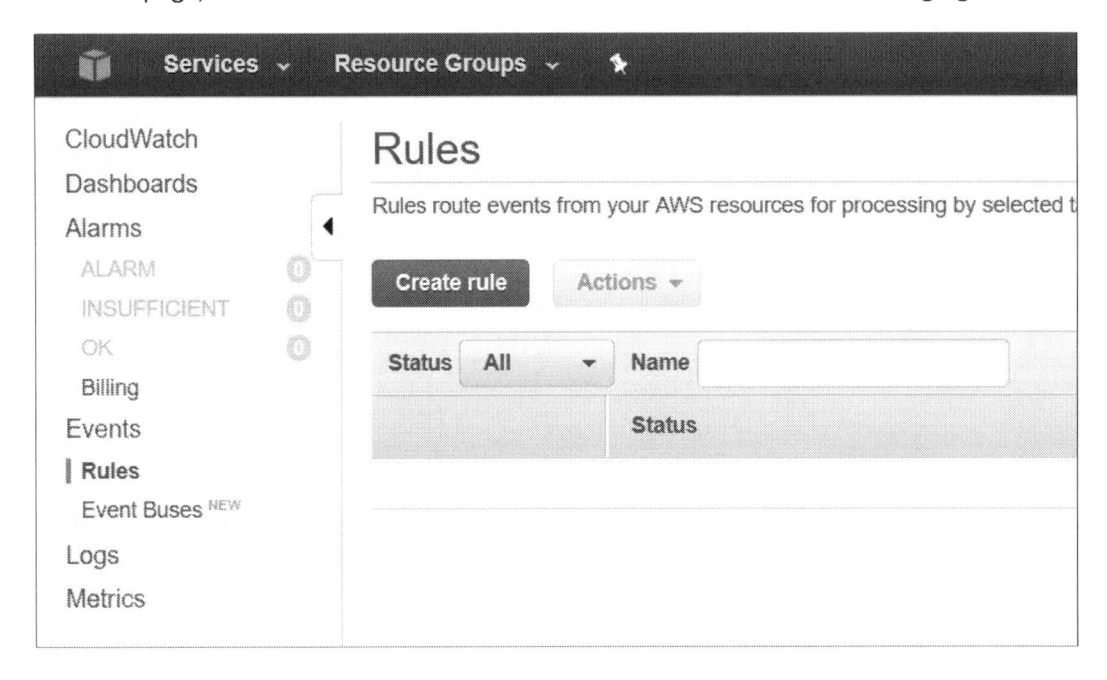

Defining Event Source

An event source can be either a pattern or a schedule. Schedule further can be configured with a fix rate of time or in the format of the cron job. Here, we will select the Schedule with cron expression. We assume that you are already familiar with the cron schedules. The AWS cron scheduler is almost same with slight differences in the syntax as what we use for Linux cron scheduler.

We recommend you to please have a look at the following cron schedule details and examples:

- http://docs.aws.amazon.com/AmazonCloudWatch/latest/events/ScheduledEvents.html

For example, in the below figure, we have configured a cron schedule that will take a snapshot of a volume on daily basis at 22:01 PM (GMT).

![Event Source screenshot showing Schedule selected with Cron expression "01 22 ? * * *" and Next 10 Trigger Dates starting Thu, 14 Sep 2017 22:01:00 GMT through Sat, 23 Sep 2017 22:01:00 GMT]

Note: Time format for a CloudWatch rule is always in the GMT format. You need to adjust the GMT format to your local time zone accordingly. For example, you need to increase your time schedule by +5.30 if your local time zone is IST and so on.

Cron Expressions Syntax and Examples

The following figure shows a few of the most common cron schedule examples. Hope, this will help you to understand Cron Expressions Rules.

Minutes	Hours	Day of month	Month	Day of week	Year	Meaning
0	10	*	*	?	*	Run at 10:00 am (UTC) every day
15	12	*	*	?	*	Run at 12:15 pm (UTC) every day
0	18	?	*	MON-FRI	*	Run at 6:00 pm (UTC) every Monday through Friday
0	8	1	*	?	*	Run at 8:00 am (UTC) every 1st day of the month
0/15	*	*	*	?	*	Run every 15 minutes
0/10	*	?	*	MON-FRI	*	Run every 10 minutes Monday through Friday
0/5	8-17	?	*	MON-FRI	*	Run every 5 minutes Monday through Friday between 8:00 am and 5:55 pm (UTC)

Image Credit: Amazon

Specifying Target

A Target defines what actions you want to perform (schedule) with the configured time schedule. The Targets can be various types, but for this exercise, we just need to select the **EC2 CreateSnapshot API**. You also need to specify the volume ID of the volume of which you want to schedule auto snapshot backup. You can add multiple targets to a single CloudWatch rule.

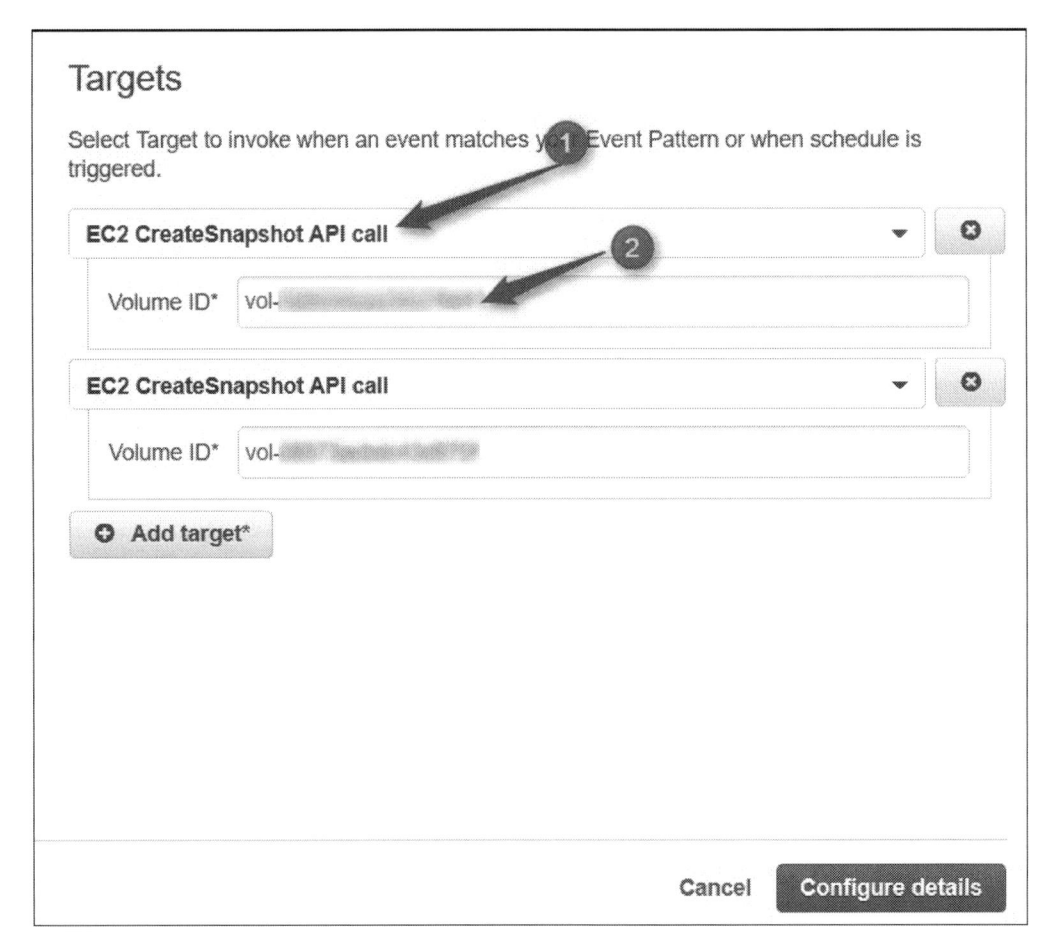

Note: CloudWatch needs permissions to perform the actions you define in the target section. For this, CloudWatch uses the IAM roles with the appropriate permissions. Most of the AWS services allow you to create IAM roles with the appropriate permissions on the configuration wizard of those services. Here, you may also need to create an IAM role for CloudWatch if you don't have already.

Configure Rule and Details

1. On the **Configure rule** details page, specify the name and description of the rule.
2. You also need to select the IAM role that has permission to create snapshots. By default, there is a preconfigured role that you can use.

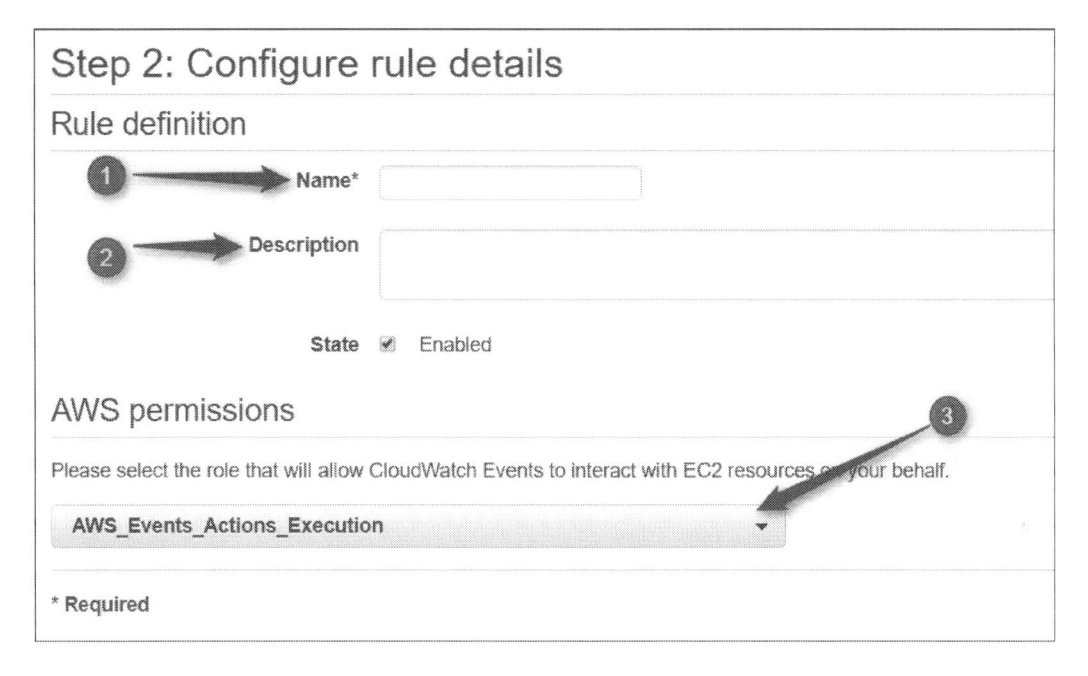

Step 2: Configure rule details

Rule definition

- ① Name*
- ② Description
- State ☑ Enabled

AWS permissions

Please select the role that will allow CloudWatch Events to interact with EC2 resources on your behalf. ③

AWS_Events_Actions_Execution

* Required

Finish the wizard once you are satisfied with your settings and values. That's all you need to do to automatically schedule snapshot backups for your EBS volumes.

When the scheduled time will come, CloudWatch will trigger the rule. Target will execute the requested action (snapshot in this case) and your snapshots for the specified volumes would be created. Snapshots will be available in the snapshot list in the EC2 dashboard.

20. Creating AMI and Recovering EC2 Instance using AMI

If you remember, there was a time when we were using Image Ghost for cloning an Operating System with all its configurations and using those on a different system. With Windows platform, we also use Sysprep Generalizing to prepare a clone image of an existing system. The same can be done on the cloud as well. However, on the Cloud, we have more advanced and flexible options especially with AWS Cloud.

Amazon Machine Image (AMI) is a complete backup image of a running or stopped instance. When you create an AMI for an instance, all the system configuration along with all the attached volumes and data are copied in the form of a single file called AMI. This AMI image or cloned VM is then stored in the S3 storage.

Recommended link:
   http://docs.aws.amazon.com/AWSEC2/latest/UserGuide/creating-an-ami-ebs.html

The AMI can be used to launch a new instance with the similar settings and configurations of the instance using which you had created this AMI. This is the best option while migrating a server from one VPC, availability zone, or region to another VPC, availability zone, or region (even across AWS accounts).

Here we will create an AMI of **My_Test_VM1** instance and then will launch a new instance in another availability zone and subnet. Before this, we will create a file and a user on the source VM so it could be verified that the settings and files are available in the destination VM created by AMI. However, the IP address of the new instance will, of course, be different from the source instance.

Creating some users and files in the source Instance

Login to **My_Test_VM1** and create a file named **My_File1** and a user named **testuser1** as shown in the following figure.

Creating Image of an EC2 instance

Now, select and right-click the **My_Test_VM1** and navigate to the **Create Image** option as shown in the following figure.

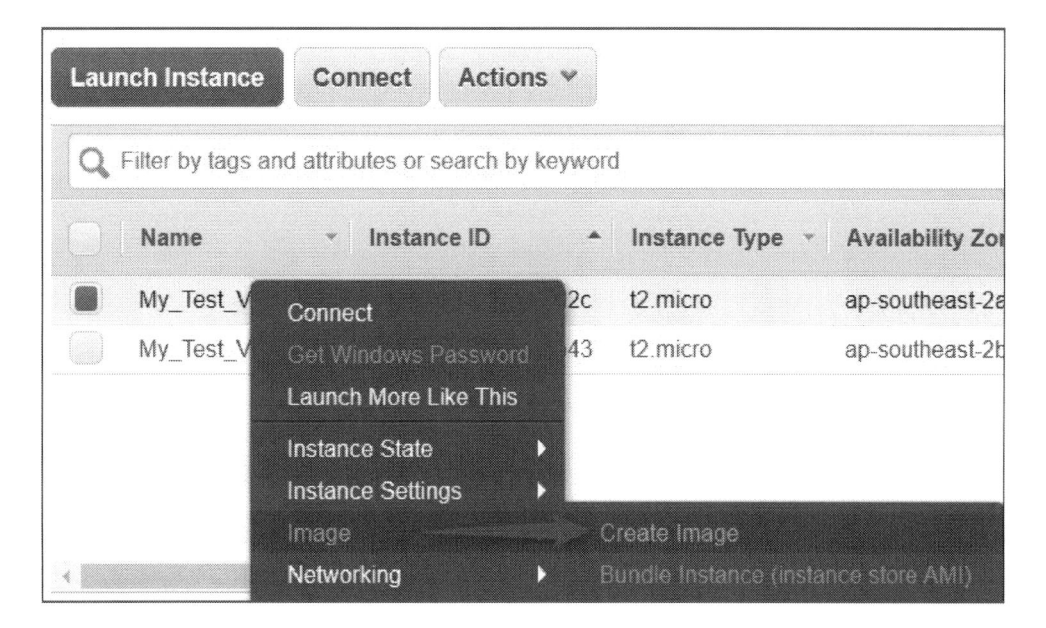

Specifying AMI settings

In the **Create Image** window, type the name and description of the AMI. Select the **No reboot** check box if you don't want to reboot the running instance while creating AMI. However, if possible, it is recommended to leave this check box cleared.

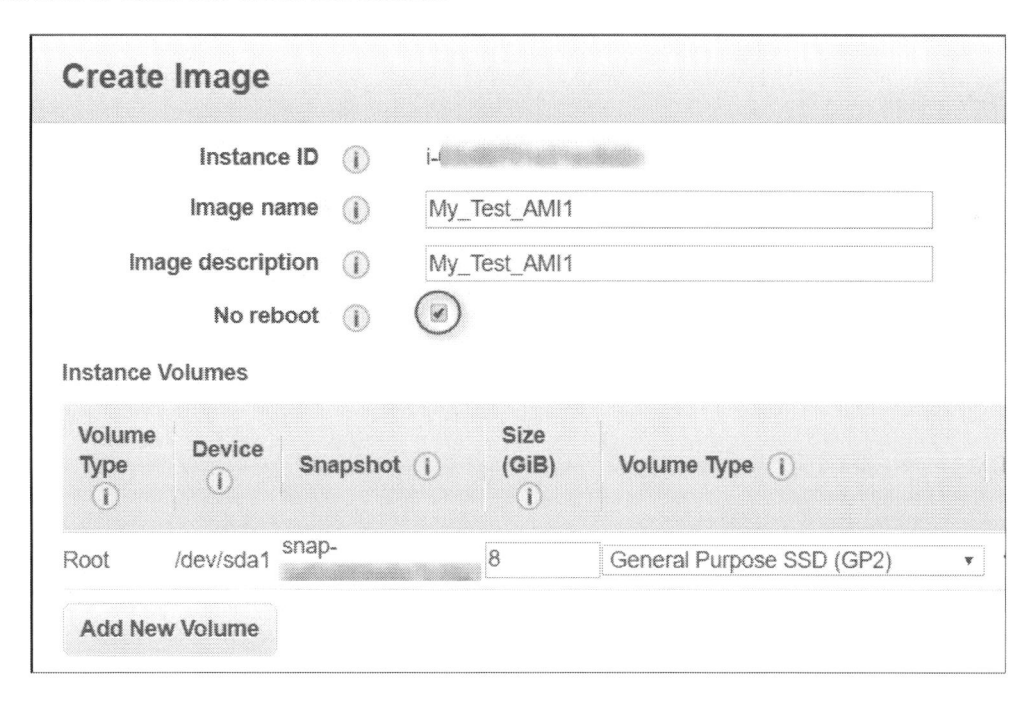

*Note: No reboot option is very important to understand. Suppose your server is servicing the service to the end-users. There might be some live transactions on-going when you start creating the AMI of your server. **If you select No reboot** option, then there might be some minor gap in the data between the running server and the*

*captured AMI, because the live transaction was happening. Hence, this is recommended to stop your VM before to take AMI. However, if you have a single server that acts as a production server, you should **always select No reboot checkbox**, else your server will be rebooted and the service will be unavailable until the server reboot process is completed. So, be careful and take appropriate action with No reboot option which suits you best.*

If required, you can modify the size of an EBS volume (Only increase) or you can also add additional volumes to the EC2 instance as per your requirement. Finally, click the **Create Image** button.

The AMI creation process will start and after few minutes, the AMI will be created and available in the AMI list as shown in the following figure.

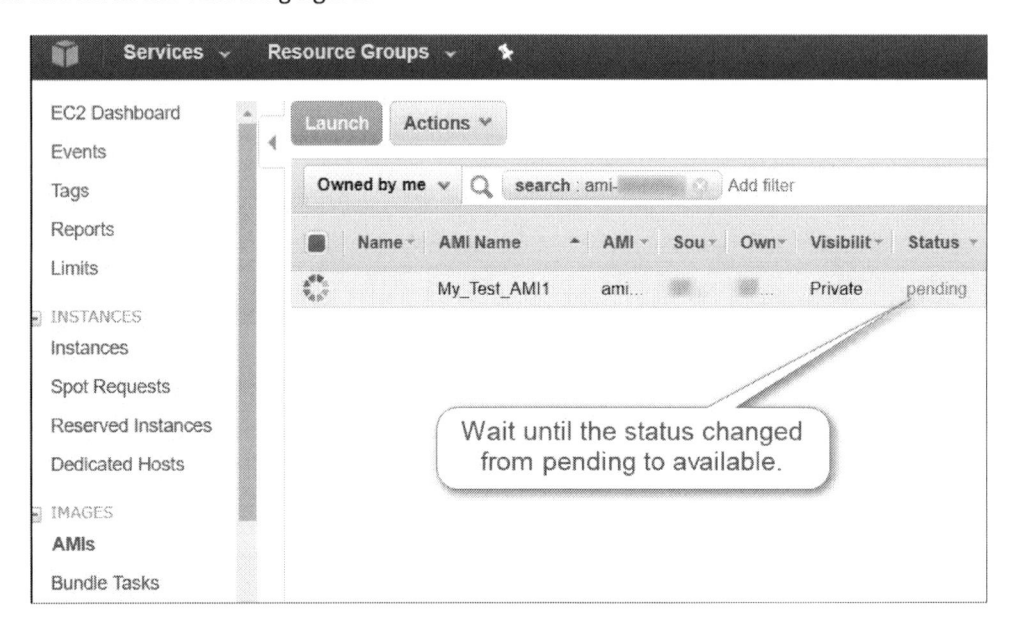

Note: Sometimes it may happen that the AMI creation process shown as available in the EC2 console, but the actual AMI creation process may still be ongoing. So, keep refreshing your AWS console until the AMI creation process changes from Pending (Red) to Available (Green).

Launching an EC2 Instance using AMI

Once the AMI creation process is done and the status shown as Available, then you can use this AMI to launch new instances. Newly launched instances using this AMI will have everything same as the source instance had, except the private IP address that will be assigned by DHCP service randomly depending on the defined subnet IP range.

1. Select the AMI and click **Launch** to launch a new instance using this AMI. The launching AMI process is almost same as launching a new instance.

2. On the **Choose instance type** page, select the instance type such as T2.Micro and proceed to the next page.

Configuring Instance Details

1. On the **Configure Instance Details** page, select the destination VPC, subnet (in which the instance will be launched) and other settings as per your need as shown in the following figure.

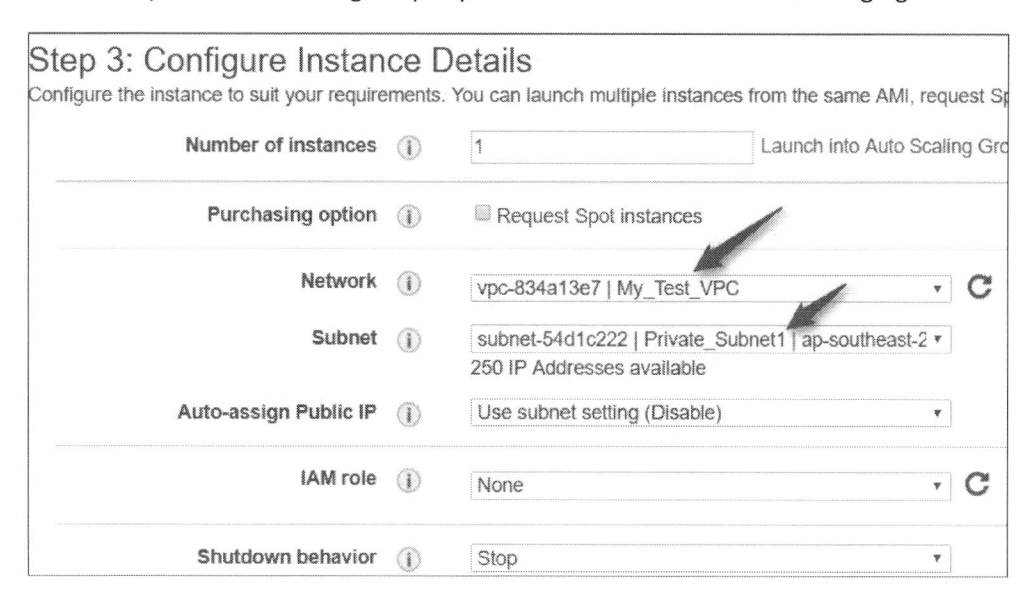

```
Step 3: Configure Instance Details
Configure the instance to suit your requirements. You can launch multiple instances from the same AMI, request Sp

    Number of instances      ⓘ    [ 1 ]                          Launch into Auto Scaling Gro

    Purchasing option        ⓘ    ☐ Request Spot instances

    Network                  ⓘ    [ vpc-834a13e7 | My_Test_VPC                  ▼ ] C

    Subnet                   ⓘ    [ subnet-54d1c222 | Private_Subnet1 | ap-southeast-2 ▼ ]
                                   250 IP Addresses available

    Auto-assign Public IP    ⓘ    [ Use subnet setting (Disable)                ▼ ]

    IAM role                 ⓘ    [ None                                        ▼ ] C

    Shutdown behavior        ⓘ    [ Stop                                        ▼ ]
```

2. On the **Storage** page, modify the storage volume size (increase only) or add new volume, if required.
3. On the **Add tags** page, specify the instance name such as **My_Test_VM3**.

> *Note: Suppose you created an AMI of a server that has 20 GB as root volume and 100 GB as Data volume. You realize that you only need the system configuration volume, but you either don't need data volume at all or want to keep the size of the data volume as low as 50 GB instead of having 100 GB. The first thing to note here is that: you cannot reduce the volume size less than 100 GB because the AMI was created with 100 GB data volume size. You can only increase the EBS volume size to more than 100 GB such as 110 GB but you cannot reduce it to 90 GB. The other thing to notice here is that: you cannot remove the 100 GB data volume that came with AMI. Because, if you will remove the data volume and when you will launch the new instance with this AMI, the system will check the /etc/fstab file where the system will expect that your data volume is available and mounted on a mount point such /data. Since you have removed the data volume, your new instance will stuck at the initialization state due to corruption in the file system.*

Configuring Security Group

On the **Configure Security Group** page, select the existing security group that you want to attach with this instance or create a new security group with the appropriate rules.

Reviewing and launching Instance

1. On the **Review** page, review the settings you have selected and click **Launch**.
2. On the **Key pair** page, select an existing key pair or create a new key pair for this instance.
3. Finally, click **Launch Instance** as shown in the following figure. The instance will be ready within a few minutes.

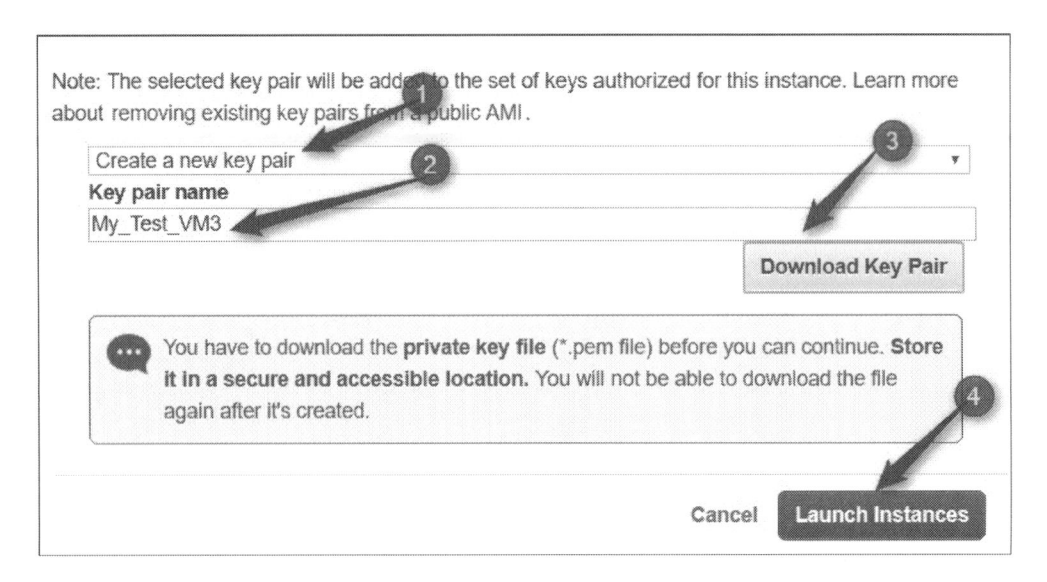

Login in to the New Instance

Now, login to your newly launched instance and verify whether the data from the source instance is available or not.

1. On the GitBash or Linux terminal, execute the following command.
- $ eval (ssh-agent)
- $ shh-add -k My_Test_VM1.pem
- $ ssh-add -k My_Test_VM3.pem
- $ ssh -A ubuntu@<my-test-vm1-public-ip>
2. After connecting the first VM, execute the following command inside the connected instance to connect private internal instance.
- $ ssh ubuntu@<my-test-vm3-private-ip>
3. As you can see in the below figure, the file and user are present that we have created in the source instance.

```
ubuntu@ip-10-50-1-93:~$ ssh ubuntu@10.50.2.158
Welcome to Ubuntu 16.04.2 LTS (GNU/Linux 4.4.0-1032-aws x86_64)

 * Documentation:  https://help.ubuntu.com
 * Management:     https://landscape.canonical.com
 * Support:        https://ubuntu.com/advantage

  Get cloud support with Ubuntu Advantage Cloud Guest:
    http://www.ubuntu.com/business/services/cloud

35 packages can be updated.
0 updates are security updates.


Last login: Sat Sep 16 08:18:37 2017 from 10.50.1.93
ubuntu@ip-10-50-2-158:~$ ls
Desktop    Downloads  My_File1  Public     Videos
Documents  Music      Pictures  Templates
ubuntu@ip-10-50-2-158:~$ cat My_File1
My cloned instance
ubuntu@ip-10-50-2-158:~$ sudo cat /etc/passwd |grep user1
user1:x:1001:1001::/home/user1:
ubuntu@ip-10-50-2-158:~$
```

That's all you need to do to create, launch, and use Amazon Machine Image (AMI).

21. Configuring CloudWatch Monitoring

Monitoring is one of the most important factors of managing IT infra in a proper way and having the pro-active solutions before anything goes wrong with your infrastructure. CloudWatch helps you to monitor operational and performance metrics for your AWS cloud resources and applications. There are hundreds of metrics that can be used with CloudWatch.

The most common metrics that every administrator would like to use are CPU, RAM, Disk, and Network consumption and usage report. However, basic CloudWatch monitoring does not support all of the metrics and also have the longer threshold value than the Advanced CloudWatch monitoring which is more expensive than the basic CloudWatch monitoring.

Quick facts about AWS CloudWatch
1. The scope of Amazon CloudWatch is limited to a specific region.
2. The default CloudWatch logs interval for most of the services is 5 minutes.
3. Advanced monitoring could be enabled with 1 minute metric update time interval.
4. Amazon CloudWatch allows you to create alarms and rules to take appropriate actions when a specific threshold value triggers.
5. By default, Amazon CloudWatch does not collect the Memory and Disk metrics.
6. Memory and Disk metrics could be configured with the Amazon CloudWatch agent on EC2 instances or on-premise servers.
7. You can create dashboards to categories and summarized the resource monitoring.

Recommended links:
- Basics of Amazon CloudWatch
- https://aws.amazon.com/cloudwatch/

Amazon CloudWatch Pricing

You should be aware of your free tier limitations for any AWS service else you might be charged by AWS if you have used any resource beyond the free tier limitations. For AWS CloudWatch, the following link explains the free tier limitations and the pricing details for the detailed monitoring if you wish to configure.

AWS CloudWatch Free Tier Limitations and Pricing
https://aws.amazon.com/cloudwatch/pricing/

Here, we will show you how to use CloudWatch to monitor CPU, Disk, and Network resource usage and get alerts when the resource utilization exceeds the limit beyond the specified values.

Selecting an Instance

In the AWS console, select the instance for which you want to enable CloudWatch monitoring. For example, let's select My_Test_VM1. You can see, by default, there is no alarms are configured.

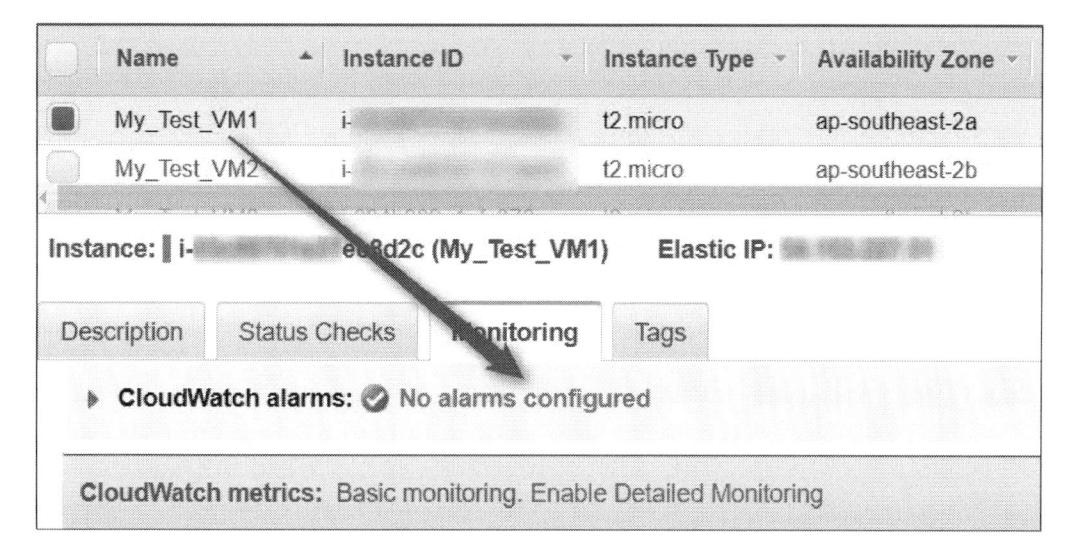

Name	Instance ID	Instance Type	Availability Zone
My_Test_VM1	i-	t2.micro	ap-southeast-2a
My_Test_VM2	i-	t2.micro	ap-southeast-2b

Instance: i-   e8d2c (My_Test_VM1)   Elastic IP:

Description | Status Checks | Monitoring | Tags

▸ **CloudWatch alarms:** ✓ No alarms configured

CloudWatch metrics: Basic monitoring. Enable Detailed Monitoring

Creating a CloudWatch Alarm

You can configure a CloudWatch alarm for your resources with the specified threshold values. Whenever the threshold value will meet the condition, an alarm will trigger. You can configure an appropriate action which will be performed when the threshold value meets. For example, sending an email to user, rebooting your EC2 instance, creating an EBS snapshot, executing a lambda function etc.

To create a CloudWatch alarm, you need to perform the following steps:

1. Click **Create Alarm** to proceed. On the **Create Alarm** window, make sure that the **Send a notification to** check box is selected.
2. Select the SNS topic, if you have already created or click to create now.
   - Type the **topic name** and **email ID** where the email alerts will be sent.
   - Select a metric such as CPU utilization, Disk reads, or Network in/out etc. that you want to enable.
   - In front of the **Is** box, select the formula and an alert value such as 60% utilization.
   - In the **Consecutive period** box select the number of minutes as threshold value till then CloudWatch wait before to send any alert.
   - In the **Name of the alarm** box, specify the name of alarm. Refer the following figure for a demonstration.

Create Alarm

You can use CloudWatch alarms to be notified automatically whenever metric data reaches a level
To edit an alarm, first choose whom to notify and then define when the notification should be sent.

☑ **Send a notification to:** CloudWatch_Alerts   cancel
With these recipients: abc@xyz.com
☐ **Take the action:** ○ Recover this instance ⓘ
○ Stop this instance ⓘ
○ Terminate this instance ⓘ
○ Reboot this instance ⓘ

Whenever: Average ▼ of CPU Utilization ▼
Is: >= ▼ 60   Percent
For at least: 1 consecutive period(s) of 1 Minute ▼
Name of alarm: My-Test-VM1-CPU-Utilization

Now CloudWatch will monitor the CPU utilization of your instance and will send an alert when the CPU utilization (threshold value) will exceed more than 60 %.

Note: Before you can get alerts from the AWS CloudWatch service, you need to create, request, and confirm your subscription using the Simple Notification Service (SNS) console. The next section covers SNS in details.

---

22. Configuring Amazon Simple Notification Service (SNS)

Amazon SNS is a web service used to coordinate and manage the delivering and sending messages to its subscribers.

Quick facts about Amazon SNS

1. It is designed to meet the needs of the leading and the most demanding applications.
2. It allows applications and end-users on different devices to receive notifications using Mobile Push notification, HTTP/HTTPS, Email/Email-JSON, SMS, SQS, or Lambda services.
3. You can use the Amazon SNS with no up-front fees or commitments.
4. It provides significant advantages over the complexity of developing your own custom messaging solutions.

Recommended links:

- Basics of Amazon SNS
  http://docs.aws.amazon.com/sns/latest/dg/welcome.html
- Getting Started with Amazon SNS
  http://docs.aws.amazon.com/sns/latest/dg/GettingStarted.html

Amazon SNS Free Tier vs Paid Pricing

The following table explains the limitations of the free tier and the pricing details for using Amazon SNS.

Notification Deliveries

Endpoint Type	Free Tier	Price
Mobile Push Notifications	1 million	$0.50 per million
Worldwide SMS	100	Learn more
email/email-JSON	1,000	$2.00 per 100,000
HTTP/s	100,000	$0.60 per million
Simple Queue Service (SQS)	No charge for deliveries to SQS Queues	
Lambda functions	No charge for deliveries to Lambda	

Image Credit: Amazon

In order to use Amazon SNS with other Amazon services such as Lambda, CloudWatch etc. you need to perform the following tasks.

Creating a Topic

The Amazon SNS topic is a category of your subscription. For example, let's assume you want to get alerts for high CPU utilization of your EC2 instances using CloudWatch alerts, you need to create an SNS topic such as CloudWatch_CPU_Alterts. Under your SNS topic, you can have multiple subscriptions such as an email list, mobile numbers, etc. where the alerts will be delivered.

To create an Amazon SNS topic, you need to perform the following steps:

1. Open the **Amazon SNS console** and click **Create new topic** under the **Topics** section.

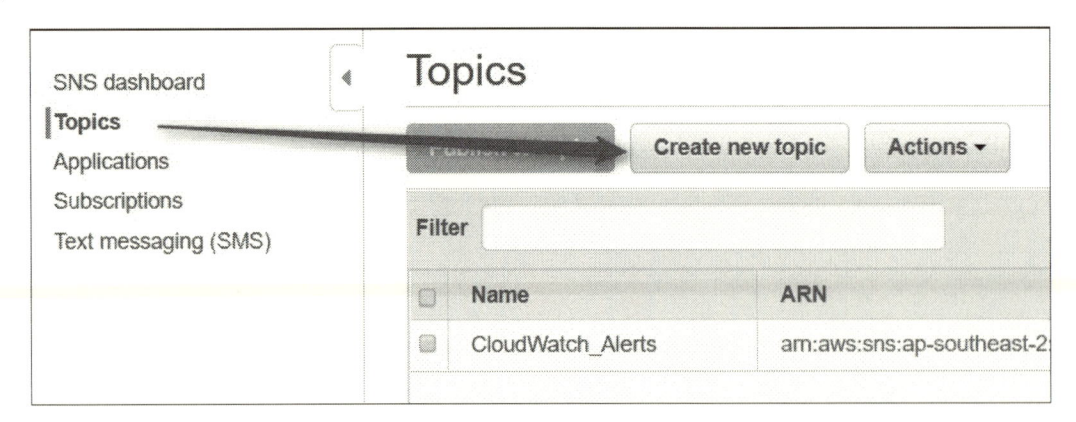

2. In the **Create new topic** dialog box, type the **Topic name** and **Display name** and then click **Create topic** as shown in the following figure.

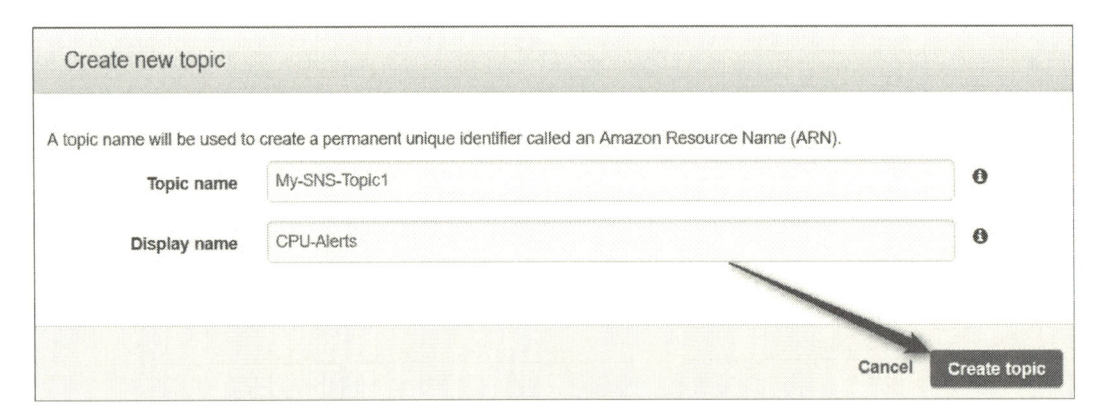

Subscribing to the topic

SNS Subscriptions are the targets such as an email list where SNS will delivered the alerts or actions.

To create an SNS subscription, you need to perform the following steps:

1. Once the topic is created, it will be listed in the topic list.
2. Select the created topic, click **Actions** and select **Subscribe to topic** as shown in the following figure.

3. On the **Create subscription** dialog box, select the protocol that you want to use with SNS. We have selected **Email** but you can also select HTTP, HTTPS, AWS Lambda, or SMS depending on your choice and need.
4. In the **Endpoint** text box, type the **Email ID** where the alerts will be sent and then click **Create subscription**.

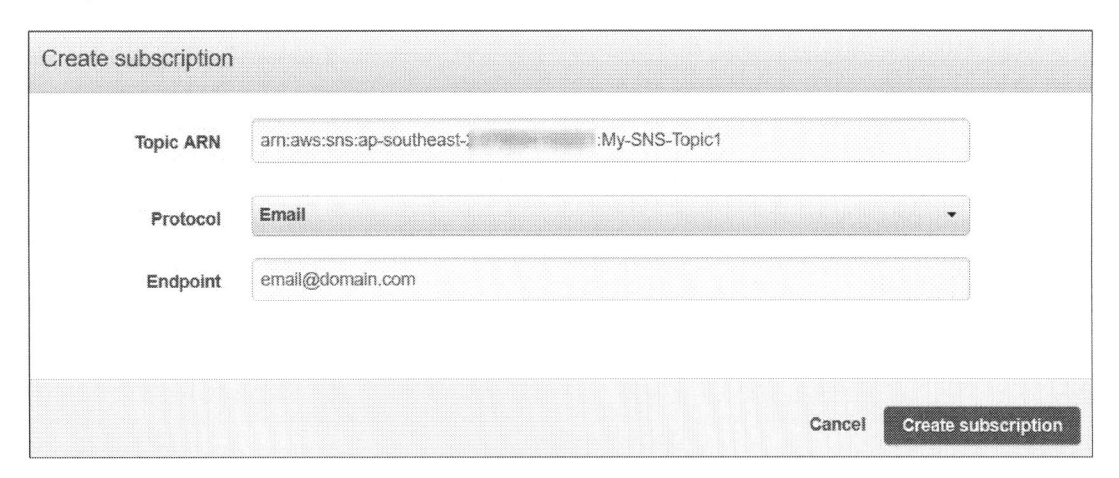

Create subscription	
Topic ARN	arn:aws:sns:ap-southeast- :My-SNS-Topic1
Protocol	Email
Endpoint	email@domain.com

Cancel Create subscription

5. Once you receive the email in your inbox, click the **confirm subscription** link to complete the subscription.

Now, your Amazon SNS topic is ready to be used for sending alerts and integration with other AWS services.

23. Configuring Centralized Log Management Using CloudWatch Log Group

Logs are very handy and useful when it comes to troubleshooting any system and application issue. In a cloud environment, it may be very difficult to login and check logs for individual systems. The best way to centralize all the EC2 instance systems' logs is CloudWatch Log group using the CloudWatch Log Agent.

You can use the CloudWatch Logs agent installer for an existing EC2 instance to install and configure the CloudWatch Logs agent. Once the installation is completed, you need to specify the log files and CloudWatch log group name where the log will be stored. Using the CloudWatch log agent, the logs are automatically sent from the instance to the log stream you have created while installing the agent.

Creating a CloudWatch Log Group

You can use CloudWatch Log Group to categorize your logs such as one CloudWatch log group for Web servers and one CloudWatch log group for database servers. Under a CloudWatch log group, you can have multiple **CloudWatch Log stream** which you can think as a sub category of a CloudWatch Log Group.

Before you can use CloudWatch Log Agent to centralize the logs, you need to create a CloudWatch Group. For this, you need to perform the following steps:

1. In the left pane, click **Logs** and then click **Create log group** as shown in the following figure.

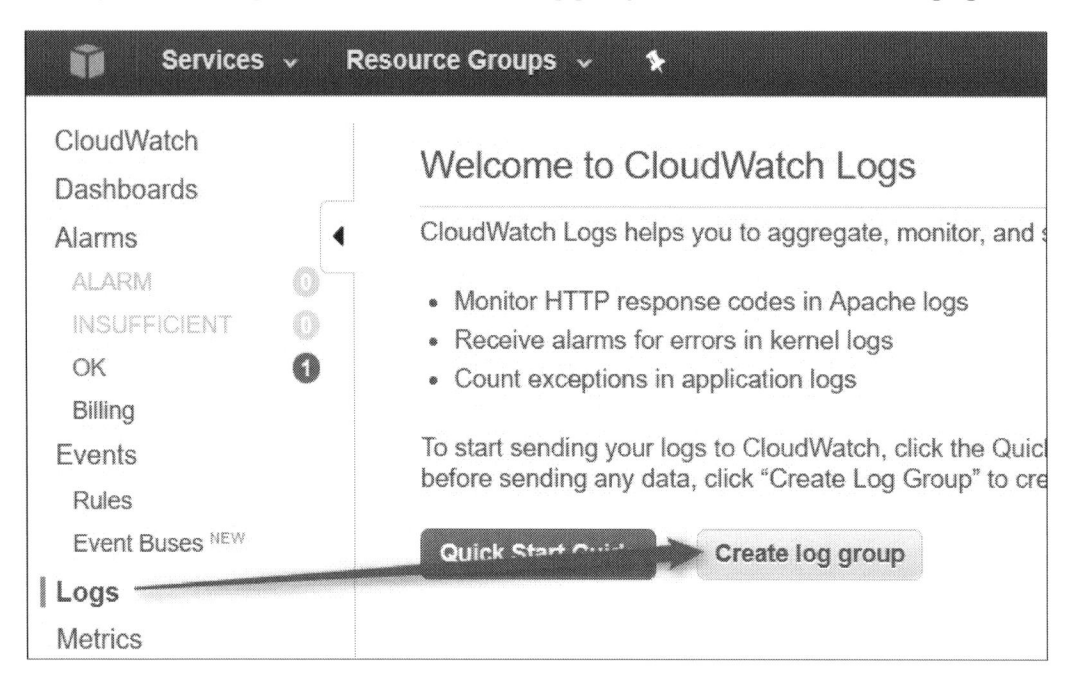

2. On the **Create Log Group** name dialog box, type the name of log group and click **Create log group**.

![Create log group dialog with Log Group Name: loggroup1]

Granting Permission to EC2 Instance to Use CloudWatch Logs

Before an EC2 instance can send the logs to the CloudWatch Log group, you need to set the permissions. Here, you have two options for assigning permission to an EC2 instance for CloudWatch Groups.

1. Using an IAM role and using AWS CLI credentials using access keys. If you have a huge number of EC2 instances to use CloudWatch logs, create and use an IAM role.
2. If you have a limited number of EC2 instances, you can configure access keys with CloudWatch agent configuration file.

> *Note: As of now, you can attach only a single IAM role to a specific EC2 instance. If an IAM role is already attached to your EC2 instance for a different purpose, such as taking database backup to an S3 bucket and you also want to send logs to CloudWatch logs group then the previously attached IAM role will be replaced with the new one. It means that your instance will not be able to upload the database backup to the S3 bucket. The solution of this problem is that: create a custom IAM role and attached both CloudWatch Log Group and S3 Bucket access permission policies to that IAM role and attach it with your EC2 instance that needs both CloudWatch and S3 bucket access.*

3. To create an IAM role for CloudWatch, open the **IAM console** and click **Roles** in the left pane.

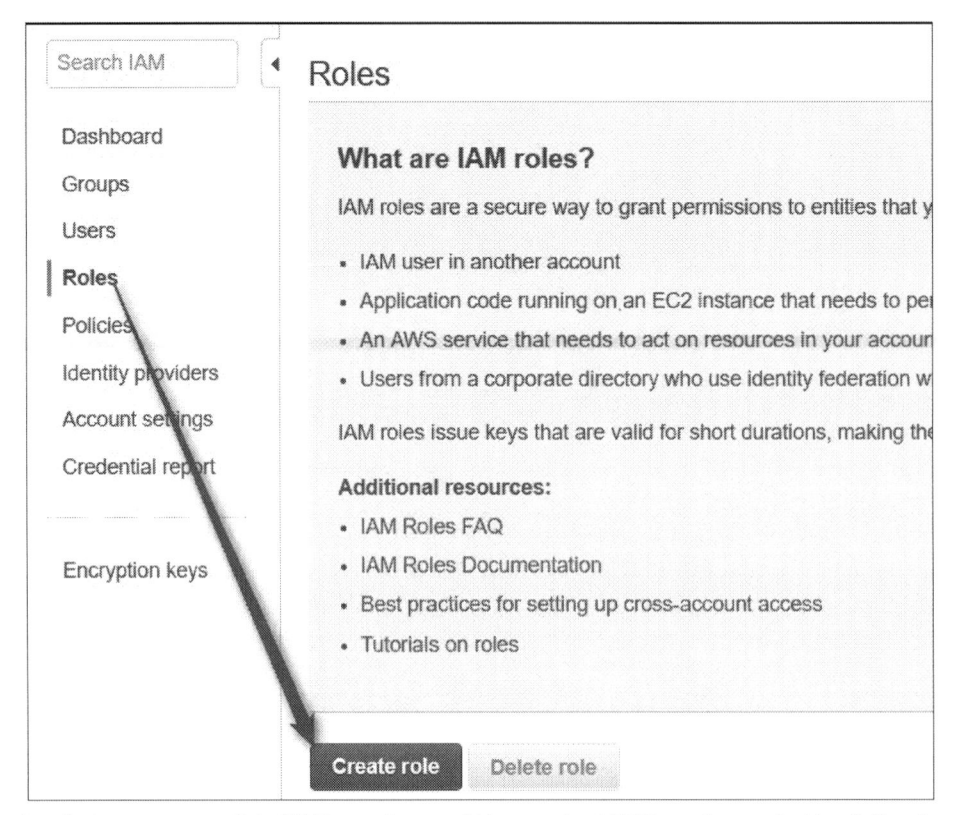

4. On the **Select role type** page, click **AWS service** and then select **EC2** as shown in the following figure.

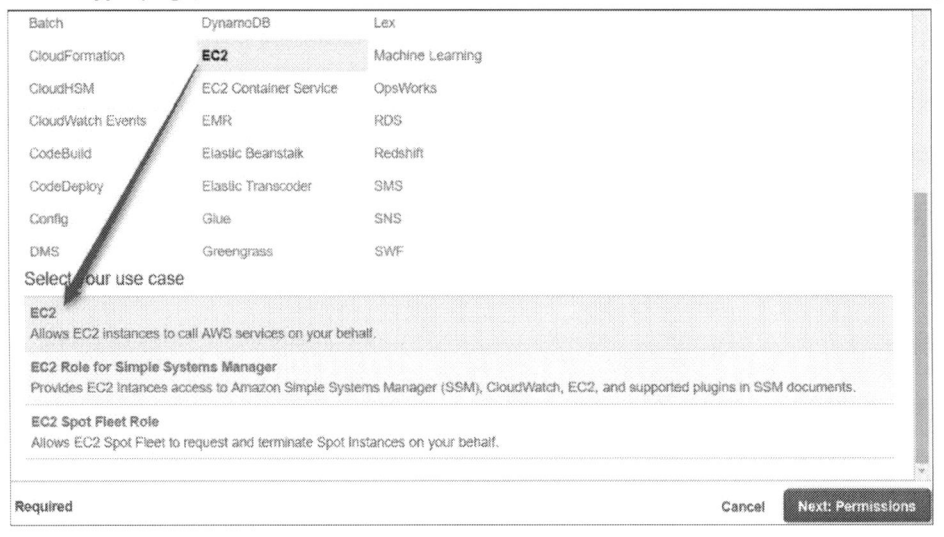

5. On the **Permission**s page, click **Create policy**. A new tab "Create policy" will be opened.
6. Click **Select** next to the **Create Your Custom Policy** option.

```
Create Policy

A policy is a document that formally states one or more permissions. Create a policy by copying

Copy an AWS Managed Policy
Start with an AWS Managed Policy, then customize it to fit your needs.

Policy Generator
Use the policy generator to select services and actions from a list. The policy generator uses yo

[Create Your Own Policy]
Use the policy editor to type or paste in your own policy.
```

7. On the **Review policy** page, specify the name and description of the policy.
8. In the Policy document text box, type the below policy carefully and click **Validate policy** to validate it.

```
{
  "Version": "2012-10-17",
  "Statement": [
    {
      "Effect": "Allow",
      "Action": [
         "logs:CreateLogGroup",
         "logs:CreateLogStream",
         "logs:PutLogEvents",
         "logs:DescribeLogStreams"
      ],
      "Resource": [
         "arn:aws:logs:*:*:*"
      ]
    }
  ]
}
```

9. Finally, click **Create Policy** to finish the wizard.

Attaching a Policy to an IAM Role

Once the policy is created, you need to attach this policy to the desired IAM role. For this, perform the following steps:

1. Switch back to the previous tab (IAM role page).
2. Select **Filter** as **Customer managed**, search the created policy and select it as shown in the following figure.

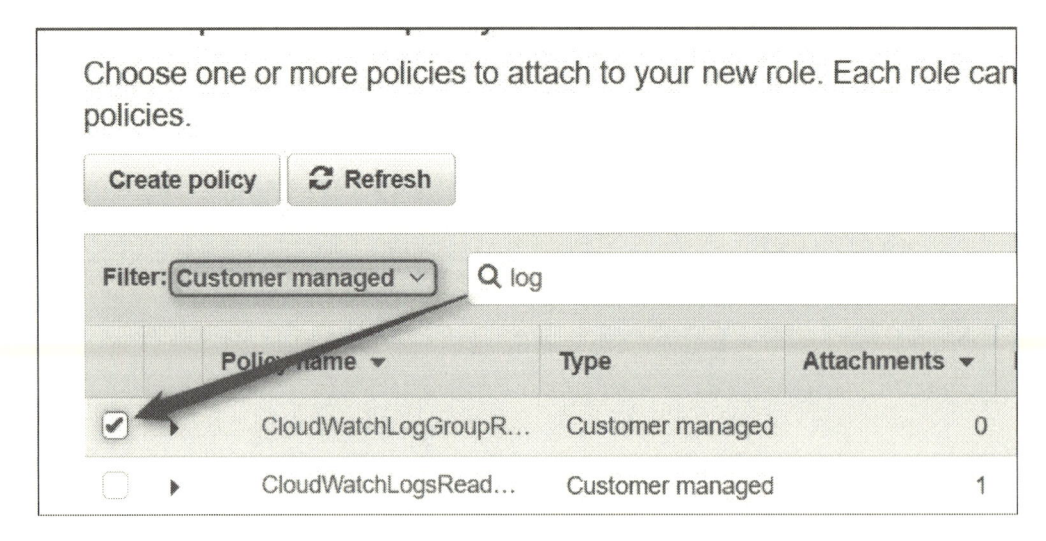

Choose one or more policies to attach to your new role. Each role can policies.

[Screenshot: Create policy / Refresh buttons. Filter: Customer managed, search "log". Policy name / Type / Attachments columns. CloudWatchLogGroupR... Customer managed 0 (checked). CloudWatchLogsRead... Customer managed 1.]

3. On the next page, specify the role name and description and finish the wizard.

Assigning Role to an EC2 Instance

To assign IAM role to an EC2 instance, perform the following steps:

1. Select the instance, click **Actions** and navigate to **Attach/Replace IAM Role** as shown in the following figure.

[Screenshot of EC2 console: Launch Instance, Connect, Actions menu expanded showing Connect, Get Windows Password, Launch More Like This, Instance State, Instance Settings (Add/Edit Tags, Attach to Auto Scaling Group, Attach/Replace IAM Role, Change Instance Type, Change Termination Protection, View/Change User Data), Image, Networking, CloudWatch Monitoring. Instances My_Test_VM1 i-03c99..., My_Test_VM3 i-034b9... Selected instance: i-03c99701e31ec8d2. Tabs: Description, Status Checks, Monitoring, Tags.]

2. On the **Attach/Replace IAM Role** page, select the role you have created earlier and click **Apply** to complete the wizard.

Attach/Replace IAM Role

Select an IAM role to attach to your instance. If you don't have any IAM roles, choose Create new
If an IAM role is already attached to your instance, the IAM role you choose will replace the exist

Instance ID i-■■■■■■■■■■■ (My_Test_VM1) 🛈

IAM role*   CloudWatchLogGroup   ▼

* Required

Installing AWS CloudWatch Log Agent

Now, connect to your EC2 instance and install the AWS CloudWatch Log Agent. The process of CloudWatch Log agent installation differs based on the Linux variant and platform. The below process explain the CloudWatch Logs Agent installation on an Ubuntu Linux instance.

> *Note: If you have different platform such as RHEL Linux, we recommend to visit the following link to know how to install CloudWatch Logs Agent on various platforms.*
>
> *https://docs.aws.amazon.com/AmazonCloudWatch/latest/logs/QuickStartEC2Instance.html*

1. On the Linux terminal, execute the following command to install the CloudWatch log agent installation script on a Ubuntu machine.
   - $curl https://s3.amazonaws.com//aws-cloudwatch/downloads/latest/awslogs-agent-setup.py -O
2. Execute the following command to configure the AWS CloudWatch log agent.
   - $sudo python3 ./awslogs-agent-setup.py --region <region-name>

```
ubuntu@ip-10-50-1-93:~$ curl https://s3.amazonaws.com//aws-cloudwatch/downloads/latest/aw
slogs-agent-setup.py -O
  % Total    % Received % Xferd  Average Speed   Time    Time     Time  Current
                                 Dload  Upload   Total   Spent    Left  Speed
100 54087  100 54087    0     0  34453      0  0:00:01  0:00:01 --:--:-- 34472
ubuntu@ip-10-50-1-93:~$ ls
awslogs-agent-setup.py  Documents  Music     Pictures  Templates
Desktop                 Downloads  My_File1  Public    Videos
ubuntu@ip-10-50-1-93:~$ sudo python3 ./awslogs-agent-setup.py --region ap-southeast-2
Launching interactive setup of CloudWatch Logs agent ...

Step 1 of 5: Installing pip ...DONE

Step 2 of 5: Downloading the latest CloudWatch Logs agent bits ... |
```

3. Here, you will we asked to specify the various settings. Let's have a look at each the following:

   AWS Access Key ID [None]: <Leave it blank>

   AWS Secret Access Key [None]: <Leave it blank>
   Default region name [ap-southeast-2]: <Your region where you have created Log Group>
   Default output format [None]: <Leave it None>

   Path of log file to upload [/var/log/syslog]: <Log's path that will flow to CloudWatch>
   Destination Log Group name [/var/log/syslog]: <You log group name>
   Choose Log Stream name: <Name of log stream inside log group name>

   Choose Log Stream name: <Refer the following figure to understand this>
   Choose Log Event timestamp format: <Refer the following figure to understand this>
   Choose initial position of upload: <Specify whether you want include logs since the beginning or from right now>

```
Choose Log Stream name:
  1. Use EC2 instance id.
  2. Use hostname.
  3. Custom.
Enter choice [1]: 3
Enter Log Stream name [None]:
Enter Log Stream name [None]: My_Test_VM1_Logs

Choose Log Event timestamp format:
  1. %b %d %H:%M:%S    (Dec 31 23:59:59)
  2. %d/%b/%Y:%H:%M:%S (10/Oct/2000:13:55:36)
  3. %Y-%m-%d %H:%M:%S (2008-09-08 11:52:54)
  4. Custom
Enter choice [1]: 1

Choose initial position of upload:
  1. From start of file.
  2. From end of file.
Enter choice [1]: 1
More log files to configure? [Y]: N

Step 5 of 5: Setting up agent as a daemon ...DONE


Configuration file successfully saved at: /var/awslogs/etc/awslogs.conf
```

Verifying Logs in CloudWatch Log Group

Now switch back to the CloudWatch console and navigate the loggroup1 CloudWatch log group. You should be able to see all the logs of EC2 instance's log file that you have selected while configuring the agent. In our case, it is **/var/log/syslogs**.

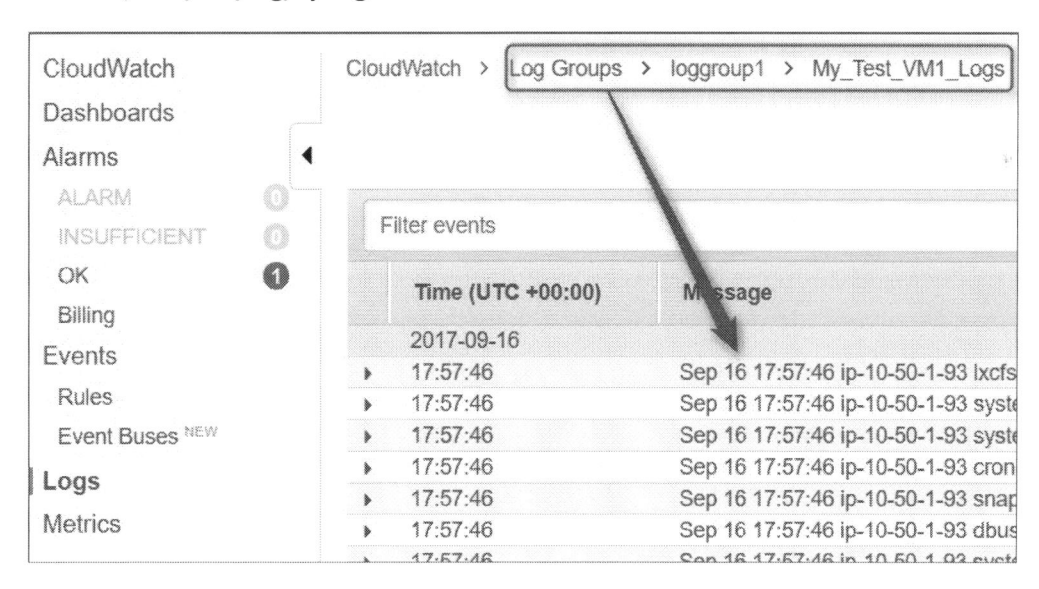

In the same way, you can redirect multiple log files in a single Log group using the different log stream names for easy identification.

Note: Once the CloudWatch Log Group Agent is installed and configured, it may take few minutes before it could send the logs to the CloudWatch Logs Group. So, if you don't see logs in the CloudWatch Logs group, you may need to wait for few minutes.

*Note: Sometimes it may happen that your EC2 instance suddenly stops sending the logs to the CloudWatch Logs Group, this usually happens due to either incorrect permission or difference in the date and time between Amazon Cloud and your EC2 instance. In this case, you can update the time of your EC2 instance using the network time protocol (NTP) using the **ntpupdate** command.*

25. Schedule Auto, Start, Stop, and Reboot EC2 Instances

When an instance is not in use, you can stop it to avoid paying unnecessary charges. Typically, every organization usage Development and Quality Audit (Dev and QA) environments for the testing and verification purposes before going to live with any code and changes. These DEV and QA instances remain idle in the nights and weekends. Auto Stop and Start Schedule can help you to save a huge amount if you are running hundreds of Dev, QA, and Productions servers for an organization.

You can either stop your EC2 instances manually or you can set a schedule to Auto Start Stop your EC2 instances. If you have a large number of running instances, the manual method cannot be possible or might be too irritating. However, you can schedule auto start-stop EC2 instances at the regular intervals using the Lambda functions.

In this article, we are going to explain a step by step guide how to start and stop your EC2 instance at a specific time, nights, and/or weekends.

To configure an Auto Start-Stop EC2 Instance schedule, you need to perform the following tasks.

Create an Auto Start EC2 Instance Lambda Function

AWS Lambda is a powerful server-less service. However, Lambda is itself a wide technology and we will cover the basics of Lambda in a separate section. Probably an entire book could be written on the Lambda functions. As of now, please follow have a look at the basics of AWS Lambda.

1. AWS Lambda is a compute service that allows us to run our code without the need of provisioning or managing servers.
2. AWS Lambda executes our code at the configured schedule or when a relevant event trigger happens.
3. The only thing we need to do with AWS Lambda is supplying our code in one of the Lambda-supported languages - these are Node.js, Java, C#, Go, and Python.
4. We only pay for the duration till our code is executed by the Lambda function else there is no charge when our code is not running.

Recommended Link:
https://docs.aws.amazon.com/lambda/latest/dg/welcome.html

To create a Lambda function to start and stop your EC2 instance at a desired schedule, you need to perform the following steps:

1. Open the **AWS Lambda Console** and click **Create a Lambda Function** as shown in the following figure to create a Lambda function.

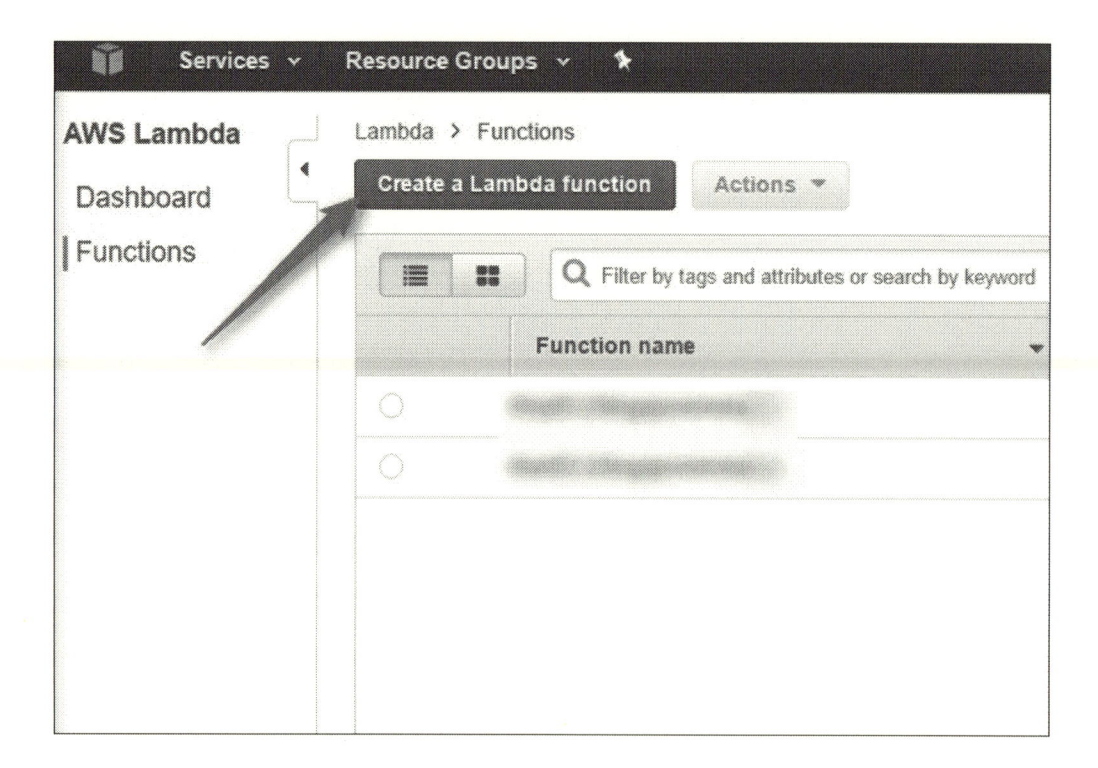

2. On the **Select Blueprint** page, click on **Blank Function** to choose it as shown in the following figure.

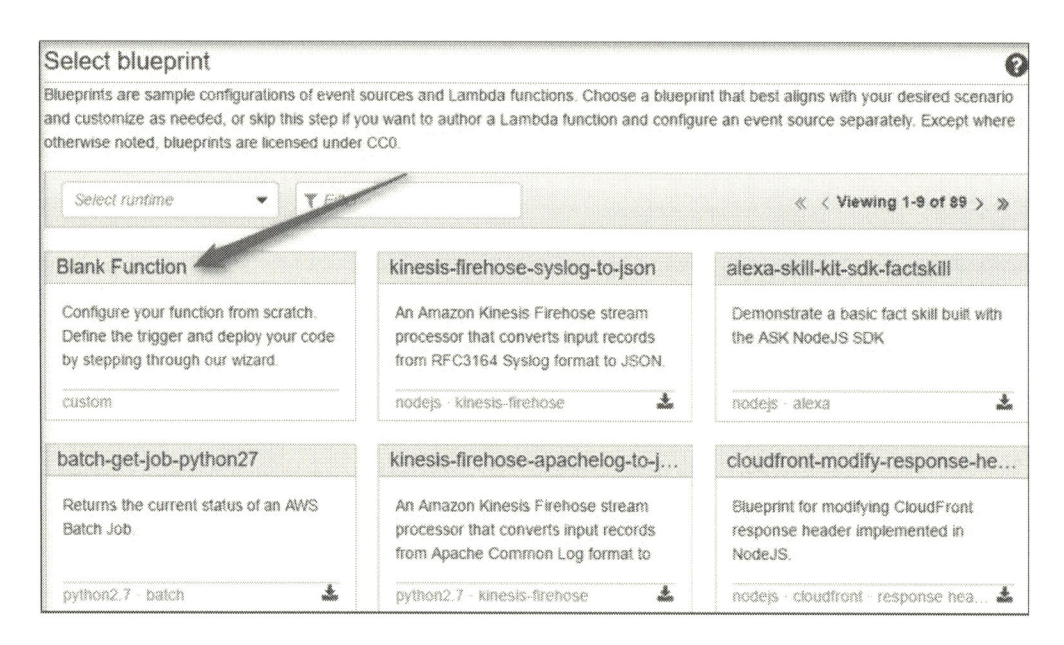

Note: There are dozens of preconfigured Lambda functions available as a ready to use. Please have a look at each of them and try to understand what they do. If you found a useful Lambda function, you can start using it for your need.

3. On the **Configure Triggers** page, click **Next** to proceed.

4. On the **Configure Function** page, set the following values:

    - Name: **AutoStartEC2Instance**
    - Description: **Auto Start EC2 Instance**
    - Runtime: **Python 2.7**.

5. On the **Code entry type** area, type the following script carefully.

    ```python
    import boto3
    # Specify the region where your instances are running. For example 'ap-southeast-1'
    region = 'ap-southeast-1'
    # Specify the instance IDs that you want to start at specific time. For example, ['i-abcd01234567', 'i-efgh01234567']
    instances = ['i-00bc7ba840f6a6520']
    def lambda_handler(event, context):
        ec2 = boto3.client('ec2', region_name=region)
        ec2.start_instances(InstanceIds=instances)
        print 'started your instances: ' + str(instances)
    ```

    Note: Replace your instance ID and region in the above python code (script) appropriately.

6. The **Configure function** page is shown in the following figure.

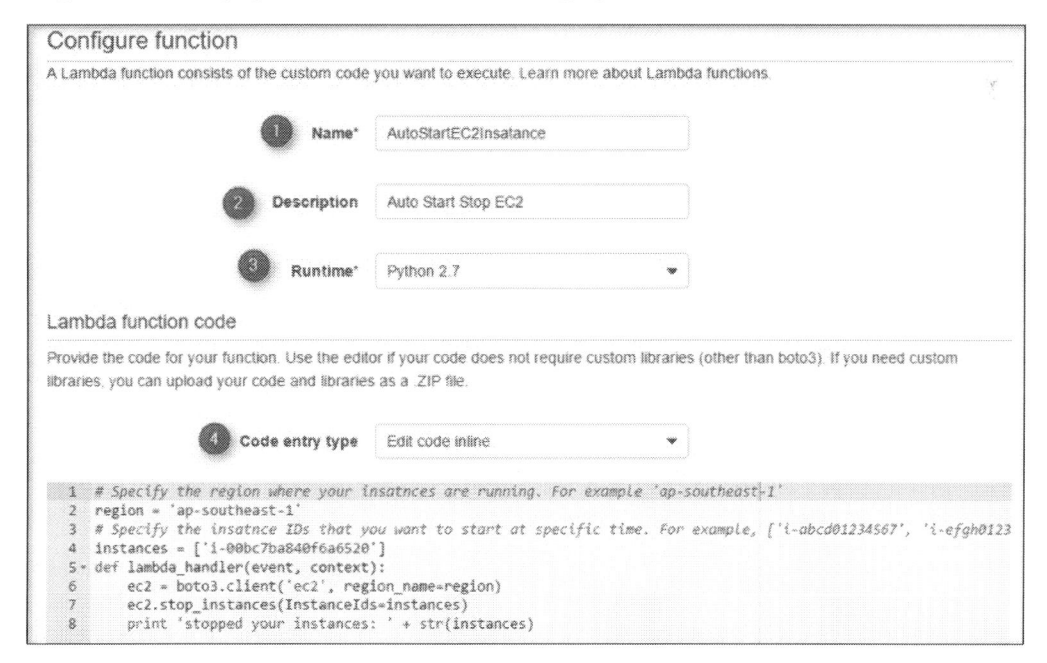

7. On the same page, scroll down to the **Lambda function and handler** section and select **Create a custom role** as shown in the following figure.

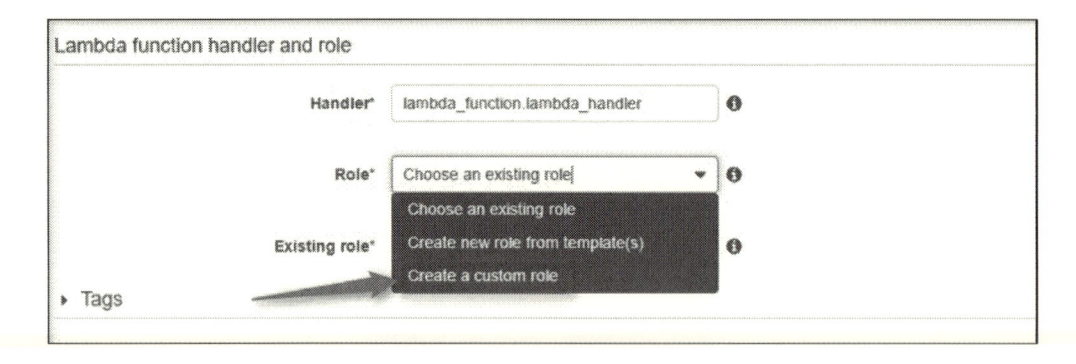

Lambda function handler and role	
Handler*	lambda_function.lambda_handler
Role*	Choose an existing role
	Choose an existing role
Existing role*	Create new role from template(s)
	Create a custom role
▸ Tags	

8. The IAM management console will be opened in a new tab, type a Role name such **AutoStartStopEC2Role**.

Note: The role should have permissions to create logs in the AWS CloudWatch and Start and Stop the EC2 instance. For this, you need to set the appropriate permissions. For this, keep following the below steps

9. Click **View policy document** and then click **Edit** to edit it.
10. Remove the existing script text and type the following script as-is in the edit policy box.

```
{
  "Version": "2012-10-17",
  "Statement": [
    {
      "Effect": "Allow",
      "Action": [
        "logs:CreateLogGroup",
        "logs:CreateLogStream",
        "logs:PutLogEvents"
      ],
      "Resource": "arn:aws:logs:*:*:*"
    },
    {
      "Effect": "Allow",
      "Action": [
        "ec2:Start*",
        "ec2:Stop*"
      ],
      "Resource": "*"
    }
  ]
}
```

11. Click **Save** to save the changes. Click **Allow** and return to the **Lambda Function** console.
12. On the same page, scroll down to the **Advanced Settings** section and set the **Timeout value** more than 1 minutes.

> ▼ Advanced settings
>
> These settings allow you to control the code execution performance and costs for your Lambda fun(
> selecting memory) or changing the timeout may impact your function cost. Learn more about how L
>
> Memory (MB)* 128
>
> Timeout* 1 min 3 sec

*Note: The **Memory** value defines how much maximum memory this Lambda function can use to execute your code. The minimum allowed value is 128 MB. Depending on the type of code and function you want to get it done by AWS Lambda, you may need to select the appropriate memory size. If you are not sure how much memory your Lambda code will take, keep it as minimum as possible.*

*The **Timeout** value defines how long the Lambda code could run before to get timed-out. Most of the lambda functions consumes less than a minute to execute. However, in a few long and complex codes that perform huge tasks, you may need to increase timeout value appropriately. You will pay as much as your Lambda function consumes the memory and execution time.*

13. Finally, click **Next** to proceed. On the **Review** page, click **Create Function** to complete the wizard.
14. To test that your function works properly, make sure that the instance you mentioned while creating the Lambda function is stopped.
15. Click on the **Test** tab and then click **Save and Test**, if everything goes fine, you will see the script execution result as succeeded.

Note: If you get any error, please check the Lambda Function script code.

16. To verify that the instance is started, go to **EC2 running instance list** and check the status of the instance you mentioned in the script.

Creating an Auto Start-Stop Event Schedule Rule

Till now, you have created the Lambda function and an IAM role, however, you have still not defined the time when this Lambda function should execute. For this, you need to create an Event scheduler and perform the following steps.

1. Open the **CloudWatch** console, click **Rules** in the left pane.
2. On the **Create Rule** page, select the **Schedule** button.

3. In the **Cron expression** box, set the desired time when you want to start your instances. In our case, we have set it to start at 01:25 GMT at daily.

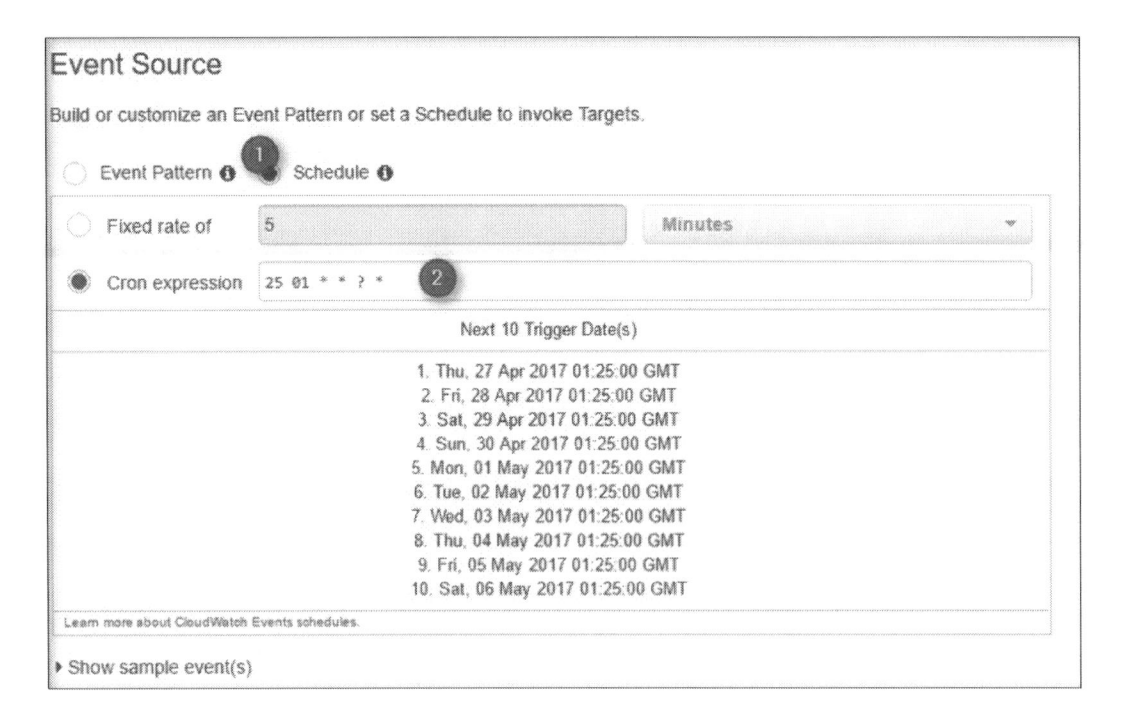

```
Event Source
Build or customize an Event Pattern or set a Schedule to invoke Targets.

  ○ Event Pattern ⓘ      ● Schedule ⓘ
  ○ Fixed rate of    5                              Minutes
  ● Cron expression  25 01 * * ? *

                   Next 10 Trigger Date(s)
                   1. Thu, 27 Apr 2017 01:25:00 GMT
                   2. Fri, 28 Apr 2017 01:25:00 GMT
                   3. Sat, 29 Apr 2017 01:25:00 GMT
                   4. Sun, 30 Apr 2017 01:25:00 GMT
                   5. Mon, 01 May 2017 01:25:00 GMT
                   6. Tue, 02 May 2017 01:25:00 GMT
                   7. Wed, 03 May 2017 01:25:00 GMT
                   8. Thu, 04 May 2017 01:25:00 GMT
                   9. Fri, 05 May 2017 01:25:00 GMT
                   10. Sat, 06 May 2017 01:25:00 GMT

Learn more about CloudWatch Events schedules.

▶ Show sample event(s)
```

4. In the right pane, select the **Lambda Function as Targets** and then select the Lambda function name you have created previously.

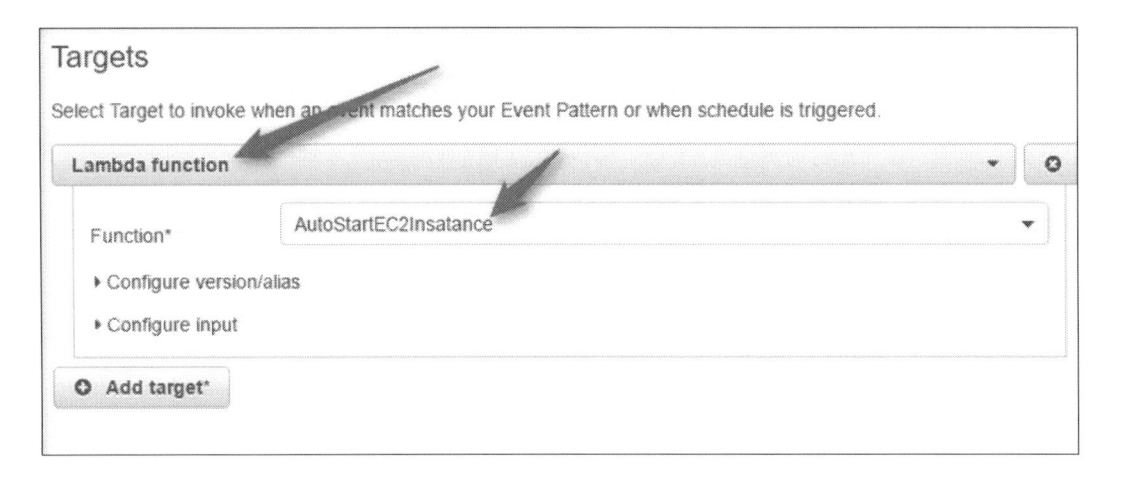

```
Targets
Select Target to invoke when an event matches your Event Pattern or when schedule is triggered.

  Lambda function                                                        ⊗

    Function*     AutoStartEC2Insatance
    ▶ Configure version/alias
    ▶ Configure input

  ⊕ Add target*
```

5. Click **Configure details** to proceed. On the **Configure details** page, specify the rule name, description, and complete wizard.

Test and Validate Auto Start-Stop EC2 Schedule

Now you have done all the steps. Just wait for the time you mentioned in the schedule expression and verify that your instance starts automatically.

Using the similar process, you can also schedule an auto stop event for specific instances at a specific time using Lambda function. The only difference is that you need to use the following

Lambda Function code as shown in the following figure. Just change the highlighted parts region and EC2 instance ID as shown in the following figure.

```
1  import boto3
2  # Enter the region your instances are in, e.g. 'us-east-1'
3  region = 'ap-south-1'
4  # Enter your instances here: ex. ['X-XXXXXXXX', 'X-XXXXXXXX']
5  instances = ['i-             ', 'i-             ', 'i-             ']
6  def lambda_handler(event, context):
7      ec2 = boto3.client('ec2', region_name=region)
8      ec2.stop_instances(InstanceIds=instances)
9      print 'stopped your instances: ' + str(instances)
```

In addition, you also do not need to create the custom IAM role as it is a one-time activity. You can use the same IAM role for this Lambda function.

26. Creating and Recovering EC2 Instance Using Snapshots

Snapshots are really helpful in the case of system or service failure and even in the case of data loss. Snapshots are actually an entire point-in-time copy of a volume. When you create a snapshot of a volume, all the settings, data of that point in that volume is stored in the S3 storage. Later, you can create a volume using this snapshot.

After creating volume from the snapshot, you can attach this volume to an EC2 instance and you will get all the data, settings as it was at the time of taking the snapshot.

Here, we will show you how to take a snapshot of an EC2 instance, create a volume using the taken snapshot, and recover instance and its data using that snapshot.

Creating Snapshot of Attached Volume

Perform the following steps to create a snapshot of a volume.

1. Select the instance of which you want to take the snapshot. Scroll-down the description tab and click the volume link such as **/dev/sda1** of which you want to take the snapshot.

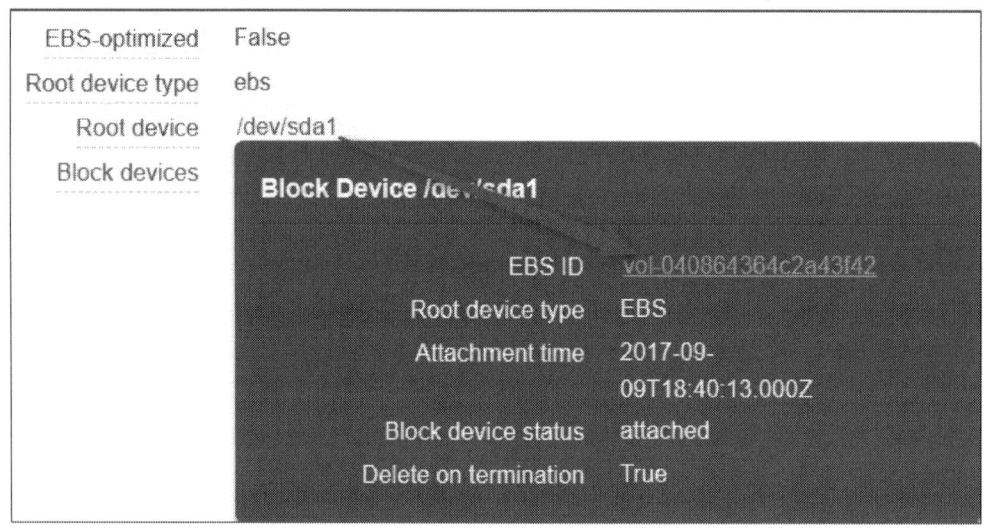

2. In the **Volume** options, click **Actions** and select **Create Snapshot**.
3. On the **Create Snapshot** window, specify the name and description and then click **Create**.

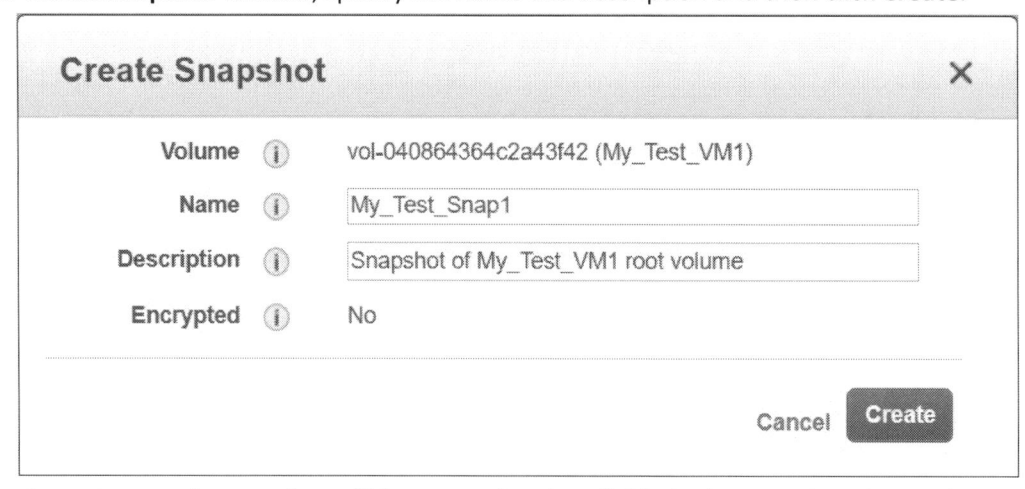

4. After a few minutes, the snapshot will be created and available in the snapshots list as shown in the following figure.

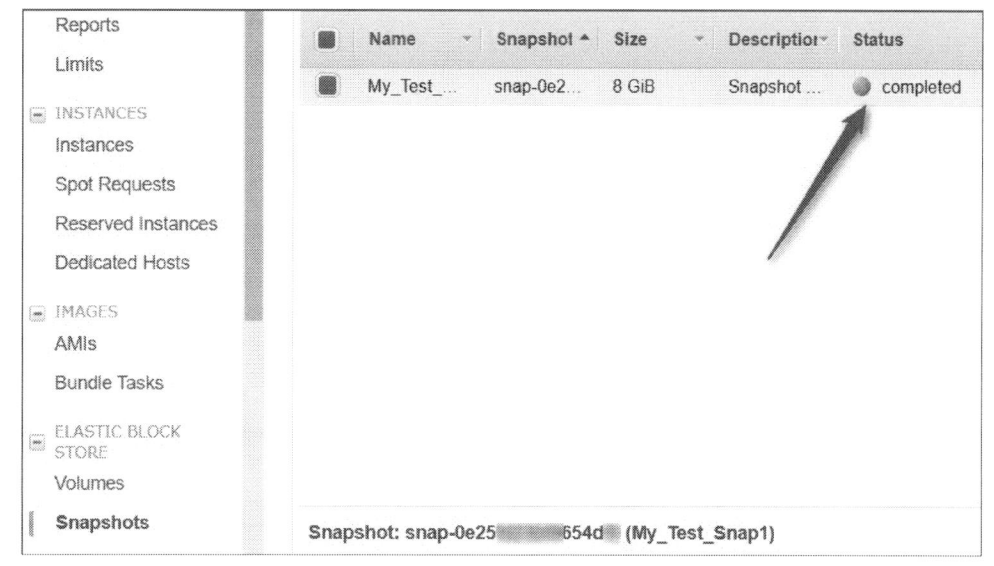

5. While the snapshot is selected, you can perform the following actions as shown in the following figure.

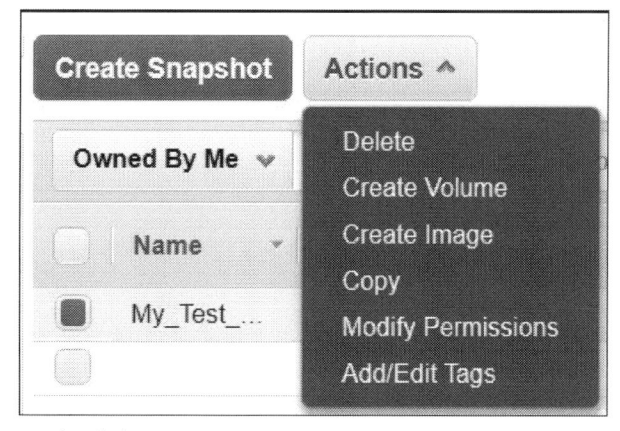

Let's have a brief look at each of them.
- **Delete**: Allows you to delete the selected snapshot.
- **Create Volume**: Allows you to create an EBS volume.
- **Create Image**: Allows you to create an AMI image.
- **Copy**: Allows you to copy the selected snapshot from one region to another region.
- **Modify Permissions**: Allows you to change the snapshot's privacy from private to public and vice versa. Additionally, you can share this snapshot with another AWS account holder.
- **Add/Edit Tags**: Allows you to add or edit the tags.

Creating Volume of EC2 Snapshot

Now, you can create a volume using this snapshot. Later, you can attach this volume to another instance and can fix the issues or copy/move its data.

Since we want to recover the instance's data in this demo, so we will Create Volume using this snapshot. For this, perform the following steps:

1. Select **Create Volume** option from the **Actions** menu.

2. On the **Create Volume** page, select the volume type, volume size, and the availability zone as shown in the following figure.

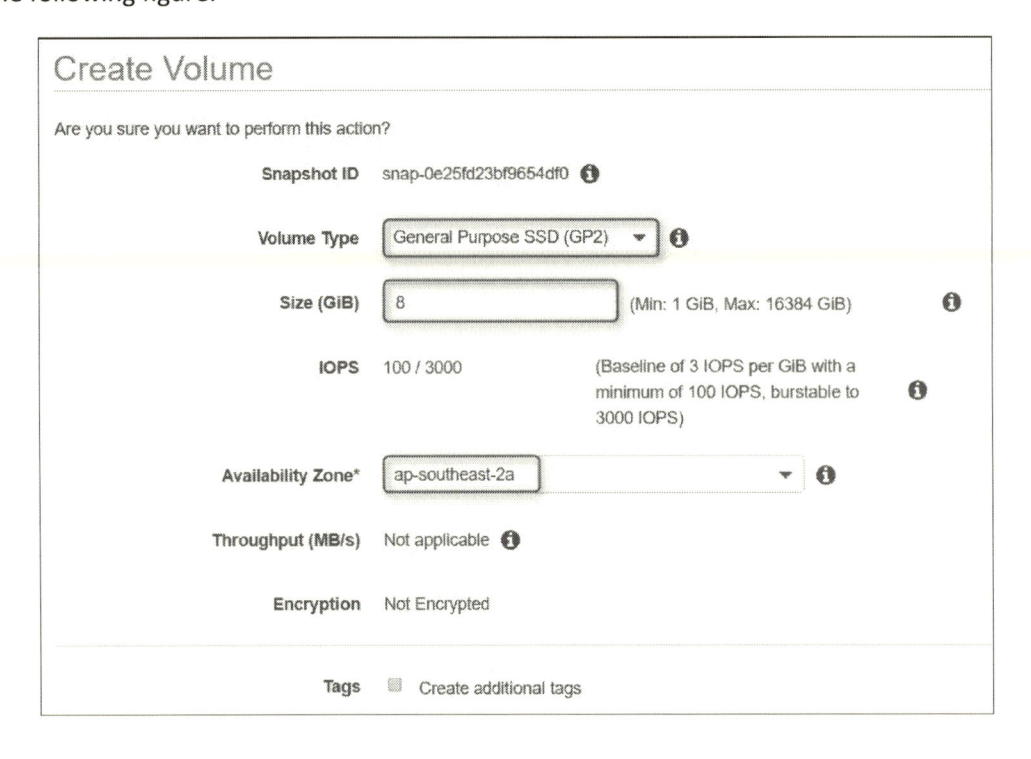

```
Create Volume

Are you sure you want to perform this action?

             Snapshot ID   snap-0e25fd23bf9654df0

             Volume Type   [General Purpose SSD (GP2) ▼]

               Size (GiB)  [8]         (Min: 1 GiB, Max: 16384 GiB)

                    IOPS   100 / 3000  (Baseline of 3 IOPS per GiB with a
                                        minimum of 100 IOPS, burstable to
                                        3000 IOPS)

         Availability Zone* [ap-southeast-2a           ▼]

        Throughput (MB/s)  Not applicable

               Encryption  Not Encrypted

                    Tags   ☐ Create additional tags
```

Note: Whenever you create an EBS volume, either fresh or from a snapshot, you must take care of your availability zone. Because volumes are availability zone specific. It means, if you have created a an EBS volume in AZ1, you cannot attach this volume to any of the instances belong to other availability zone such as AZ2. So, please select the appropriate target AZ while creating an EBS volume.

3. Finally, click **Create** button to finish the wizard. The volume will be created after a few minutes.

Attaching Volume to an Instance

To attach a volume to an instance, you need to perform the following steps:

1. Select the volume, click **Actions** and select **Attach Volume** to attach it to another instance.

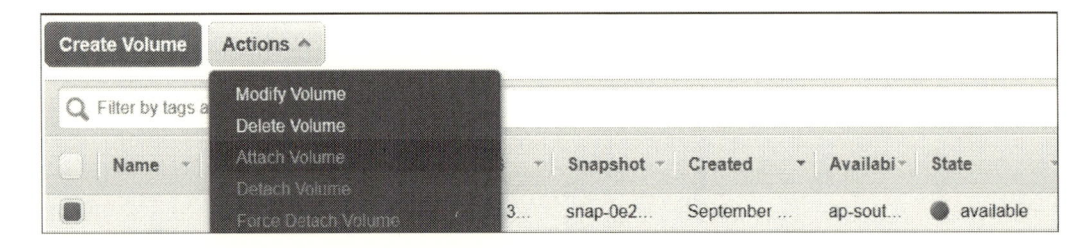

```
Create Volume   Actions ▲

Q Filter by tags a   Modify Volume
                     Delete Volume
     Name      ▼     Attach Volume              ▼  Snapshot ▼  Created    ▼  Availabi ▼  State
                     Detach Volume
     ☐               Force Detach Volume        3...  snap-0e2... September...  ap-sout...  ● available
```

2. In the **Attach Volume** window, type the instance name to which you want to attach this volume.
3. In the **device** box, notice the device name such as **/dev/sdf**.

Note: If you want to attach this volume as the root volume to the selected instance, detach the current attached root volume from that instance and set the device name as /dev/sda1.

Attach Volume

Volume	vol-0331f49d37941039a in ap-southeast-2a	
Instance	i-03c99701e31ec8d2c	in ap-southeast-2a
Device	/dev/sdf	
	Linux Devices: /dev/sdf through /dev/sdp	

Note: Newer Linux kernels may rename your devices to /dev/xvdf through /dev/xvdp internally, even /dev/sdp.

4. Finally, click **Attach** to attach the volume.

Note: The instance must be in the same availability zone in which the volume has been created.

Mounting the Attached Volume

Now, you have the volume attached to an EC2 instance, but cannot use it (in a Linux system) until you mount it on a mount point.

To mount and use the attached volume, you need to perform the following steps:

1. Start the instance to which you have attached this volume and connect it.
2. Execute the **sudo fdisk -l** command to view the device later.
3. Create a mount point and mount the noted volume (output from fdisk -l).
4. Now, all the data on the mounted volume will be available for you. Perform the actions, whatever you want to do. Please refer the following figure for quick steps.

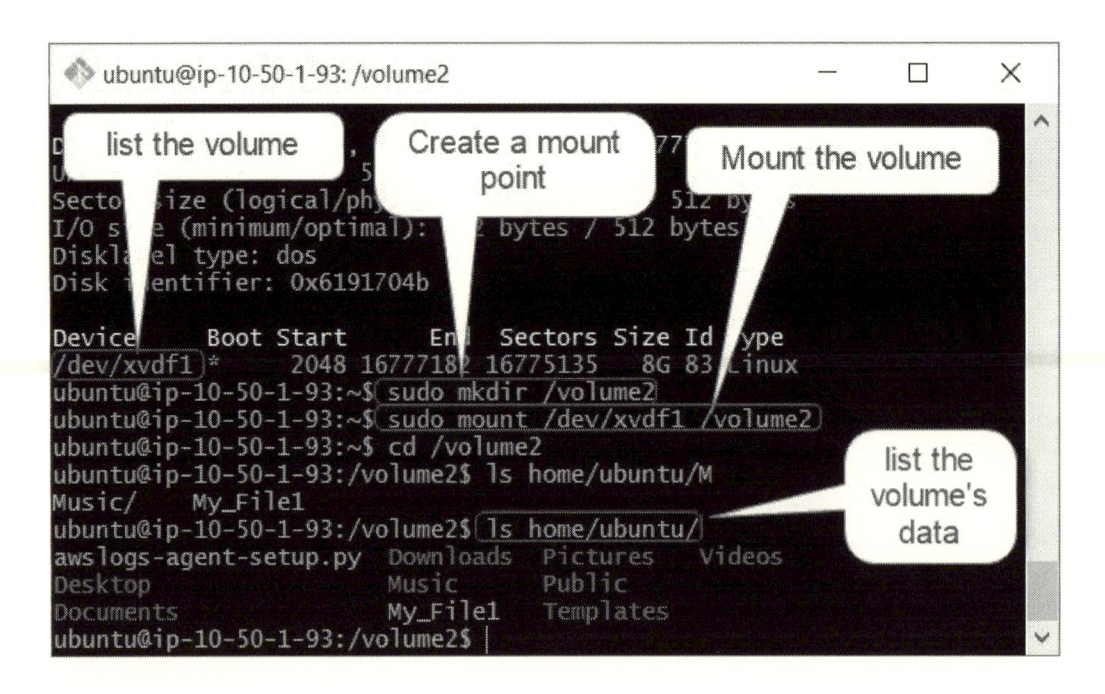

That's all you need to create a snapshot, create a volume using the snapshot, and recover the data using the EC2 snapshot.

27. Working with IAM User Properties

We have already discussed the basics of IAM users and its usage and role. Here, we will explain some of the major properties of an IAM user that will help you to control the AWS resources more accurately, securely, and appropriately. There are various IAM user properties options that you should know. The following four tabs are available for an IAM user:

Permissions

This tab shows what permissions have been granted to the selected IAM user. You can add or remove the permissions using this tab as shown in the following figure.

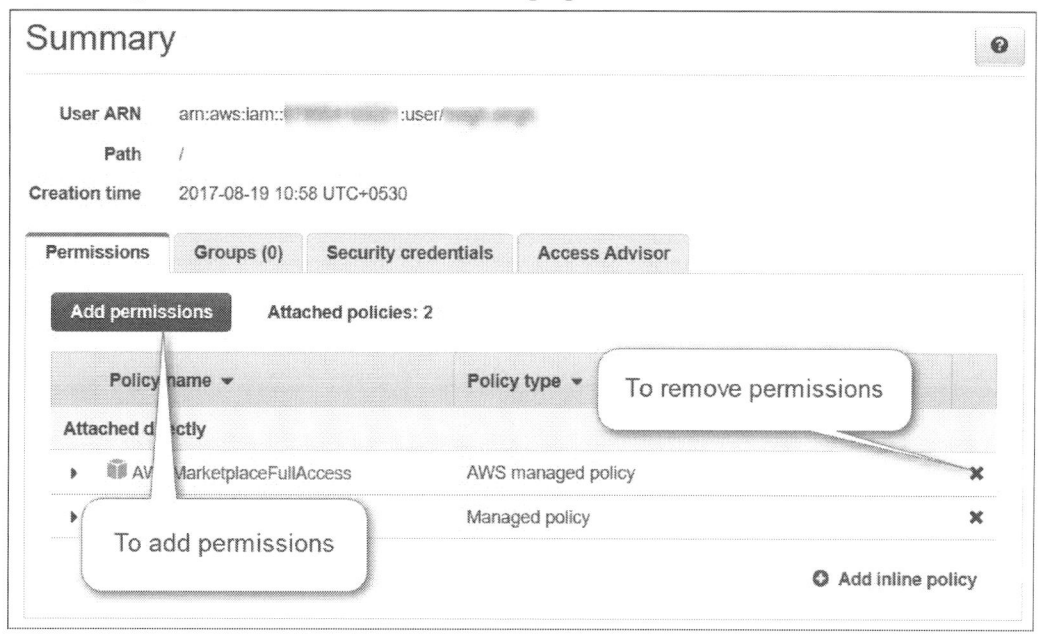

Groups

This tab allows you to add the selected user to a specific group for better control and management.

Security Credentials

This is the most important tab that holds the key features for an IAM user. Here you can do the following actions:
- Enable or disable console login for the selected user
- Change the console password for the selected user
- Enable or disable Multi-factor authentication
- Create and remove CLI-based access keys
- Manage CodeCommit credentials etc.

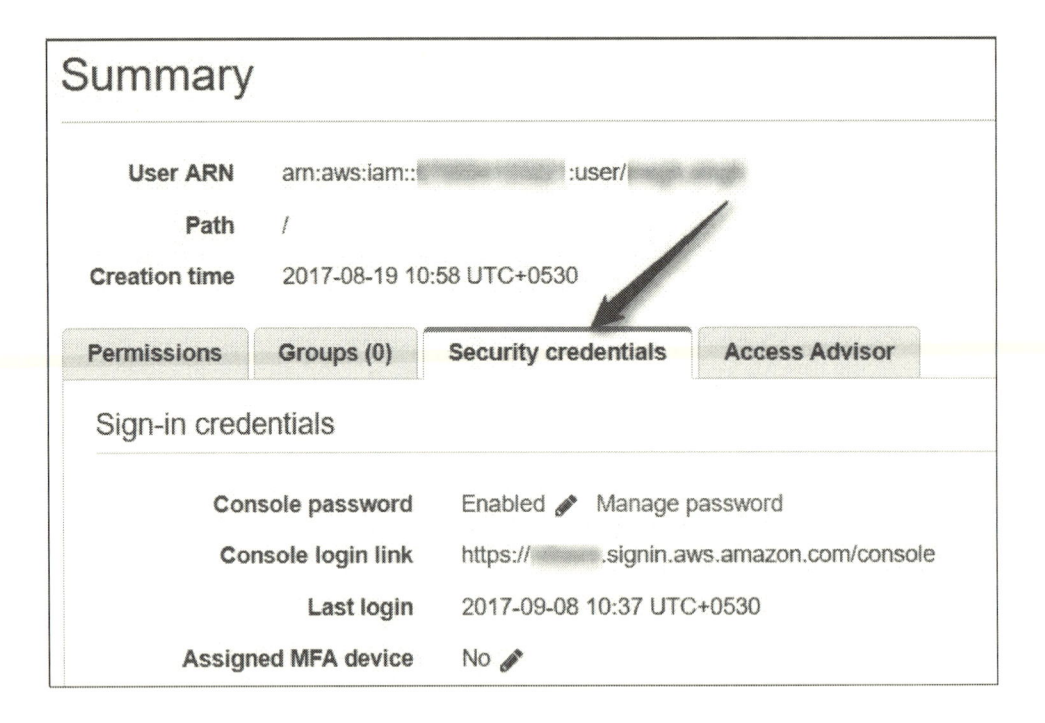

Summary

User ARN	arn:aws:iam::██████:user/██████
Path	/
Creation time	2017-08-19 10:58 UTC+0530

Permissions | **Groups (0)** | **Security credentials** | **Access Advisor**

Sign-in credentials

Console password	Enabled ✏ Manage password
Console login link	https://██████.signin.aws.amazon.com/console
Last login	2017-09-08 10:37 UTC+0530
Assigned MFA device	No ✏

Access Advisor

This tab allows you to track the activities performed by this user. However, if you want more details and tracking for an IAM user, you should use the CloudTrail that is covered in a later section.

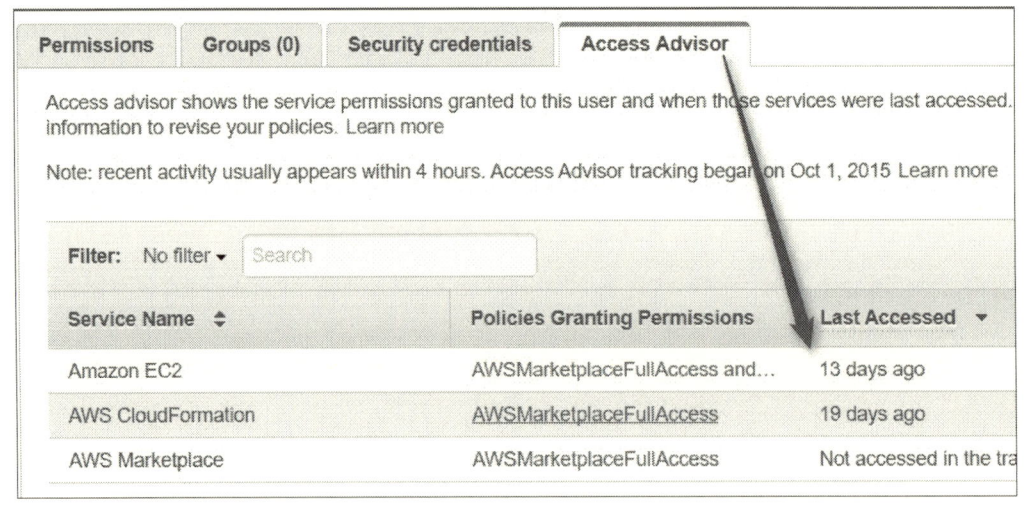

Permissions | **Groups (0)** | **Security credentials** | **Access Advisor**

Access advisor shows the service permissions granted to this user and when those services were last accessed. information to revise your policies. Learn more

Note: recent activity usually appears within 4 hours. Access Advisor tracking began on Oct 1, 2015 Learn more

Filter: No filter ▾ | Search

Service Name ⇕	Policies Granting Permissions	Last Accessed ▾
Amazon EC2	AWSMarketplaceFullAccess and...	13 days ago
AWS CloudFormation	AWSMarketplaceFullAccess	19 days ago
AWS Marketplace	AWSMarketplaceFullAccess	Not accessed in the tra...

28. Creating and Using an IAM Role

You can use IAM roles to delegate access and permissions to your AWS resources. The usage of IAM roles in AWS is very wide. There are various scenarios and requirements where IAM roles can be used. Even you can create a role that allows an IAM user to manage other AWS account managed by your organization. Various CloudFormation templates and services require roles to be created in order to use them. We have already used IAM roles with AWS Lambda functions, CloudWatch Log group in our previous sections. But these were created by the AWS services itself. Here, we will create our own custom IAM roles.

Here, we will show you how to create and use an IAM role to manage AWS resources.

The following steps need to be followed in order to create an IAM role:

1. In the **IAM console**, click **Roles** and then click **Create role** as shown in the following figure.

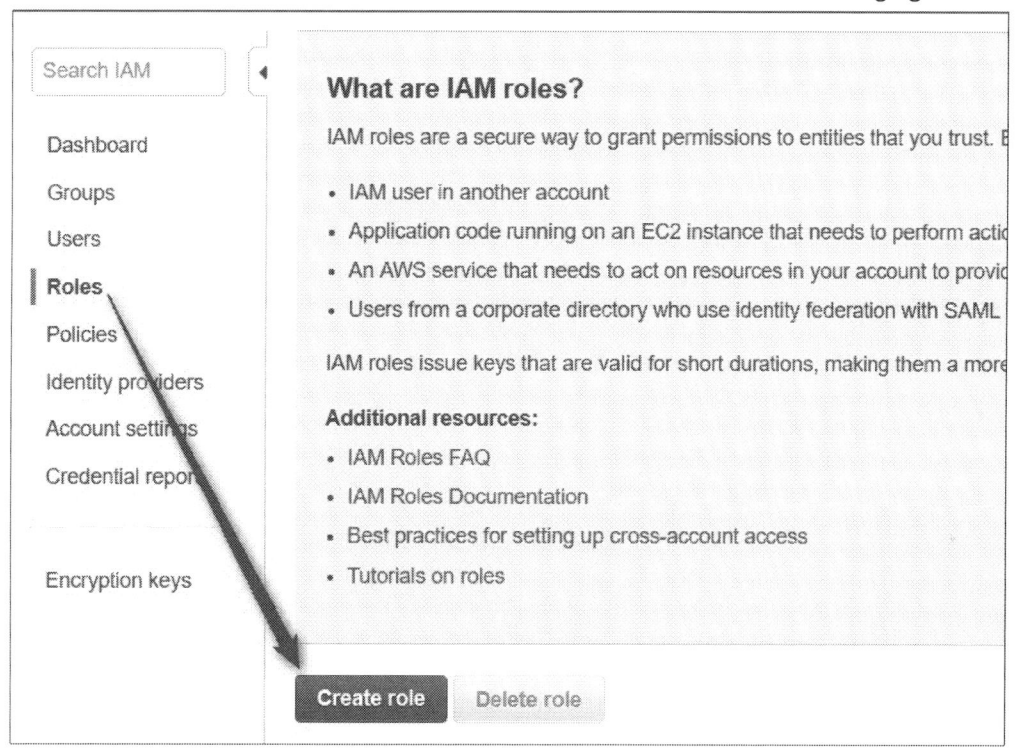

2. On the **Select role type** page, select the type of role, for example, **EC2** under the AWS service as shown in the following figure.

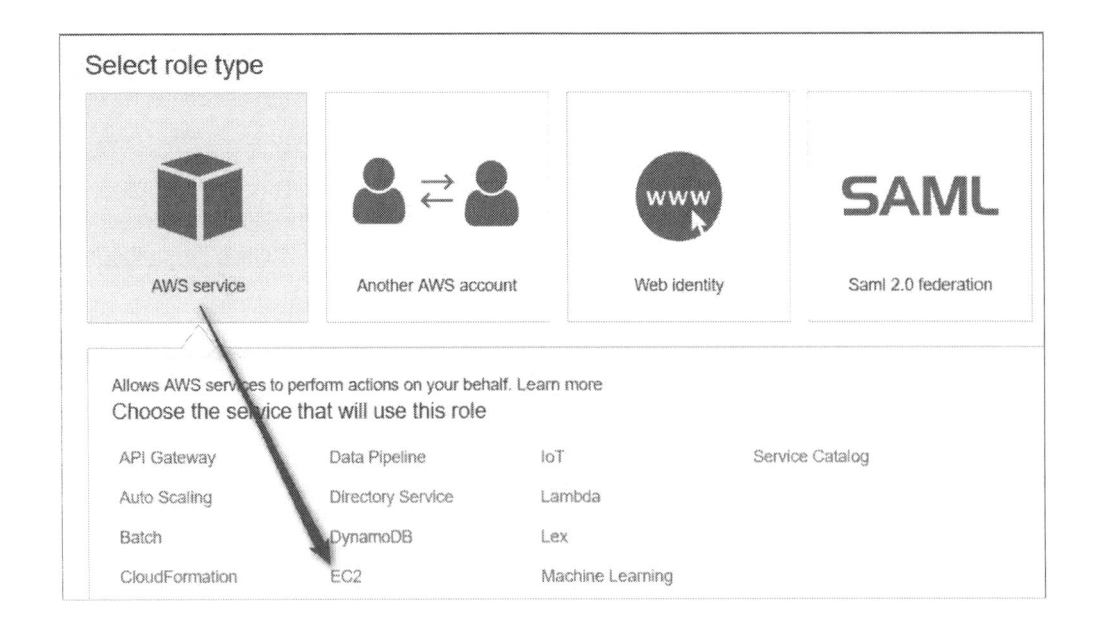

Select role type

AWS service	Another AWS account	Web identity	Saml 2.0 federation

Allows AWS services to perform actions on your behalf. Learn more
Choose the service that will use this role

API Gateway	Data Pipeline	IoT	Service Catalog
Auto Scaling	Directory Service	Lambda	
Batch	DynamoDB	Lex	
CloudFormation	EC2	Machine Learning	

Note: Role type defines what type of role you want to create and what is the purpose of creating this role. There are various types of Role Types that you can choose depending on what tasks, services, and actions you are going to perform with this IAM role.

---

3. Depending on the selected role type, you may be further asked to select your use case as shown in the following figure. For this demo, we will select EC2.

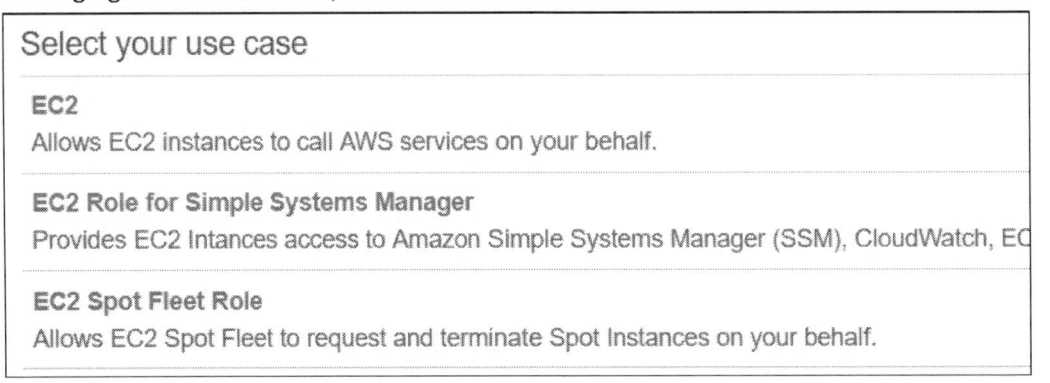

Select your use case

EC2
Allows EC2 instances to call AWS services on your behalf.

EC2 Role for Simple Systems Manager
Provides EC2 Intances access to Amazon Simple Systems Manager (SSM), CloudWatch, EC

EC2 Spot Fleet Role
Allows EC2 Spot Fleet to request and terminate Spot Instances on your behalf.

4. On the **Attach permission policy** page, search and select the policy you want to attach to this role. For example, if you want that this role should be allowed to perform CloudWatch related jobs, select the CloudWatchFullAccess permission as shown in the following figure.

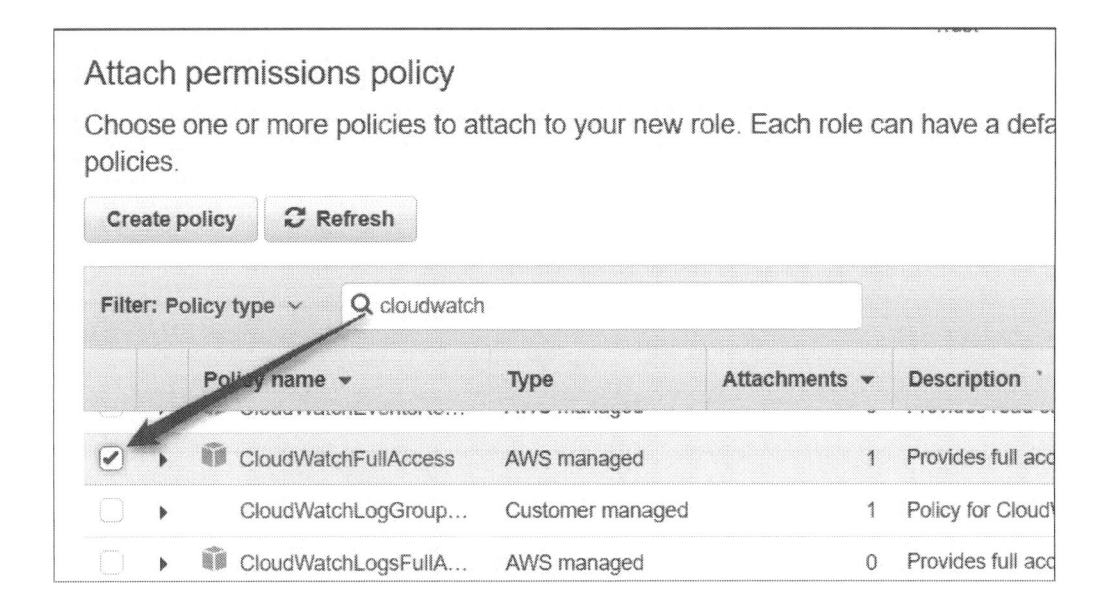

Attach permissions policy

Choose one or more policies to attach to your new role. Each role can have a defa policies.

Policy name	Type	Attachments	Description
☑ CloudWatchFullAccess	AWS managed	1	Provides full acc
☐ CloudWatchLogGroup...	Customer managed	1	Policy for Cloud
☐ CloudWatchLogsFullA...	AWS managed	0	Provides full acc

Note: There are hundreds of pre-configured policies for the various AWS resource usage and control. However, you may not find the appropriate policy as per your exact custom need. Here comes the custom policy as a handy feature, but you have to be familiar with the policy document and how to create and configure new custom policy.

5. In the **Review** page, specify the **Role and Description** and finish the wizard.

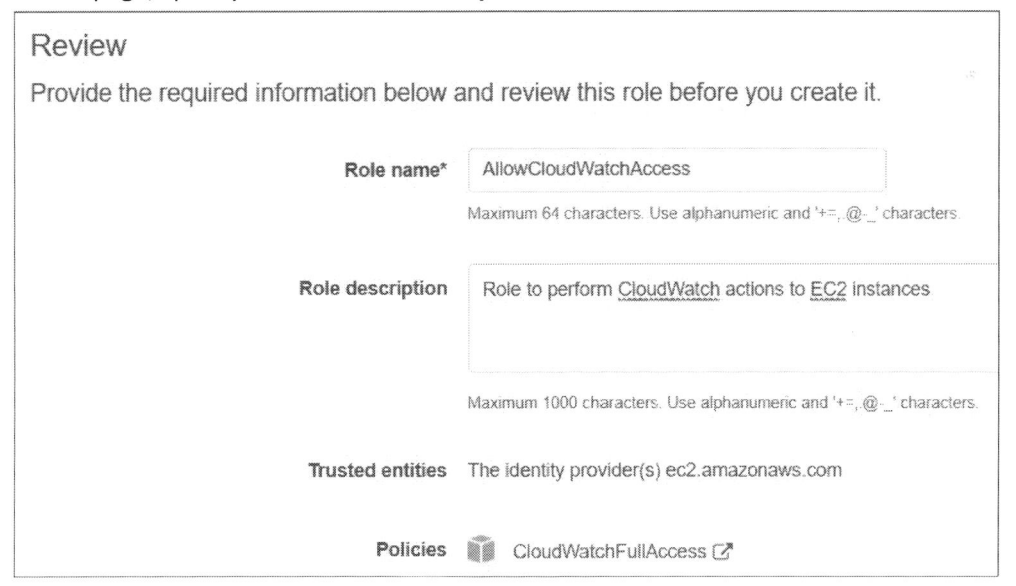

Review
Provide the required information below and review this role before you create it.

- **Role name*:** AllowCloudWatchAccess
  - Maximum 64 characters. Use alphanumeric and '+=,.@-_' characters.
- **Role description:** Role to perform CloudWatch actions to EC2 instances
  - Maximum 1000 characters. Use alphanumeric and '+=,.@-_' characters.
- **Trusted entities:** The identity provider(s) ec2.amazonaws.com
- **Policies:** CloudWatchFullAccess

Attaching IAM role to an EC2 Instance

Once the EC2 Role is created, you can attach it to the desired EC2 instance. To do this, perform the following steps:

1. Select an **EC2 instance** and navigate to **Attach/Replace IAM Role** as shown in the following figure.

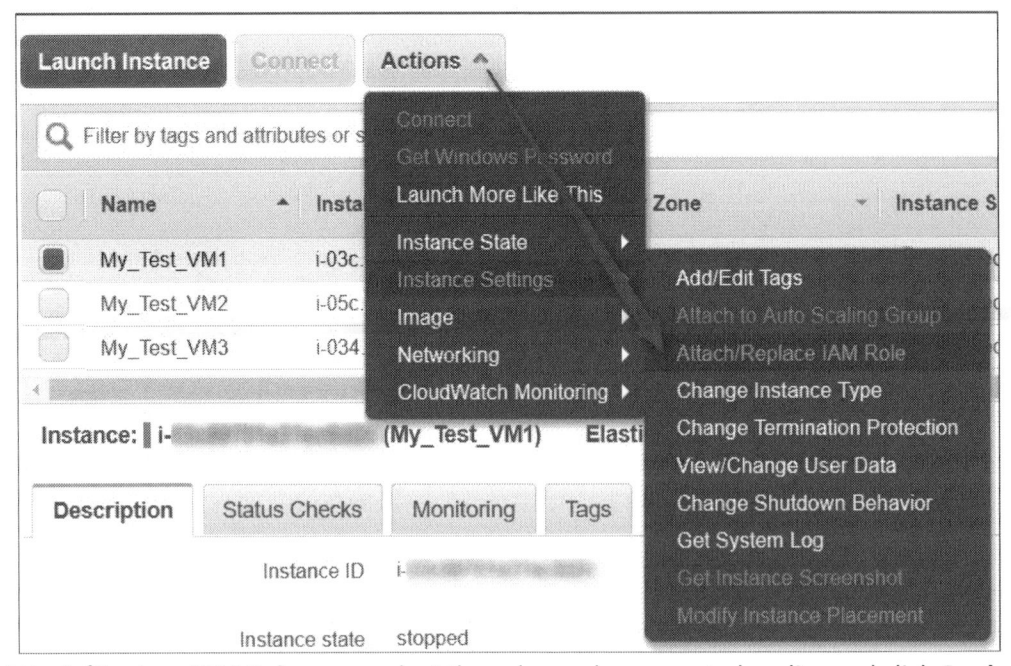

2. In the **Attach/Replace IAM Role** page, select the role you have created earlier and click **Apply**.

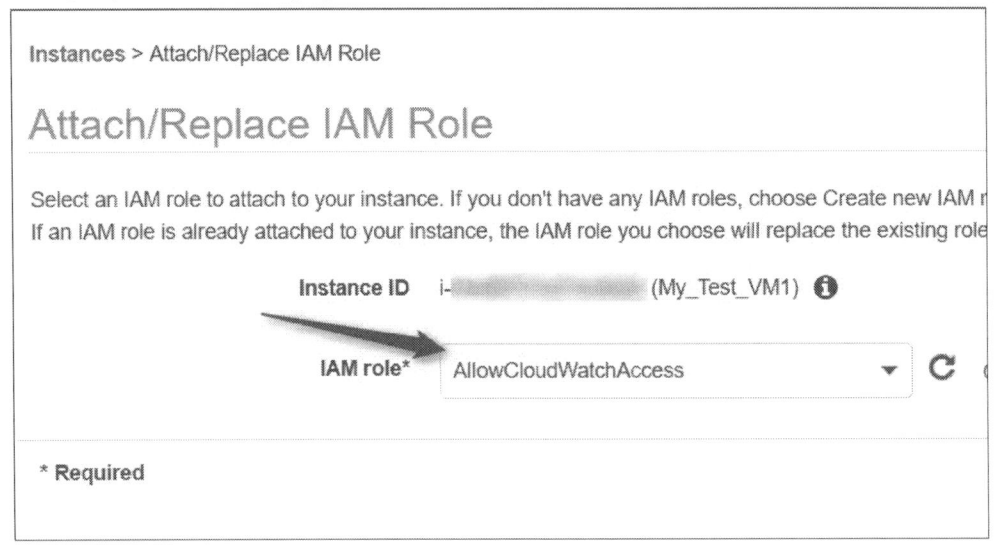

3. In the **Description** tab, you will see that the role is applied to the selected instance. This instance now can perform the CloudWatch related functions without the need of AWS CLI-based access keys at all.

29. Configuring Password Policies for IAM Users

Security is always a major area where you should always focus seriously. Keeping strong password for IAM users will only make malicious users to crack the password harder and harder. As per the AWS official document, you should perform the following actions for a strong password policy:

1. The minimum password length should be set to 8 or greater.
2. The password should require specific character types, including uppercase letters, lowercase letters, numbers, and non-alphanumeric characters.
3. All IAM users should be able to change their own passwords.
4. All IAM users should change their password after a specified period of time.
5. All IAM users should be prevented from reusing previous passwords.

Changing IAM Password Policy Settings

Changing IAM password policy is very simple, just navigate to account settings in the IAM console. The following figure shows the sample of a decent IAM password policy.

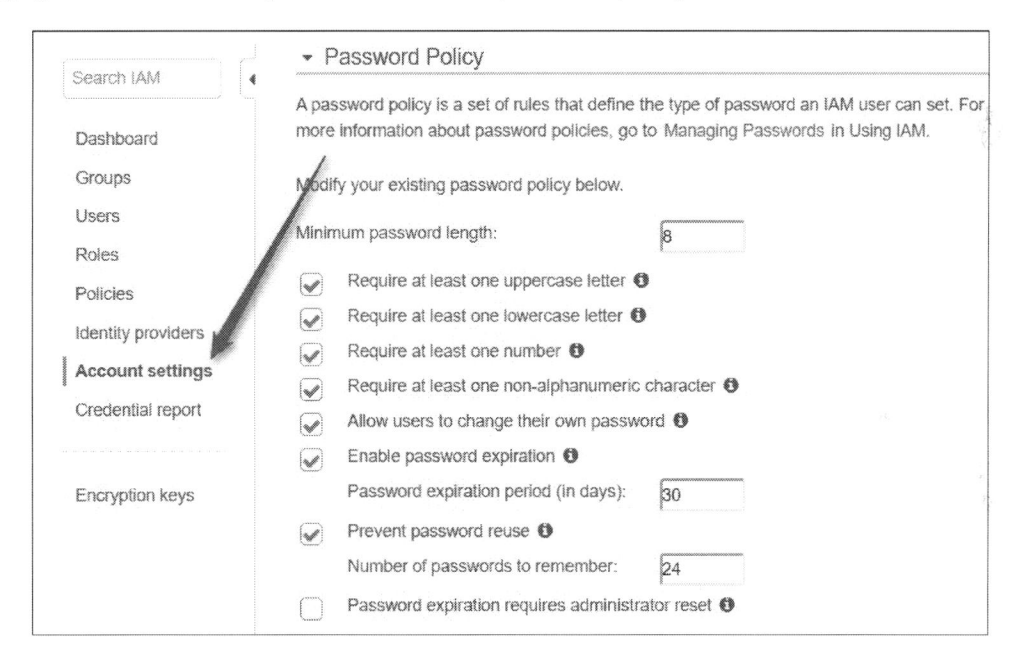

After setting the appropriate values for your IAM password policy, just click **Apply** to make it effective.

30. Installing and configuring AWS CLI

The AWS CLI is an open source tool built on top of the AWS SDK for Python (Boto) that provides commands for interacting with AWS services. You can perform almost all the AWS tasks using the AWS CLI that you perform using the AWS console. The AWS CLI tool is available for both Linux as well for Windows systems. Here, we will explain how to manage AWS Resources using AWS CLI.

You can download and install AWS CLI for Windows XP or later systems. Once you have installed it on a Windows machine, you need to setup credentials method to authorize your Windows machine to perform AWS actions.

Download AWS CLI for Windows System

Depending on the architecture you are using for your Windows machine, click the appropriate download link and download the AWS CLI MSI installer for your Windows system.

- Download AWS CLI Installer for Windows 32-bit systems
  https://s3.amazonaws.com/aws-cli/AWSCLI32.msi
- Download AWS CLI Installer for Windows 64-bit systems
  https://s3.amazonaws.com/aws-cli/AWSCLI64.msi

Installing AWS CLI on Windows System

The installation process of AWS CLI on Windows is pretty simple and straightforward, just click the executable MSI installer file and follow the on-screen instructions to proceed.

Just finish the installation using the default selections.

Installing AWS CLI on Linux system

Depending on the Linux variants you are using, the installation commands for installing AWS CLI in Linux system may vary. But if you are familiar with any one of the Linux variants such as Ubuntu, you should not face any major issue to install it on a different variant such as Red Hat Linux.

For example, to install AWS CLI on an Ubuntu machine, execute the following command:

- *$sudo apt-get install awscli -y*

This is the simplest way to install the AWS CLI tool. But for any reason, if the above method does not work for you, visit the following link and follow the steps to install it with pip method.

- Installing AWS CLI on Linux with Pip
  http://docs.aws.amazon.com/cli/latest/userguide/awscli-install-linux.html

Setup Credentials for AWS CLI

Before you could use the AWS CLI interface to manage the AWS resources, you must set up the proper credentials for the AWS CLI interface. If you are using your local system to perform AWS actions, you must have AWS Access Key ID and AWS Secret Keys with the appropriate permissions to the resources you wish to manage.

For example, if you want to manage S3 buckets using AWS CLI from your local system (Windows or Linux), you first need to create an AWS Access Keys under the Security Credentials tab of an IAM user. These keys need to be configured on your local machine using the **aws configure** command as shown in the following figure.

The following configuration values are needed to setup AWS CLI based credentials:

- AWS Access Key ID: **<You IAM user's access key>**
- AWS Secret Access Key: **<You IAM user's secret key>**
- Default region name: **<You default region such ap-south-1>**
- Default output format: **<Default output such as JSON>**

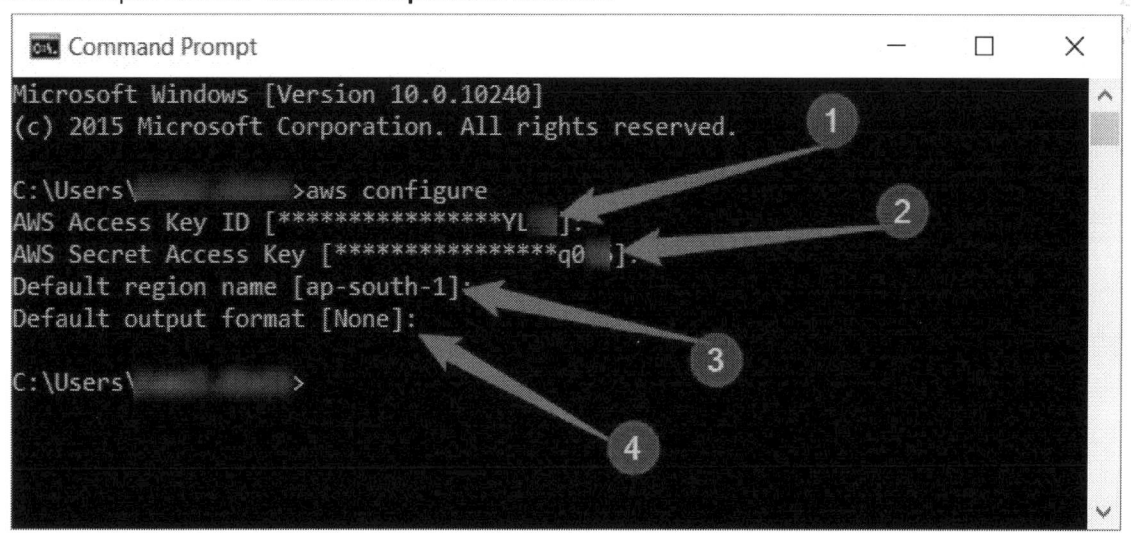

Setting up AWS CLI credentials method will remain same for both Linux and Windows systems. Once the credentials are set, you can perform the actions for which your IAM user is allowed.

31. Configuring OpenVPN Server to Securely Access Instances

We assume that you are already familiar with the usage and importance of VPN server and its features. If not, let me explain the basics of the VPN server.

VPN stands for Virtual Private Network. VPN allows you to access your private network (on premise or on-cloud) over the public network using a secure virtual tunnel. There are various protocols used to secure the traffic over the VPN tunnel such as PPTP, L2TP, IPSec, etc. Most of the Cloud Service Providers also provide their own VPN as managed service such as AWS VPN Gateway and Azure VPN Gateway. However, you can also use a third party VPN solution such as OpenVPN.

OpenVPN is not part of any AWS certification exam or syllabus, this is just a bonus lab for the professionals working (or want to work) on production servers.

Why to Use VPN?

In order to access EC2 instance from your local system, you have to enable the SSH port for EC2 instance publicly.

> *Note: This topic is not a part of AWS Certified Solutions Architect –Associate Exam. This is just for the best practices while using the AWS EC2 instances in the real world.*

Allowing SSH or RDP over the public network might be a little bit risky action in term of security. One more issue you may face that if you have a public subnet and private subnet based VPC network, you cannot access SSH or RDP of your private subnet's EC2 instances directly from your local machine. Here comes OpenVPN as a highly secure and handy mechanism for connecting and managing EC2 instances securely.

The most popular and easy to use VPN solution for AWS cloud is the OpenVPN server solution.

We will use the following network for this lab exercise.

- **VPC**: My_Test_VPC
- **Subnets**:
  - **My_Public_Subnet1**- Belongs to the availability zone1.
  - **My_Private_Subnet1** – Belongs to the availability zone2.
- **Instances**
  - **My_Test_VM1** - Belongs to the public subnet1 and have an elastic IP attached.
  - **My_Test_VM2** - Belongs to the private subnet1 and do not have any public IP.
- **Internet Gateway**: My_Test_IGW1 - Attached to the public subnet1

Launching Pre-configured AMI from AWS Market Place

Here, we will use a pre-configured OpenVPN AMI from the AWS Marketplace and will launch it in My_Public_Subnet1.

> *Note: Almost all Cloud Service Providers such as AWS and Azure provide a marketplace where hundreds of pre-configured solutions (applications, services, servers) are available as ready to use. Few of them are free to use, few of them are*

trial based, and few of them are paid. You can search and find the appropriate pre-configured AMIs and can launch directly to your AWS account as per your need. Please be very careful with the pricing model of these (third-party) pre-configured solutions before to use/launch them.

To launch the OpenVPN server from the AWS Marketplace, you need to perform the following steps.
1. In the EC2 dashboard, click **Launch Instance** and select **AWS Marketplace** in the left pane.
2. In the search box, type **OpenVPN** and select **OpenVPN Access Server** as shown in the following figure.

![Step 1: Choose an Amazon Machine Image (AMI) showing AWS Marketplace search for openvpn with OpenVPN Access Server result]

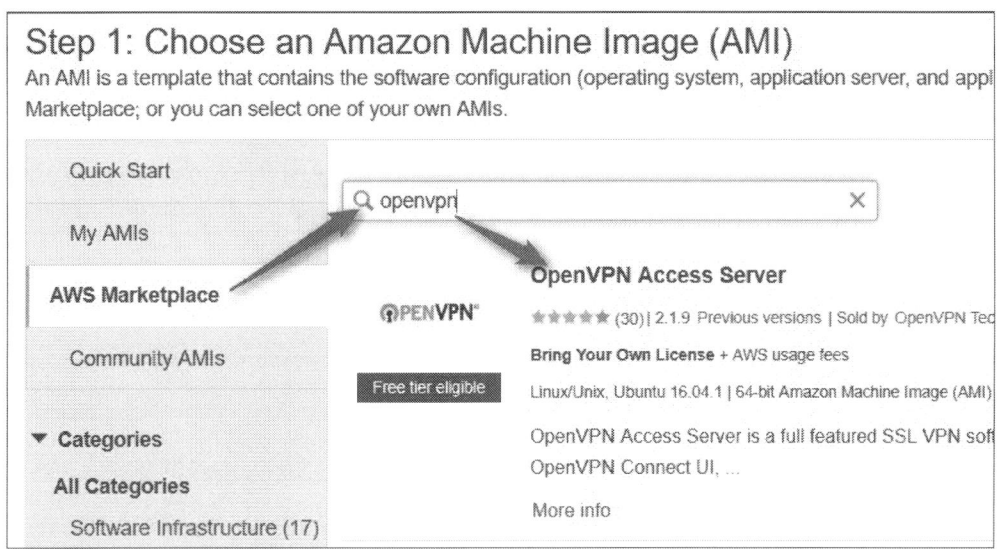

3. Review the instance type and pricing fee for this AMI and then click **Continue** to proceed. You will get two VPN users for free to use with OpenVPN Access Server.
4. On the **Choose Instance Type** page, select the **T2 Micro** option.
5. On the **Configure Instance Details** page, select the **VPC** and your public subnet as shown in the following figure.

![Step 3: Configure Instance Details showing Network vpc-834a13e7 | My_Test_VPC and Subnet subnet-13967474 | Public_Subnet1 | ap-southeast-2]

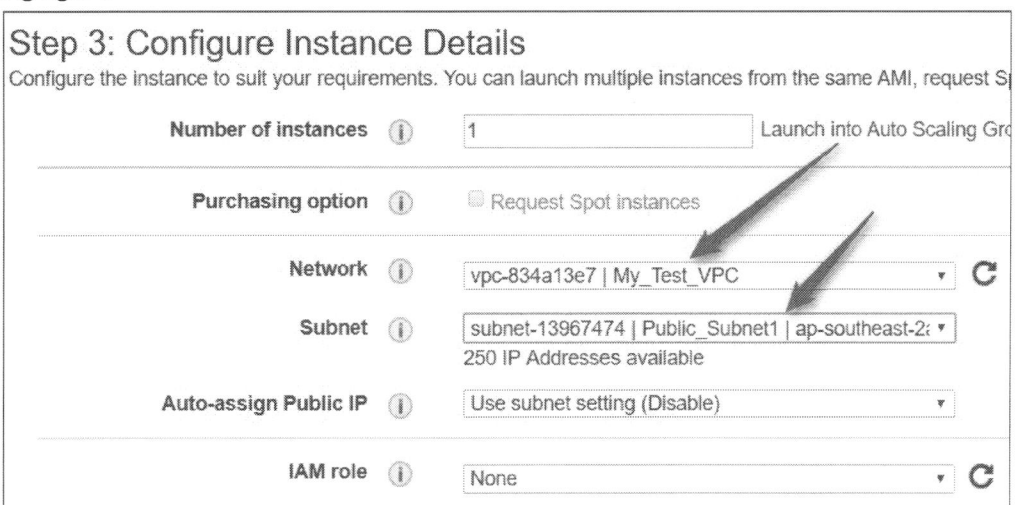

6. On the **Storage** page select the default storage size.
7. On the **Add Tags** page, assign the name as My_Test_VPN1 as the name of the instance.

8. On the **Configure Security Group** page, specify the name of description of the security group.
9. Finally, click **Review and Launch** button to launch it.
10. Specify My_Test_VPN1 as the key pair name and click Launch. Wait for a few minutes to complete the launch process.

Assigning Elastic IP

Depending on your public subnet settings, OpenVPN server may or may not get public IP. To assign an Elastic IP for your OpenVPN server, just generate an Elastic IP and associate it with your VPN server (My_Test_VPN1).

Configuring OpenVPN Initial Settings

The following steps need to be performed to configure OpenVPN server for the first time:
1. Once the instance is ready and the EIP is attached, connect it using the following command
    - *$ssh -i <key-name> openvpnas@<public-ip-address>*
    - You will be prompted to accept the license agreement and you know what you have to do here.
    - Since this is your primary Access Server node, press **enter** to accept the default setting.
    - Press **enter** to accept the default setting for network interface option.
    - Press **enter** to accept the default port for the OpenVPN Access server.
    - Press **enter** to accept the default Web Admin UI port for your server.
    - Keep reviewing the prompts asked by the wizard and choose the appropriate option. For the lab exercise, accepting and keeping the default options are enough.
2. One the wizard is finished, you will get the URLs that will be used to manage the OpenVPN server.

```
openvpnas@openvpnas2: ~                                    —    □    ×
Generating init scripts auto command...
Starting openvpnas...

NOTE: Your system clock must be correct for OpenVPN Access Server
to perform correctly.  Please ensure that your time and date
are correct on this system.

Initial Configuration Complete!

You can now continue configuring OpenVPN Access Server by
directing your web browser to this URL:

https://          :943/admin
Login as "openvpn" with the same password used to authenticate
to this UNIX host.

During normal operation, OpenVPN AS can be accessed via these URLs:
Admin  UI: https://          :943/admin
Client UI: https://          :943/

See the Release Notes for this release at:
   http://www.openvpn.net/access-server/rn/openvpn_as_2_1_9.html
openvpnas@openvpnas2:~$
```

*Note: If you selected any wrong option and want to reconfigure OpenVPN options, you can execute the **sudo open-init --ec2** to re-launch the OpenVPN initial configuration prompts.*

3. Execute the following command to set the password for your Web UI OpenVPN user.
   - *$sudo passwd openvpn*
4. Now, open the browser and log in to your OpenVPN Web Admin UI with username as openvpn.
   - https://<public-ip-address>/admin
5. You will be asked to accept the license agreement, at the first time login.
6. In the **Web Admin** console, you can configure various options for OpenVPN Access server.

The most common and initial configuration options for OpenVPN Access server are described as follow:

Activating License

By default, you will get two users free license for the OpenVPN server, if the number of users are more than two, you can purchase the license. To activate the license, click **License** in the left pane, type license key and click **Add A New License Key** to activate as shown in the following figure.

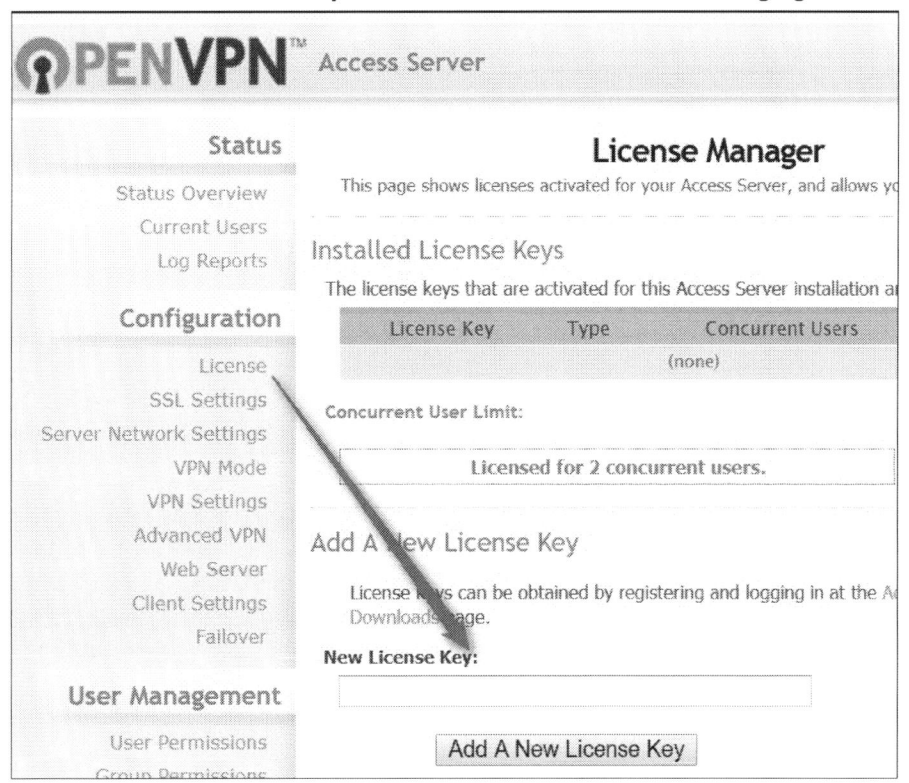

Creating OpenVPN user accounts.

By default, one user "OpenVPN" is already created when you configure your OpenVPN server. This user has admin privileges and should be used to perform the Web Admin UI actions. For the other users who want to connect your AWS infra using the OpenVPN server, a separate user should be created.

For this, just click **User Permissions** under **the User Management** section.

Type a username, set the desired password, and click **Save Settings** to create VPN user as shown in the following figure.

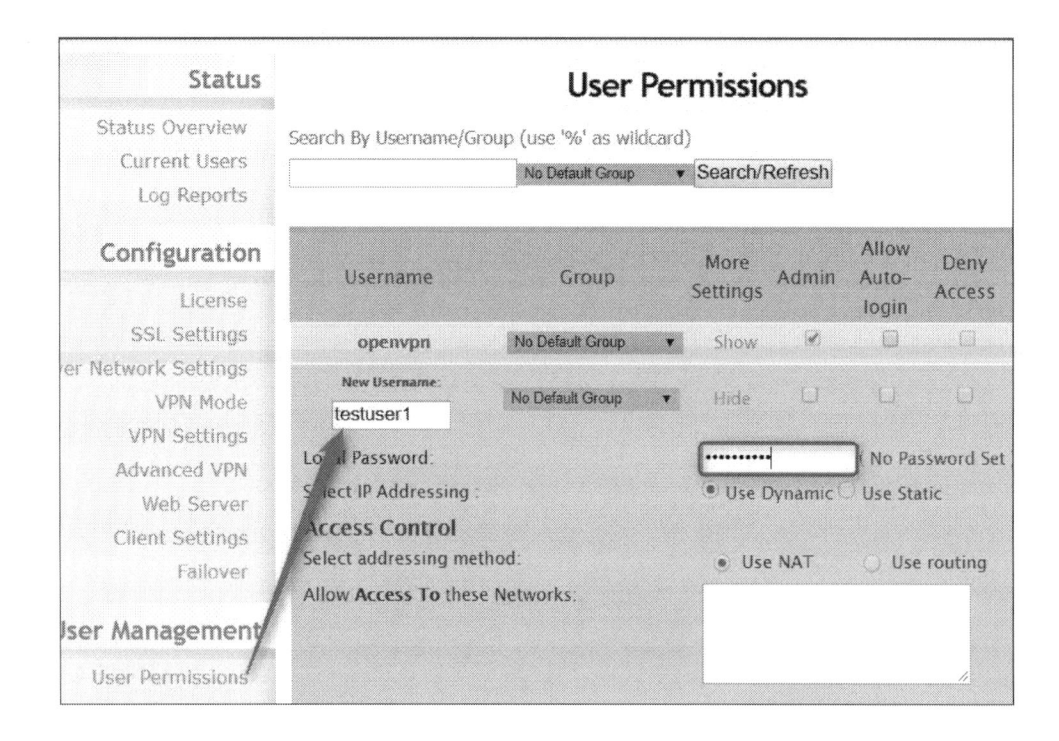

Configuring VPN Settings

Now your OpenVPN server is ready to be used. However, you may also want to configure few other OpenVPN server settings such as what IP address should get a client when connected. What private subnets are allowed to connect through OpenVPN server? These settings can be configured in the **VPN Settings** section.

You can customize the dynamic IP address range for a client under the **VPN IP Network** section as shown in the following figure.

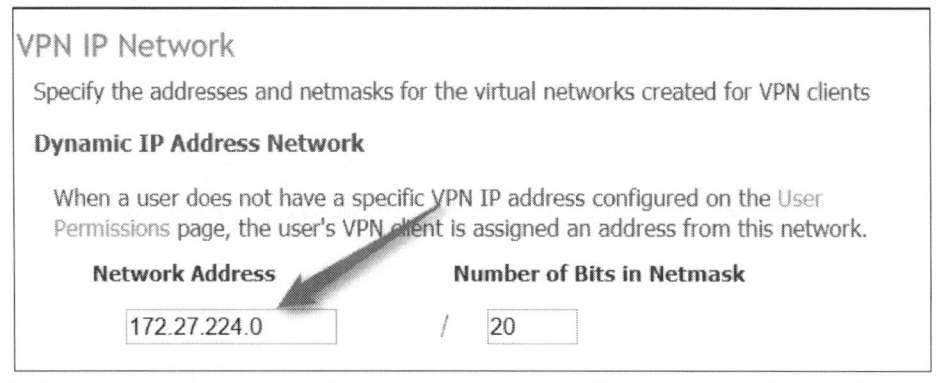

You can specify the private subnet under the **Routing** section as shown in the following figure.

> Routing
>
> Should VPN clients have access to private subnets (non-public networks on the server side)?
>
> Subnets added here will be available Globally. If Group ACLs are desired then those changes should be made in Group/User Permissions
>
> ○ No
>
> ◉ Yes, using NAT
>
> ○ Yes, using routing (advanced)
>
> Specify the private subnets to which all clients should be given access (as '*network/ netmask_bits*', one per line):
>
> 10.50.0.0/16

Note: As per the above figure, VPN users will only be allowed to connect/use resources of 10.50.0.0/16 CIDR range. However, it also depends on the security groups rules, whether the incoming port/protocol for the OpenVPN server is allowed or not, in the EC2 instance's security group.

Enabling Google Authenticator for VPN Clients

If you wish to enable two-factor authentication for your VPN users, you can enable **Google Authenticator Support** feature as shown in the following figure.

Client Settings

This page can be used to configure the Client Web Server or modify Access Server client settings.

Client Web Server

Configure Client Web Server access.
- ☐ Restrict Client Web Server access to Access Server administrators

Note: checking the above box does not prevent users from accessing their client configuration using the XML-RPC/REST API. Use the following option to disable this as well.

Configure XML-RPC/REST API. Note: The XML-RPC/REST API must be enabled to support general Client functionality. Also note that changing this setting will restart the web server.
- ○ Disable API
- ● Enable limited API
- ○ Enable complete API

Configure Google Authenticator support

Google Authenticator is a time-based one-time password authentication system. When enabled, users will be required to provide one-time passwords in addition to other login credentials when connecting to the VPN. Users will need to run the Google Authenticator app on their mobile phone, and key it by scanning a QR code from the Client Web Server.

- ☑ Require that users provide a Google Authenticator one-time password for every VPN login

That's all you need to set up your OpenVPN server with the basic settings. Now, you can connect to this OpenVPN server using the OpenVPN Client tool and can access the private EC2 instances (other resources such as RDS databases) directly.

- Click here more detail about OpenVPN Access Server
  https://docs.openvpn.net/getting-started/

32. Connecting OpenVPN Server

Since we have configured OpenVPN server in the previous lab exercise, here we will explain the process how to connect the OpenVPN server using the OpenVPN client app.

Two-Factor Authentication

If the two-factor authentication is enabled for the OpenVPN access server, then you should consider the following else you may skip this.

Before you can connect to the VPN server, you need to download two step authentication application such as Google Authenticator on your mobile. Depending on your mobile platform, you can download it for iPhone store, Android store, and also for Blackberry mobile. If you are using Windows phone, you can use Authenticator+ app available in the Windows store.

Alternatively, you can also use two factor google chrome extension for Google Chrome browser. But it is not as secure as having mobile based two-factor authentication.

Once you have installed the Two steps Authentication app, you need to perform following steps:

Setting up Two Factor Configuration

1. Use the below URL to open the VPN connection
- https://<openvpn-public-ip>
2. On the **OpenVPN** window, type your VPN username and password.
3. Select the **Login** and click the **Go** button.

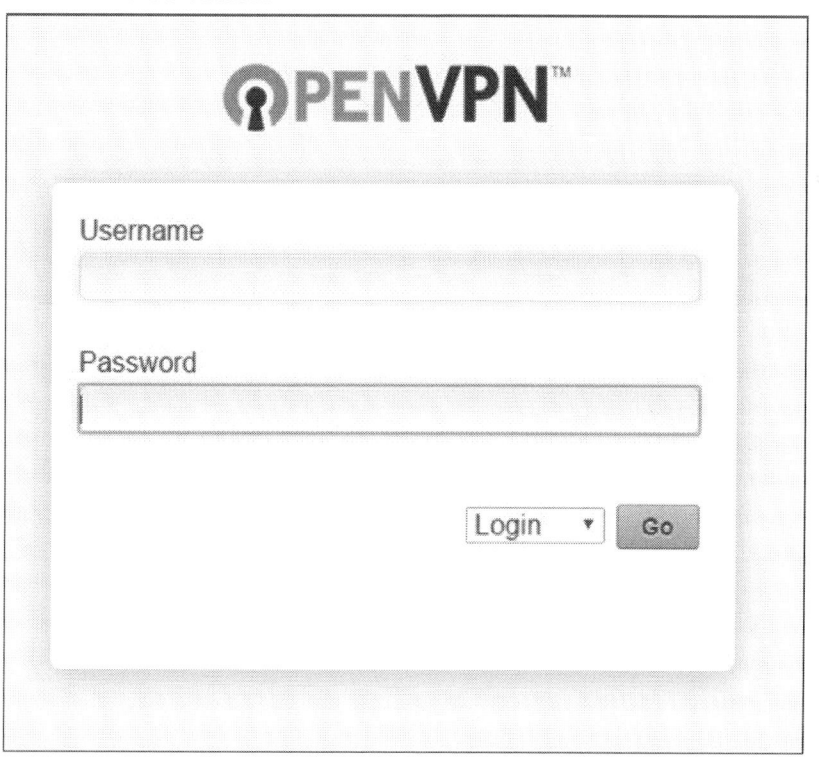

4. On the next window, you will see the link from where you can download the OpenVPN client app.
5. If the two-factor authentication is enabled, scroll-down and scan QR code using **Google Authenticator**. Alternatively, you can also enter secret key manually if you have a problem with scanning the QR code.

6. Click **I Scanned the QR code** to proceed.
7. Next, you need to download the OpenVPN client tool depending on the platform Windows/Linux/MAC you are using. For the future reference, you also need to **download the connection profile file** by clicking **yourself (user-locked profile)** link.

> Logout
>
> To download the OpenVPN Connect app, please choose a platform below:
>
> - OpenVPN Connect for Windows
> - OpenVPN Connect for Mac OS X
> - OpenVPN Connect for Android
> - OpenVPN Connect for iOS
> - OpenVPN for Linux
>
> Connection profiles can be downloaded for:
>
> - Yourself (user-locked profile)

Setting Google authentication app, downloading client profile, installing OpenVPN client connect tool all these are a one-time activity.

Connecting Using OpenVPN Client Tool

We assume you have downloaded and installed OpenVPN client on your machine. Depending on the OS platform, you may need to adjust some settings.

For Linux Platform

For Linux platform (Ubuntu), you need to execute the following commands to connect OpenVPN.

- *$sudo apt-get install openvpn*
- *$sudo openvpn --config <path of user connection ovpn file>*

For Windows OS

For the Windows-based system, you need to perform the following steps:

1. Open the OpenVPN client application, type the public IP address of your OpenVPN Access Server and then click **Connect**.

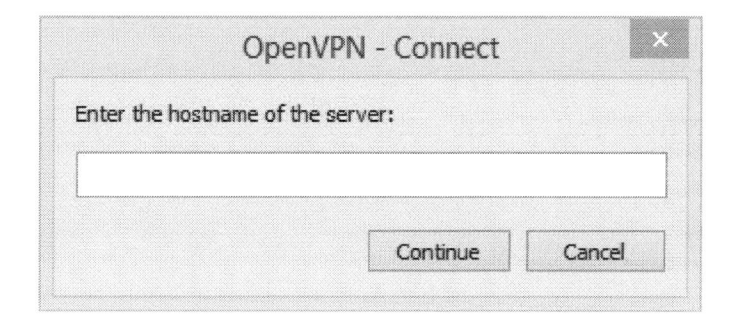

2. If your system is behind a proxy server, you need to set the Proxy address before to proceed next. For this, on the **OpenVPN Client** app, click **Options**, select **HTTP Proxy** and then set the appropriate proxy address.
3. On the **Connect** window, type your username and password and proceed to the next.

4. If the **Google Authenticator** feature is enabled then you will need to type the authenticator dynamic code before to click **Connect**.
5. Now, you should be connected to your OpenVPN Access server and should get a private IP address for your local system.

Now, you can connect your internal private EC2 instances from your local system. But before this, make sure that your instances' security groups are configured to allow incoming traffic from the OpenVPN server network.

33. Configuring Linux Bastion Server for Securely Access SSH of Private Instances

Bastion server is nothing but just a Linux secured server acting as a jump server. It allows you to connect your internal private servers securely. The Bastion server is typically configured in the Private subnet and only accessible through OpenVPN connection. If you don't have OpenVPN server, then you can launch Bastion server in a public facing subnet. You should allow SSH connections of your internal EC2 instances towards Bastion server. DevOps users will first connect to Bastion server and then will connect to internal EC2 instances depending on what instances are allowed for to use for a specific user.

We will use the following scenario to demonstrate how to use Bastion server to connect internal private EC2 instances.

In the below figure you can see:
- There is one VPC with two availability zones.
- The VPC consists of two subnets: one is public and another is the private subnet.
- The VPC has an OpenVPN server configured and running, which is placed on the public subnet.
- The VPC has one instance that belongs to the internal private subnet and does not have any public IP associated.

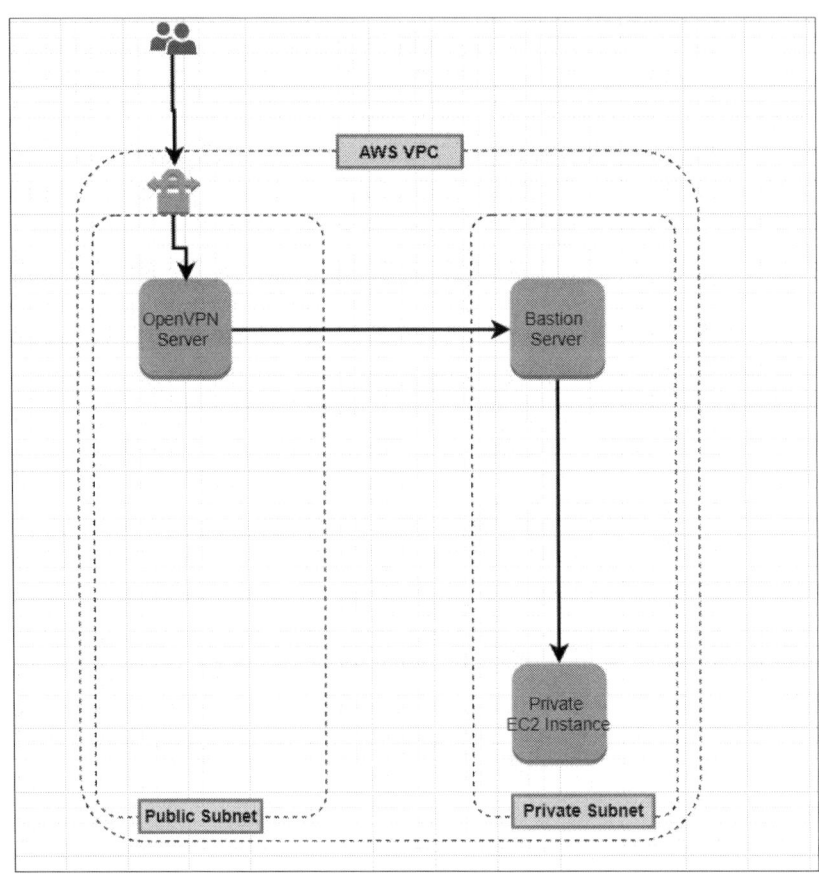

We will launch the bastion server on the private subnet and will connect the internal private EC2 instance using this bastion.

We assume that you have already configured and running the OpenVPN access server.

Launching a New Bastion Server

Now, launch a new Ubuntu Linux instance with the following settings:
- **Amazon Machine Image**: Ubuntu 16.04
- **Instance type**: T2 Micro
- **VPC**: My_Test_VPC
- **Subnet**: Private Subnet1
- **Storage**: Default size (8 GB)
- **Instance Name**: My_Test_Bastion1
- **Security Group**: My_Test_Bastion_SG1
- **Key pair Name**: My_Test_Bastion1

Configuring Security Groups

Once the bastion server is launched, you need to update the security group rules as per the network diagram shown above.

The following points explain the security group requirements in details:

1. My_Test_VPN_SG1 (security group attached to OpenVPN server)

    The SSH port of this security group should only be allowed for your IP location. For this, edit the security group inbound rule and select My IP for SSH as shown in the following figure.

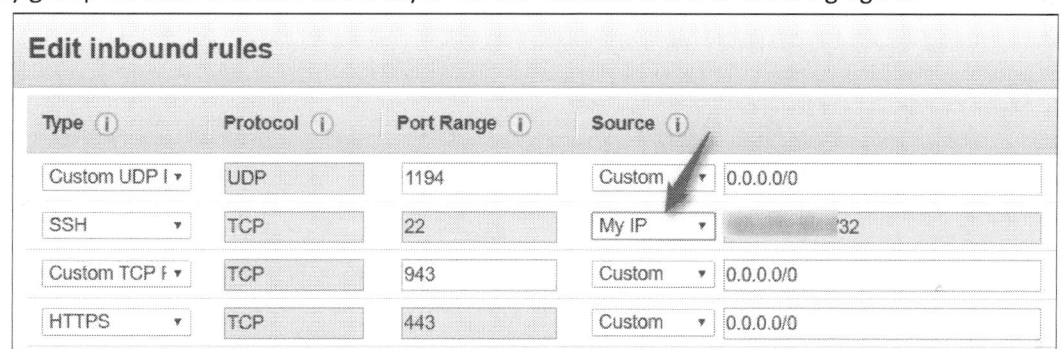

Type	Protocol	Port Range	Source	
Custom UDP I	UDP	1194	Custom	0.0.0.0/0
SSH	TCP	22	My IP	/32
Custom TCP I	TCP	943	Custom	0.0.0.0/0
HTTPS	TCP	443	Custom	0.0.0.0/0

2. My_Test_Bastion_SG1 (Security group attached to bastion server)

    The Bastion server's SSH should be allowed for OpenVPN network. For this, select the bastion server's security group and click Edit inbound rule.

3. In the **Source** drop-down, select **Custom** and specify the security group ID of OpenVPN server's attached security group as shown in the following figure.

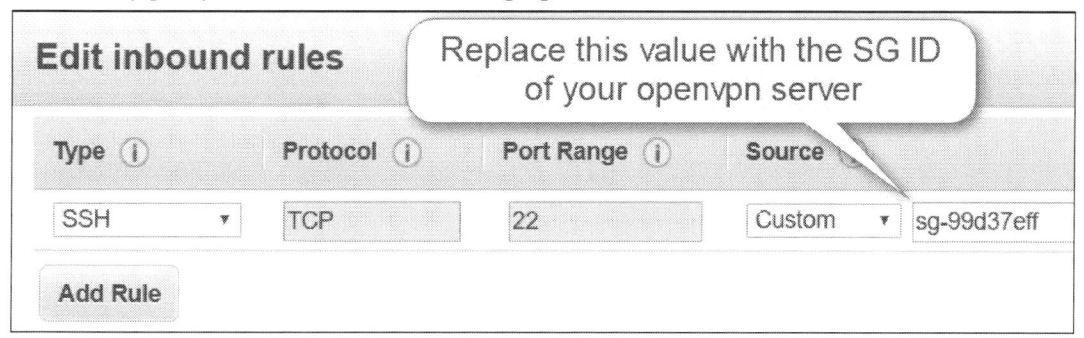

    Edit inbound rules

    Replace this value with the SG ID of your openvpn server

Type	Protocol	Port Range	Source	
SSH	TCP	22	Custom	sg-99d37eff

    Add Rule

4. My_Test_VM_SG (Security group attached to private instance).

Now, your internal private instances SSH should only be allowed for Bastion server. Anyone who wants to connect your internal instances should come through the bastion server. For this, you need to allow SSH of the private instance for My_Test_Bastion_SG1.

5. Edit the inbound rule and paste the bastion server's SG ID in the source custom value in front of SSH port as shown in the following figure.

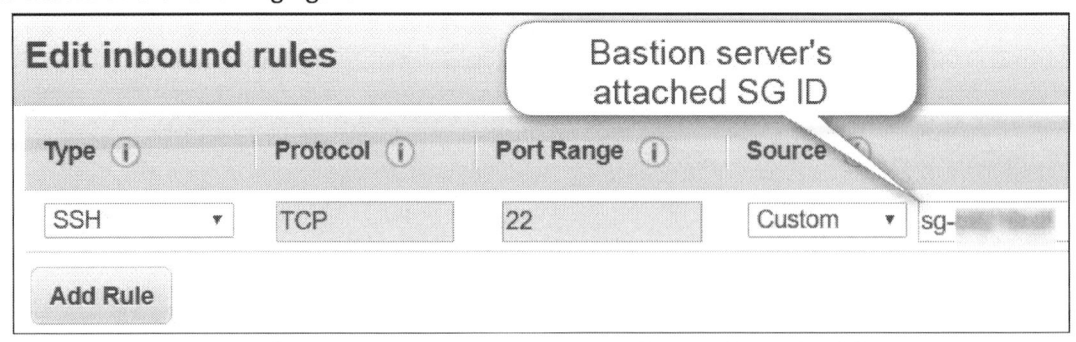

Edit inbound rules

Type	Protocol	Port Range	Source
SSH	TCP	22	Custom ▼ sg-

Add Rule

(Bastion server's attached SG ID)

Now, if you want to access SSH of your private instance, you need to perform the following process:

1. Connect to your OpenVPN server using the VPN username, password, and optionally google authenticator code (if enabled).
2. Once you are connected to OpenVPN server, you will get a private IP address.
3. From your local system's terminal, you can connect now Bastion server.
4. From bastion server's terminal, you can connect to your private EC2 instances.

Connecting SSH using Bastion Server

From your local system's terminal, execute the following command to enable SSH agent forwarding server. This will allow you to add SSH keys of Bastion and Internal EC2 instance using SSH Agent service. Thus eliminating the manual copying of SSH access keys on individual servers.

- $eval $(ssh-agent)
- $ssh-add -k <bastion-server-ssh-key>
- $ssh-add -k <internal-instance-ssh-key>
- $ss -A user@<bastion-server-private-ip>

For example, if your bastion server key is My_Test_Bastion1.pem, private instance's key is My_Test_VM2, and the bastion server IP address is 10.50.2.147 then you need to execute the following commands. (Assuming your instance's username is ubuntu)

- $eval $(ssh-agent)
- $ssh-add -k My_Test_Bastion1.pem
- $ssh-add -k My_Test_VM2.pem
- $ssh -A ubuntu@10.50.2.147

From the bastion server terminal, you can access all the private instances whose SSH ports are allowed in the inbound rule for Bastion server's security group.

For example, if your private instance's username is ubuntu and IP address is 10.50.2.115, then execute the following command on bastion server's terminal.

- $ssh ubuntu@10.50.2.115

You should be connected even without mentioning the .pem key as you have already added that with the SSH forwarding agent service.

34. Working with S3 Buckets

The Amazon Simple Storage Service (S3) is one of the most popular and premier AWS Cloud services. Amazon S3 is an object storage solution designed for storing and retrieving any amount of data from anywhere. Amazon S3 stores data for millions of applications used by market leaders in every industry. S3 buckets are typically folders used to store your data. You can create your own customized folder structure inside an S3 bucket.

We assume that you are already familiar with the basics of Amazon S3 storage, its permissions, and policy concepts. However, here we would like to highlight a few of the basic features of S3 storage.

- You can upload a maximum of a 5 GB of a single file to S3 bucket.
- You can upload any amount of data to S3 storage.
- By default, all the S3 buckets are private until unless you make them publicly manually.
- You can host a static website using the S3 storage and server-less architecture.
- S3 buckets are region specific.
- S3 bucket names are globally unique across all the AWS accounts.

S3 Storage class is further divided into multiple storage classes. Understanding the key differences between various S3 storage classes is very important for any AWS exam point of view (even to work on AWS cloud platform). The following figure explains the basic features and differences provided by various S3 storage classes. Please try to understand them as much as possible.

	S3 Standard	S3 Standard-IA	S3 One Zone-IA	Amazon Glacier
Designed for Durability	99.999999999%	99.999999999%	99.999999999%†	99.999999999%
Designed for Availability	99.99%	99.9%	99.5%	N/A
Availability SLA	99.9%	99%	99%	N/A
Availability Zones	≥3	≥3	1	≥3
Minimum Capacity Charge per Object	N/A	128KB*	128KB*	N/A
Minimum Storage Duration Charge	N/A	30 days	30 days	90 days
Retrieval Fee	N/A	per GB retrieved	per GB retrieved	per GB retrieved**
First Byte Latency	milliseconds	milliseconds	milliseconds	select minutes or hours***
Storage Type	Object	Object	Object	Object
Lifecycle Transitions	Yes	Yes	Yes	Yes

Image Credit: Amazon

Recommended links:
- Getting Started With Amazon S3
  http://docs.aws.amazon.com/AmazonS3/latest/user-guide/what-is-s3.html

Here, we will show you how to create, rename, and delete S3 buckets and how to upload and download data in S3 buckets using the console-based GUI interface as well using the AWS CLI tool.

Creating an S3 Bucket Using the AWS Console

To create an S3 bucket using the AWS console is pretty simple, just follow the following steps:

1. Login to **AWS console** and navigate to the S3 page.
2. Click **Create bucket** to create a new S3 bucket as **Create bucket** dialog box will be displayed as shown in the following figure.

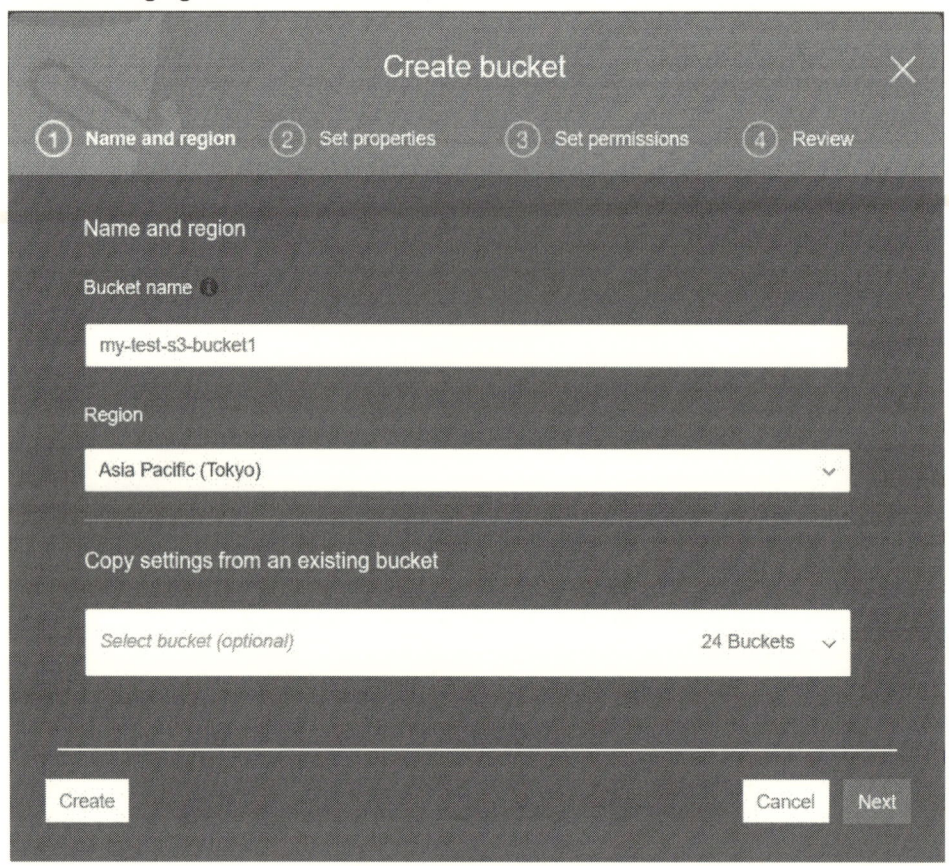

3. Specify a unique name for your S3 bucket and click **Next**.
4. On the **Set Properties** page, you can define the versioning, tagging, and logging which we will cover in a separate section.
5. On the **Set Permissions** page, you can specify the permissions that you want to assign for this bucket. We will cover permissions in the upcoming section.
6. Review the options you have selected and finish the wizard to complete the process. Your S3 bucket will be created.

Creating Folders under S3 Bucket

Now, you can create your folder structure inside the S3 bucket. For this, just perform the following steps:

1. Click the **S3 bucket** and click **Create folder**.
2. Specify the folder name and click **Save** to save it as shown in the following figure.

Upload Content/Files/Data in S3 Bucket
1. To upload data in an S3 bucket, open the desired S3 bucket and navigate to the folder where you want to upload data.
2. Click **Upload** and drag-n-drop the files you want to upload or click **Add files** and browse the location.
3. Select files you want to upload as shown in the following file.

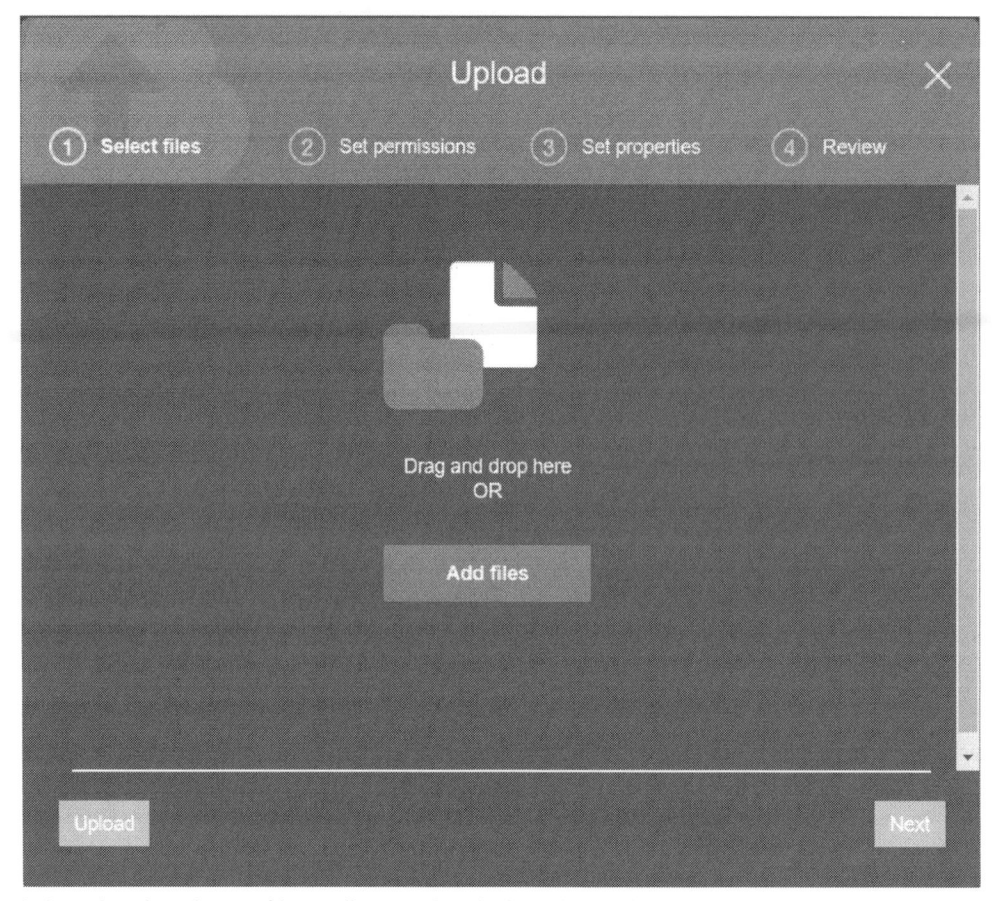

4. Finally, click **Upload** and your files will we uploaded to the S3 bucket.
5. Select any of the uploaded files and click **More** to view all the available actions that you can perform as shown in the following figure. Try each one of them to understand their functionality.

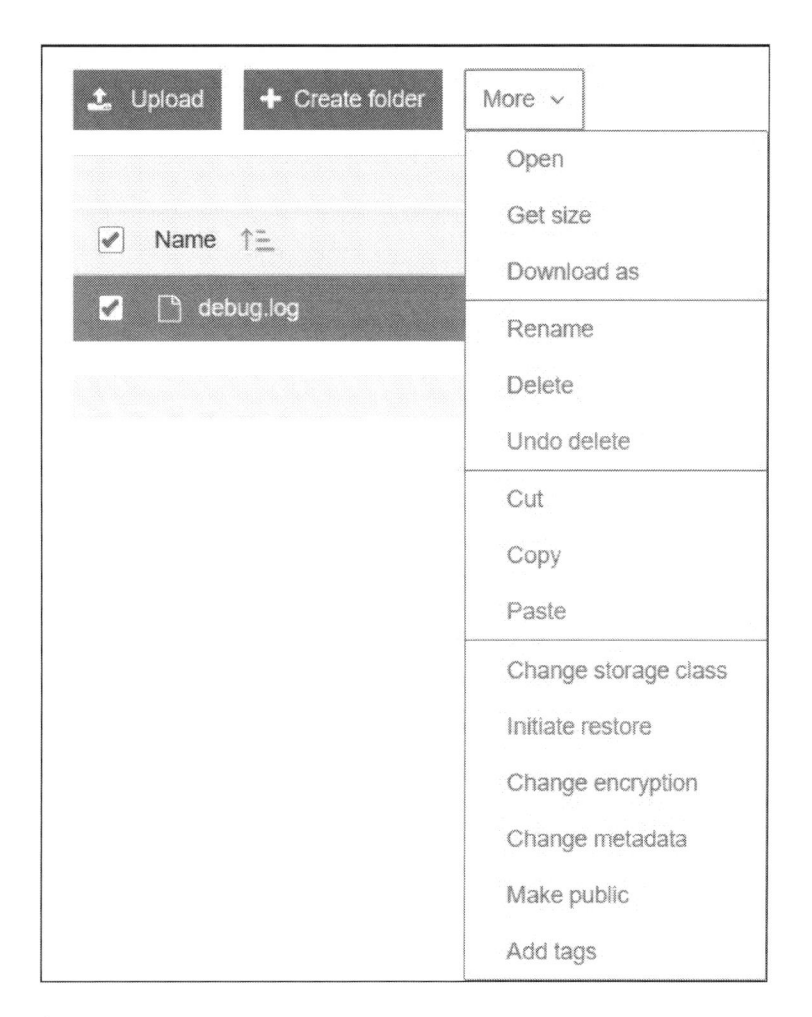

Deleting S3 Bucket
Deleting an S3 bucket using the console is pretty simple and straightforward.
1. Just select the S3 bucket you want to delete and click **Delete bucket** option.
2. On the **Delete bucket** dialog box, type the exact bucket name in the text box and click **Confirm** to delete it as shown in the following figure.

Delete bucket

Are you sure you want to delete the bucket "my-test-s3-bucket1" ?

Type the name of the bucket to confirm:

Amazon S3 buckets are unique. If you delete this bucket, you may lose the bucket name to another AWS user.

Cancel Confirm

35. Configuring Permissions and Policy for S3 Buckets

Manage permissions for S3 buckets is a little bit complicated and requires some study before you could implement proper permissions. But once you become familiar with the various custom-scenario-based S3 bucket policies, you are really on the track of becoming an AWS Cloud expert.

There are various ways to protect your S3 buckets from unauthorized access. Some of the basic security scenarios are:
- Restricting specific S3 buckets for specific IP location(s).
- Restricting specific IAM user to access specific S3 buckets.
- Restricting specific S3 bucket to access from specific domains.

Recommended links:
- S3 Buckets User Access Policy Examples
  http://docs.aws.amazon.com/AmazonS3/latest/dev/example-policies-s3.html

Customizing S3 Bucket Policies

To customize and manage permissions for an S3 bucket, you need to perform the following steps:

1. Navigate the S3 bucket for which you want to customize permissions.
2. Select the **Permissions** tab to view the assigned permissions for the selected bucket.
3. Permission tab has few other sub tabs such as **Access Control List** and **Bucket policy**.

Access Control List Tab

This tab allows you to add or remove IAM user to list and write objects in this bucket.

To add an IAM user to allow list and write objects in this bucket, perform the following steps:

1. Click **Add account** and enter the user's canonical id or email address.
2. Select the permissions that you want to assign to this user and click **Save** as shown in the following figure.

Bucket Policy Tab

Here, you can create a custom policy for the selected bucket. The scenarios for the custom policy depends on the organization's need and may have a wide range of custom requirements. In the next section, we have covered few example scenarios to manage custom S3 bucket policies.

36. Configuring S3 Bucket Policies for Specific IAM Users

Here we are going to configure the custom S3 bucket policy for the following scenarios:

- Allow a specific IAM user, such as **my-test-user1** to access a specific S3 bucket such as **my-test-s3-bukcet1**.
- Create a role that allows accessing **my-test-s3-bucket1** S3 bucket to multiple EC2 instances.

Creating Custom S3 Policy for a Specific IAM User

For the first scenario, you need to perform the following steps:

1. Create an IAM user named **my-test-user1** using the IAM management console. Since we have already covered the process of creating IAM users, so we are going to skip it here.
2. Create a custom policy that allows only **my-test-s3-bucket1** for my-test-user1.
3. Click **Policies** and then click **Create Policy** in the IAM console.
4. In the **Create Policy** page, select **Create Your Own Policy**.
5. Specify the Policy name and description as per your wish.
6. In the **Policy Document** text area, paste the following policy code and replace the bucket name, if required.

```
{
   "Version": "2012-10-17",
   "Statement": [
     {
       "Effect": "Allow",
       "Action": [
         "s3:ListBucket"
       ],
       "Resource": [
         "arn:aws:s3:::my-test-s3-bucket1"
       ]
     },
     {
       "Effect": "Allow",
       "Action": [
         "s3:PutObject",
         "s3:GetObject"
       ],
       "Resource": [
         "arn:aws:s3:::my-test-s3-bucket1/*"
       ]
     }
   ]
}
```

7. Finally, click **Create Policy** to create it.

> Note: The above policy will allow (after attaching) to get and put the objects in this S3 bucket.

Attaching Policy to IAM Role, Group, or User

The created policy will not affect anything until unless it is attached to an entity such as IAM user or group. To attach a policy to an IAM user, role, or group, you need to perform the following steps:

1. Select the created policy and then go to the **Attached entities** tab.
2. Click **Attach** to attach it to an IAM user, role, or group as shown in the following figure.

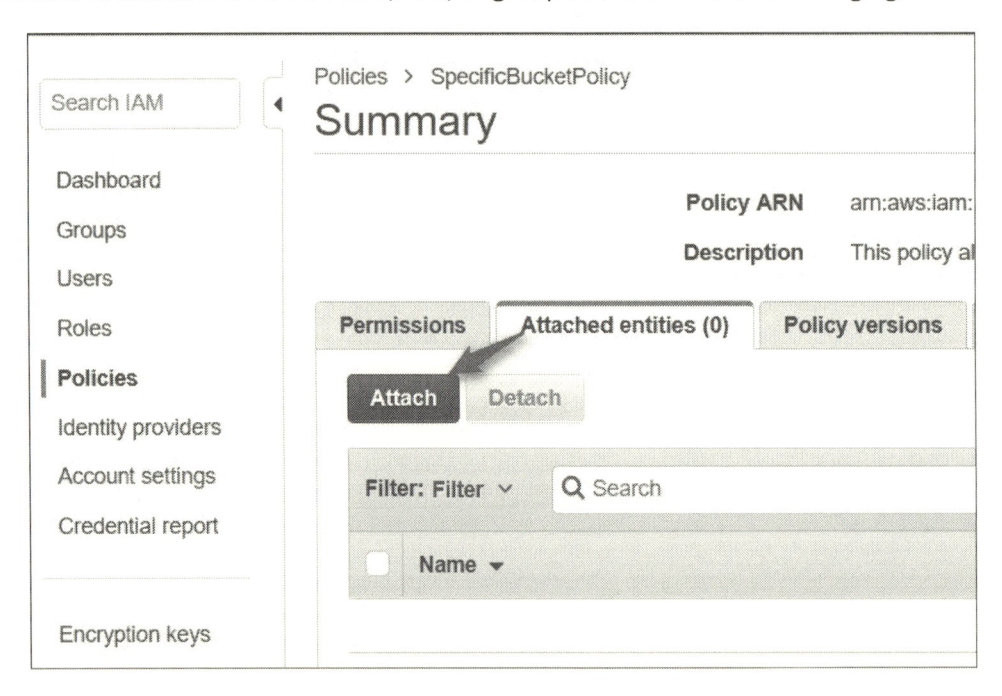

3. In the **Attach Policy** window, select the IAM user, group, or role to which you want to attach it. For this demo, select **my-test-user1** and click **Attach Policy**.
4. Now, you have created a custom S3 bucket policy and attached to the IAM entity (IAM user).

Verifying Custom S3 Bucket Policies

To test and verify whether my-test-user1 is able to view, download, and upload content to my-test-s3-bucket1, login to the AWS console with my-test-user1 and click the below link.

https://s3.console.aws.amazon.com/s3/buckets/<your-bucket-name>

You should be able to view the content of the selected S3 bucket. If you will try to access this bucket with a different IAM user, you will get an Access Denied error.

Verifying S3 Bucket Policy Using AWS CLI Tool

Here we will test and validate the above-created policy by the following methods:

1. Create an EC2 role and attach the above-created policy (specific-bucket-policy) to this role.

Create role

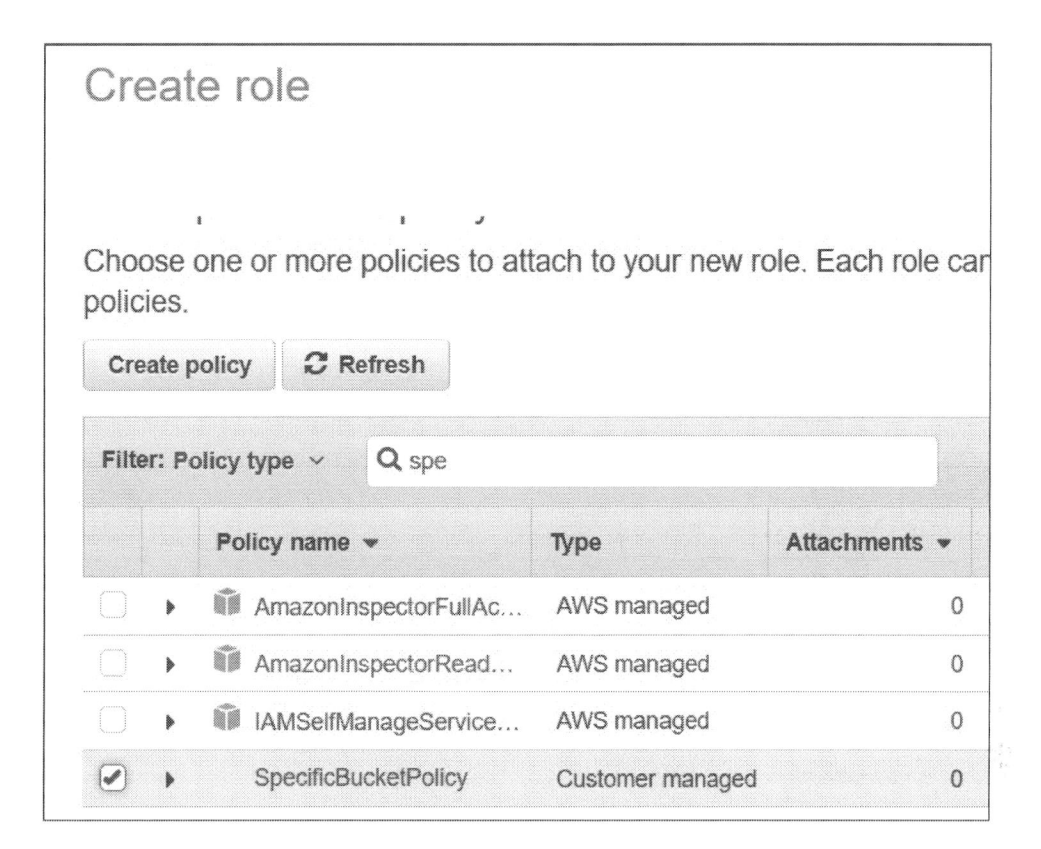

Choose one or more policies to attach to your new role. Each role can policies.

	Policy name	Type	Attachments
☐ ▶	AmazonInspectorFullAc...	AWS managed	0
☐ ▶	AmazonInspectorRead...	AWS managed	0
☐ ▶	IAMSelfManageService...	AWS managed	0
☑ ▶	SpecificBucketPolicy	Customer managed	0

2. Attach this role to one of the test VMs such as My_Test_VM1.

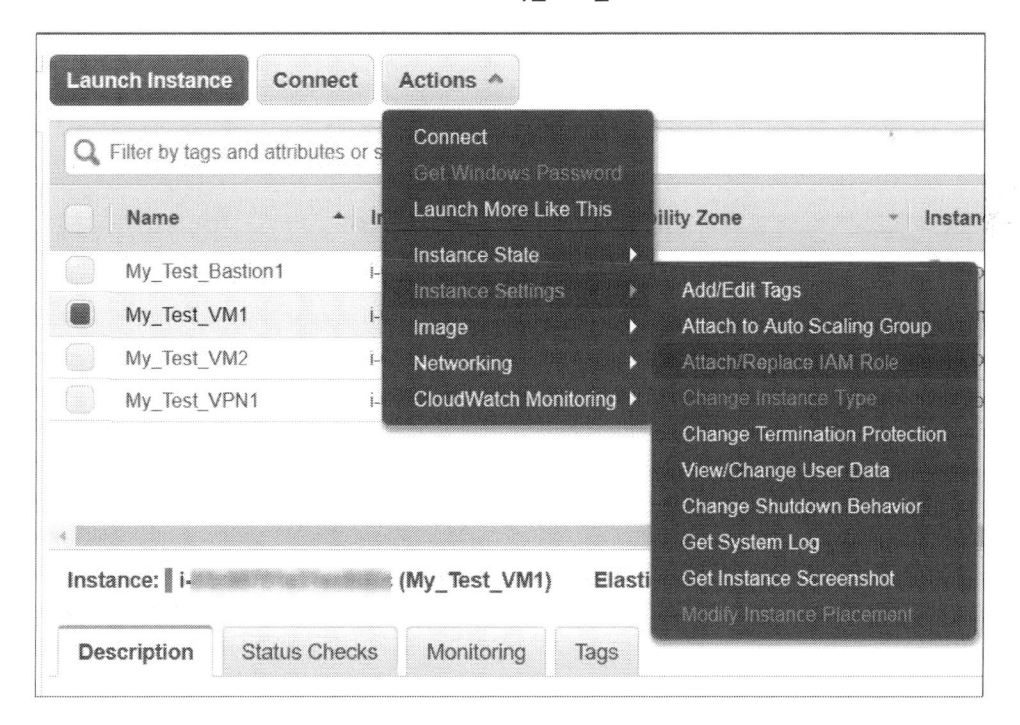

3. Install the AWS CLI tool on the test VM, if not installed already.
4. List my-test-s3-bucket1 content using the command as shown in the following figure.

```
ubuntu@ip-10-50-1-93:~$ aws s3 ls my-test-s3-bucket1
                           PRE my-test-folder1/
ubuntu@ip-10-50-1-93:~$
```

5. Create and upload a text file named **my-test-file1** to a folder named my-test-folder1 under my-test-s3-bucket1 as shown in the following figure.

```
ubuntu@ip-10-50-1-93:~$ cat >my-test-file1
This is my first test file.

^Z
[1]+  Stopped                 cat > my-test-file1
ubuntu@ip-10-50-1-93:~$
ubuntu@ip-10-50-1-93:~$ aws s3 cp my-test-file1 s3://my-test-s3-bucket1/my-test-folder1/
upload: ./my-test-file1 to s3://my-test-s3-bucket1/my-test-folder1/my-test-file1
ubuntu@ip-10-50-1-93:~$ aws s3 ls my-test-s3-bucket1/my-test-folder1/
2017-09-30 17:46:59          0
2017-09-30 17:52:15        108 debug.log
2017-10-01 07:30:22         29 my-test-file1
```

6. Download a file named debug.log from s3 bucket location (my-test-folder1 under my-test-s3-bucket1) to the current working directory of local system as shown in the following figure.

```
ubuntu@ip-10-50-1-93:~$ aws s3 cp s3://my-test-s3-bucket1/my-test-folder1/debug.log ./
download: s3://my-test-s3-bucket1/my-test-folder1/debug.log to ./debug.log
ubuntu@ip-10-50-1-93:~$ ls
awslogs-agent-setup.py  Desktop    Downloads  My_File1       Pictures  Templates
debug.log               Documents  Music      my-test-file1  Public    Videos
ubuntu@ip-10-50-1-93:~$
```

Here, we have explained how to allow a specific IAM user, role, and group to access specific one or more S3 buckets using the custom policies.

37. Configuring S3 Bucket Versioning and Logging.

There are various other configuration options for S3 buckets apart from S3 bucket policies. Here, we are going to explain a few of the most common options.

Configuring S3 Bucket Versioning

If you usually keep changing and modifying files and content stored in the S3 buckets, you can enable S3 versioning to keep multiple versions of the modified files. If the versioning feature is enabled for an S3 bucket, S3 keeps all versions of modified objects of that bucket. You can view and restore the previous version whenever required (also depends on S3 bucket object expiration settings).

Recommended links:

- Click here to know more about the object versioning.
  http://docs.aws.amazon.com/AmazonS3/latest/dev/ObjectVersioning.html

To enable or disable versioning for S3 bucket objects, you need to perform the following steps:
1. Select the desired S3 bucket and select the **Properties** tab.
2. Click the **Versioning feature** box to enable it.
3. Select **Enable versioning** radio button and then click **Save** as shown in the following figure.

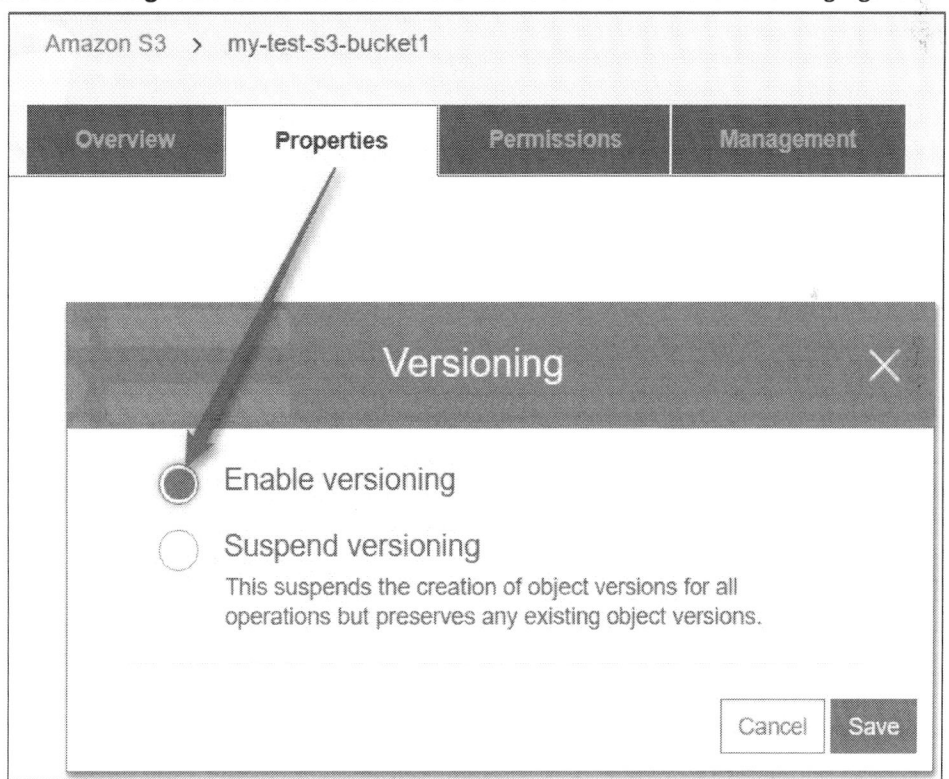

Note: Once you enabled versioning on an S3 bucket, it cannot be disabled as of now. However, you can suspend it whenever required.

Configuring Logging for S3 Buckets

Sometimes, it may be very useful to track the activities performed by users for particular S3 buckets. For this, you can configure logging for your S3 buckets. Each access log record provides details about a single access request, such as the requester, bucket name, request time, request action, response status, and error code, if any. You can track the access activities for the S3 buckets if you have enabled the logging feature for your S3 buckets.

- S3 Bucket Access Logging
  https://docs.aws.amazon.com/AmazonS3/latest/dev/ServerLogs.html

To enable logging for an S3 bucket, you need to perform the following steps:
1. Select the **S3 bucket** and then select **Properties**.
2. Click **Logging** to enable it.
3. On the **Logging** window, select the target bucket and then click **Save** as shown in the following figure.

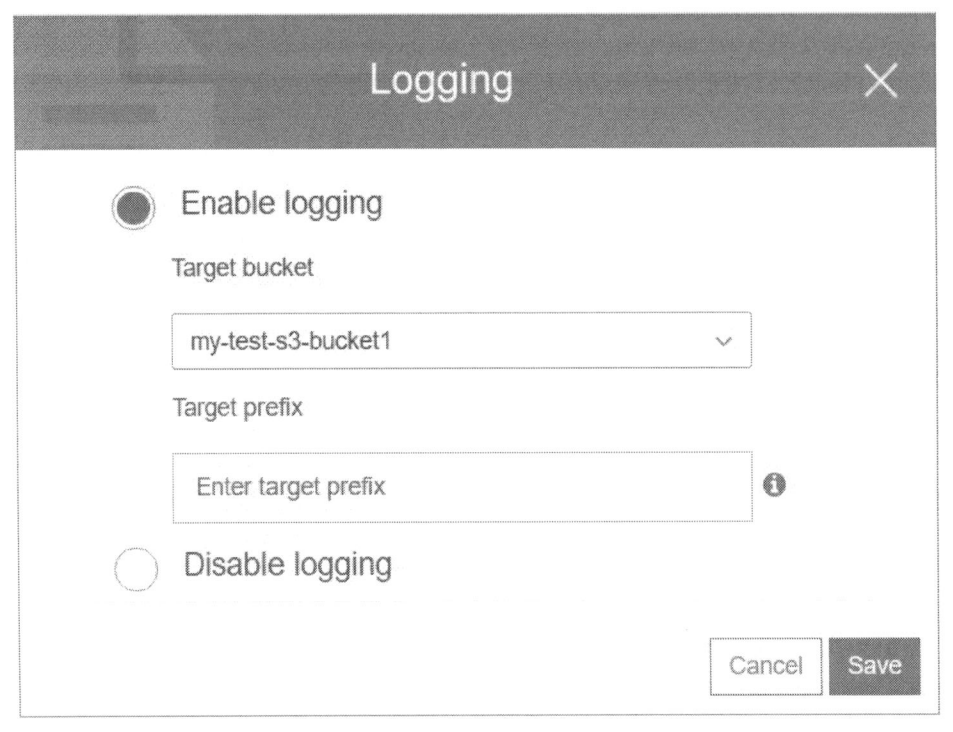

38. Configuring S3 Bucket Alerting and Notifications

In the previous labs, we have done various hands-on labs with the S3 buckets. Here, we will explore one more interesting hands-on lab called S3 Bucket Alerting and Notifications.

Sometimes, IT admins may wish to receive alerts such as emails whenever there are any changes happening with an S3 bucket. These changes may be putting a new object, renaming an existing object, or deleting an object inside an S3 bucket. Before configuring notification for S3 buckets, we assume that you have already created an SNS topic with the appropriate mail list of users who will receive the notifications.

Recommended links:

- S3 Bucket Notifications
  https://docs.aws.amazon.com/AmazonS3/latest/user-guide/enable-event-notifications.html

To configure notification or events for an S3 bucket, you need to perform the following steps.

1. Select the **Properties** tab of the desired S3 bucket.
2. In the **Advanced Settings** section, click the **Events** box.
3. Click **Add notification** to configure the notification options. Here you can configure the following options:
   - **Name**: Name of the notification rule.
   - **Events**: Type of events for which you want to enable notifications. For example, select **Object Created (All).**
   - **Prefix**: If the bucket has multiple folders, you can limit the notifications by limiting it to specific prefix as the folder name.
   - **Suffix**: Specify the file type or extensions such as .txt, .exe, .jpg to limit the notifications.
   - **Send to**: Select the preconfigured SNS topic where the notification will be sent.

Events

+ Add notification   Delete   Edit

Name	Events	Filter	Type

New event

Name

e.g. MyEmailEventForPut

Events

- [ ] RRSObjectLost
- [ ] Put
- [ ] Post
- [ ] Copy
- [ ] Complete Multipart Upload
- [ ] Delete
- [ ] Delete Marker Created
- [ ] ObjectCreate (All)
- [ ] ObjectDelete (All)

Prefix

e.g. images/

Suffix

e.g. .jpg

Send to

Select notification destination

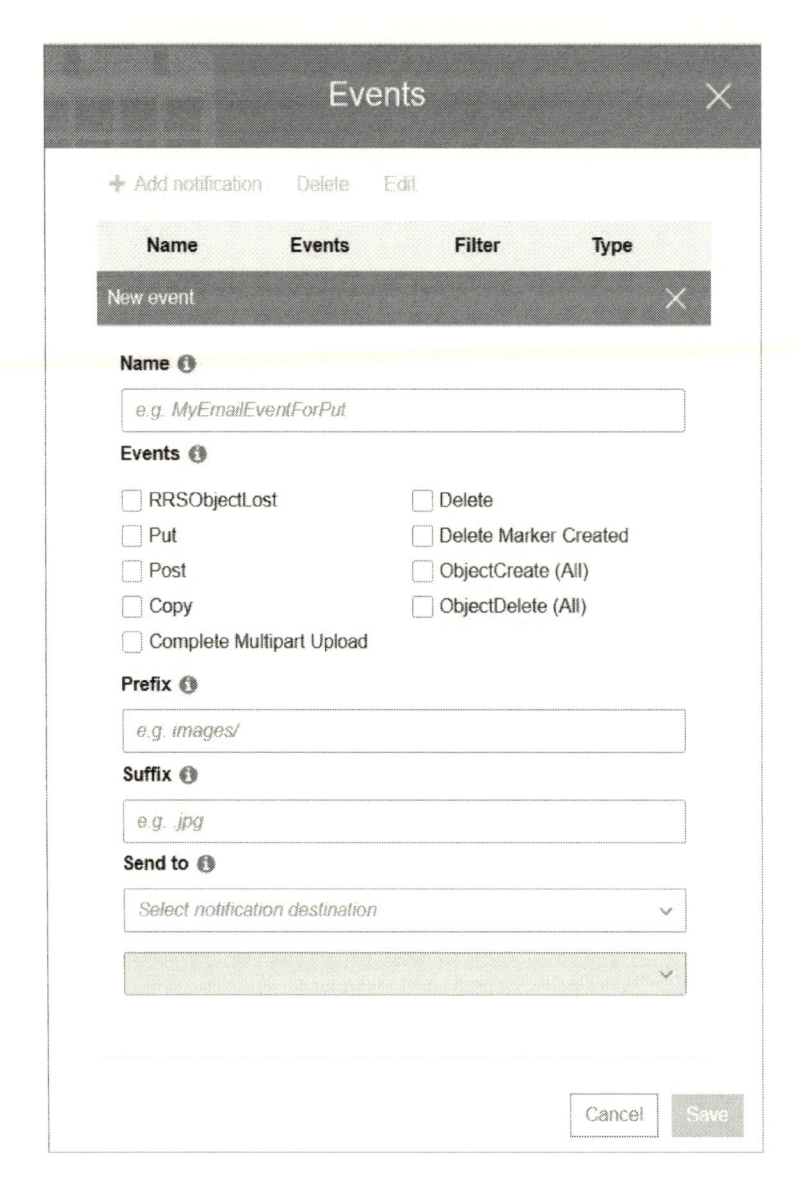

Cancel Save

4. Finally, click **Save** to save the settings.

Now, whenever any changes will happen as per your selected event types such as **Put**, **Copy**, **Delete,** etc. in your selected S3 bucket a notification will be sent through the selected SNS topic.

39. Configuring S3 Bucket Lifecycle Rule

S3 buckets can store objects and content as long as you do not delete them manually. But there might be some scenarios when you may want to delete the data of a bucket after the specific days. One such example is given as below.

Suppose you are taking the regular backups of your MongoDB database to an S3 bucket on a daily basis. After a few months, there will be a huge number of backup copies and you would require deleting older copies manually which might be a tedious job. Here comes S3 Lifecycle rule as a handy feature.

You can create a Lifecycle rule that defines the lifecycle of the S3 objects. The lifecycle can be defined as:

- How many days should the objects remain in an S3 bucket?
- After how many days these objects should go into Glacier storage?
- After how many days the objects should be deleted permanently from AWS cloud?

Let's create a Lifecycle rule that will automatically delete the object after 30 days from an S3 bucket.

To create and configure S3 lifecycle rule, you need to perform the following steps:

1. Select an S3 bucket for which you want to create lifecycle rule and select the **Management** tab.
2. Click the **Add lifecycle rule** to add a new lifecycle rule.

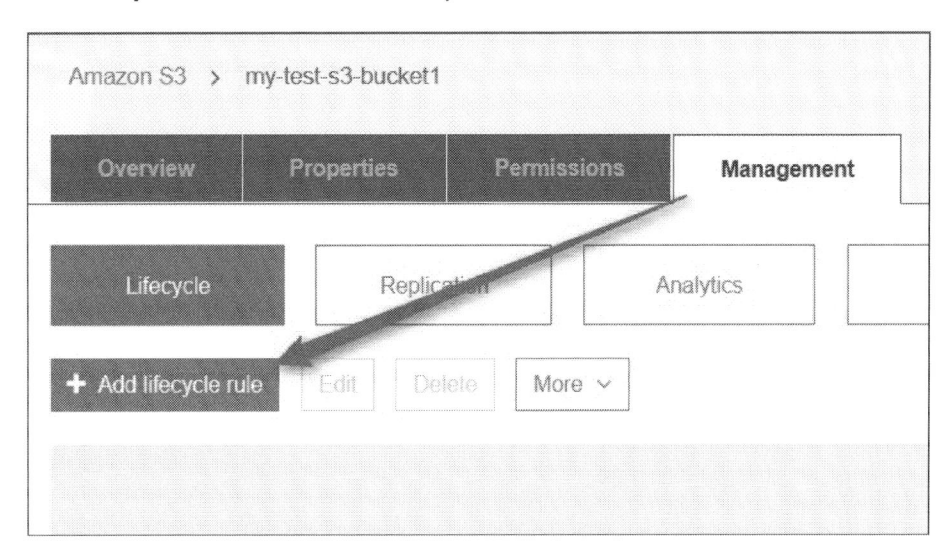

3. On the **Lifecycle rule** dialog box, specify the name and scope as shown in the following figure.

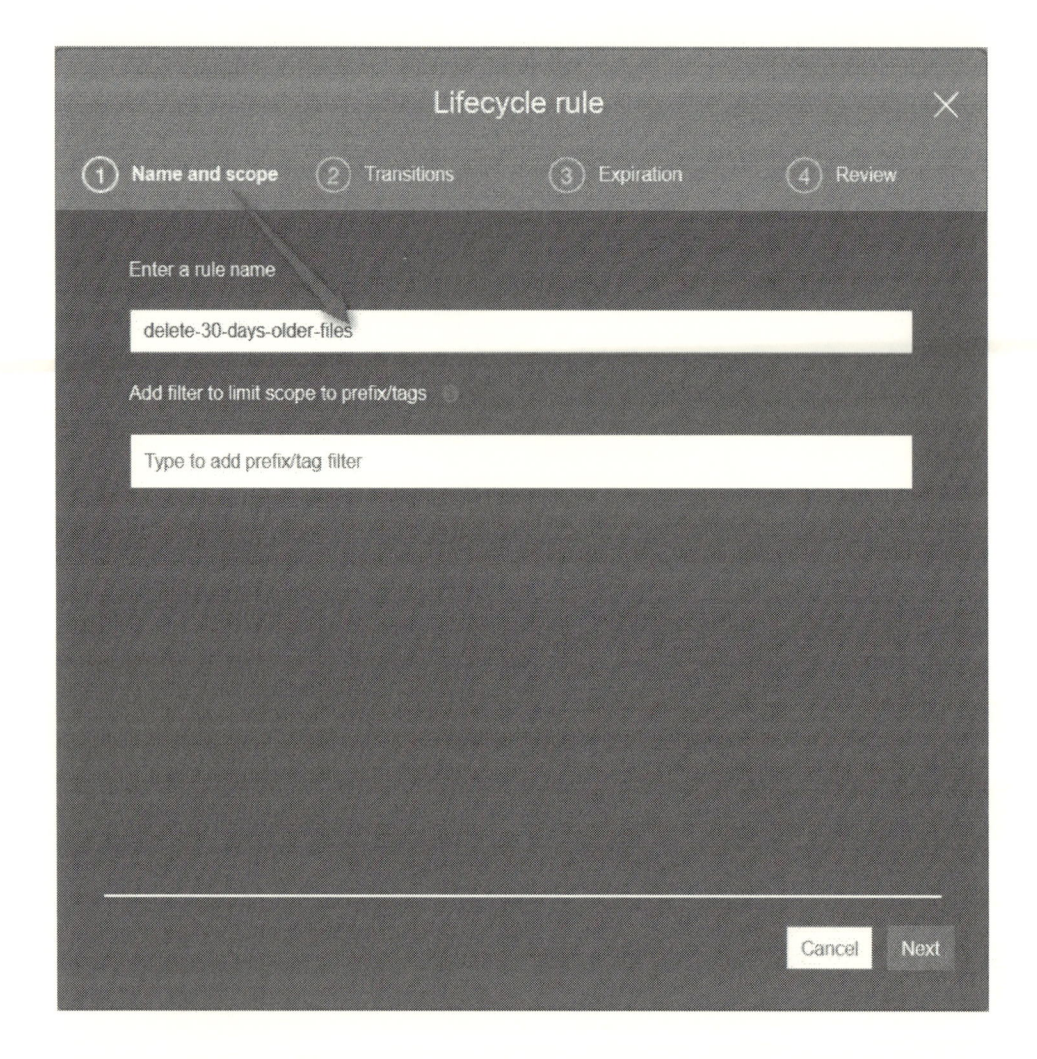

4. On the **Transitions** page, select the current versions or previous versions or both as per your S3 bucket settings and requirements, and proceed to the next page.
5. Click **Add transition** and select the destination where objects should go after deletion. Also, select the number of days after which objects should be moved to transition storage.

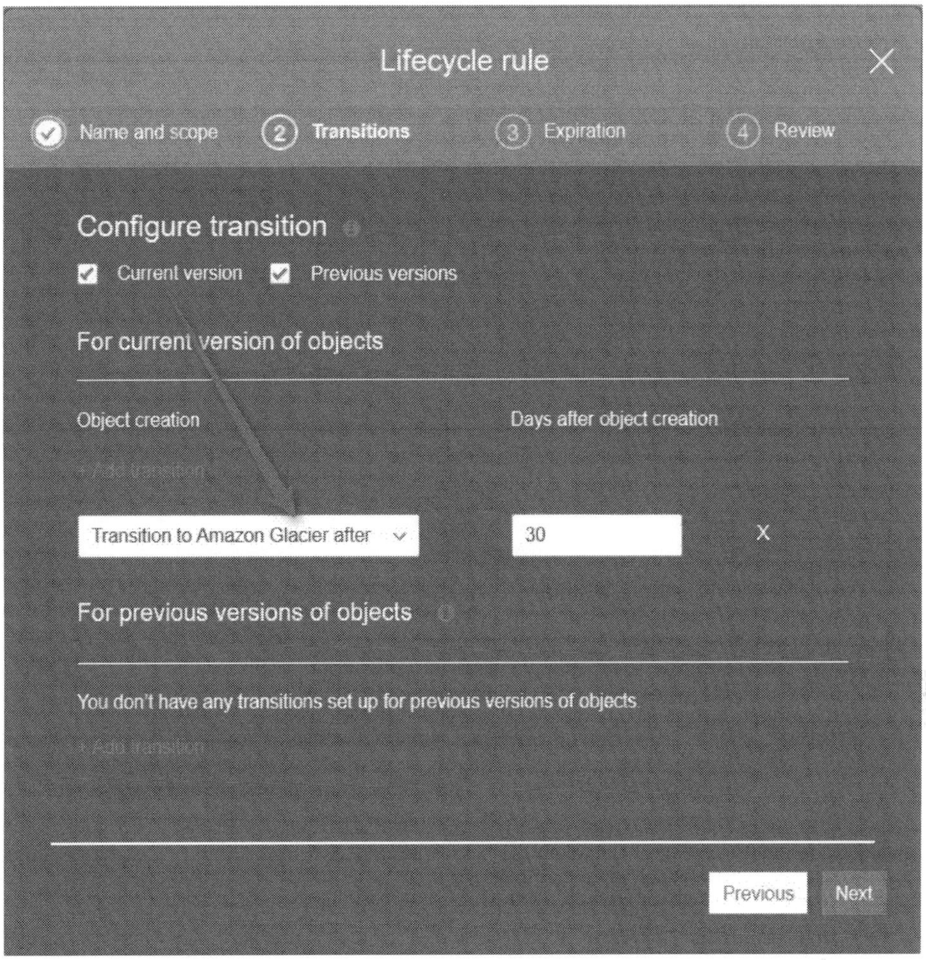

Lifecycle rule
Name and scope
2 Transitions
3 Expiration
4 Review
Configure transition
Current version
Previous versions
For current version of objects
Object creation
Days after object creation
Transition to Amazon Glacier after
30
For previous versions of objects
You don't have any transitions set up for previous versions of objects
Previous
Next

6. On the **Expiration** page, specify the number of days after which object should be deleted permanently from the transition storage, which is **Standard –IA** and **Amazon Glacier** also. This setting should be greater than the previously defined value, in our case 30 days.

Lifecycle rule

- Name and scope
- Transitions
- **3 Expiration**
- 4 Review

Configure expiration

☑ Current version ☑ Previous versions

☑ Expire current version of object

After [31] days from object creation

☑ Permanently delete previous versions

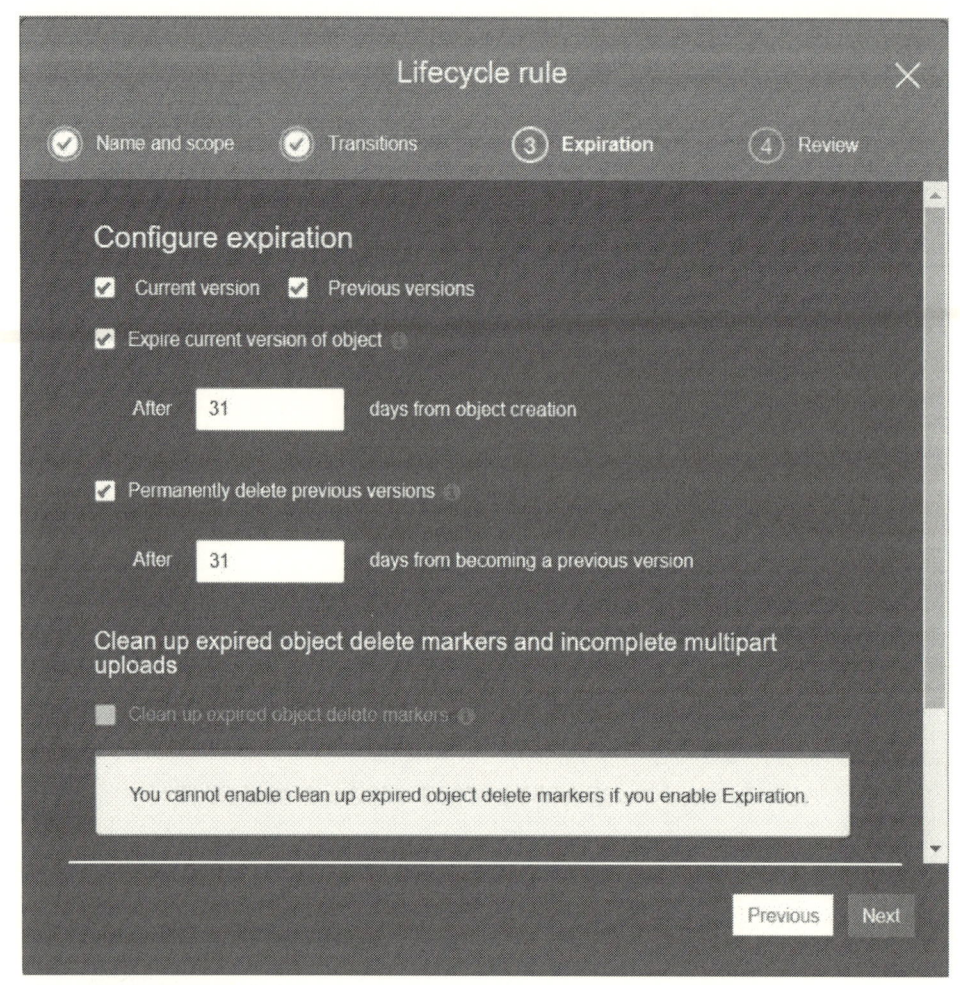

After [31] days from becoming a previous version

Clean up expired object delete markers and incomplete multipart uploads

☐ Clean up expired object delete markers

> You cannot enable clean up expired object delete markers if you enable Expiration.

[Previous] [Next]

7. On the **Review** page, review all the settings you have selected, click **Previous** to modify any settings and finally finish the wizard.
8. Now, the objects will be moved to the transitions storage after the specified days and then will be permanently deleted from the transition storage after the specified days automatically.

40. Implementing Cross-Region S3 Replication

Replication is a process of synchronizing and updating content between two objects, places, or services. By default, S3 buckets store a single copy of its objects in the region where it is created. But what will happen if that region becomes unavailable due to any reason? Your bucket and its entire data will be inaccessible until the source region becomes available again. Here comes cross-region replication (CRR) as a solution for this. Cross-region replication is a bucket-level feature that enables automatic, asynchronous copying of objects across buckets in different AWS regions.

Configuring cross-replication of S3 bucket

In order to configure cross-region S3 replication, let's consider the following:

- Create an S3 bucket in the destination region where you will replicate your source S3 bucket.
- Make sure that the versioning is enabled for both the source and destination buckets.
- Let's assume our source bucket **my-test-s3-bucket1** is in Tokyo region and the destination bucket is **my-dest-s3-bucket1** is in Sydney region. Create these two buckets before to proceed to this lab. Since the S3 buckets are globally unique you may need to adjust the names accordingly.

Creating Replication Rule

To configure cross-region S3 bucket replication, you need to perform the following steps:

1. Select the source s3 bucket and select the **Management** tab.
2. Click **Replication** and then click **Add rule** as shown in the following figure.

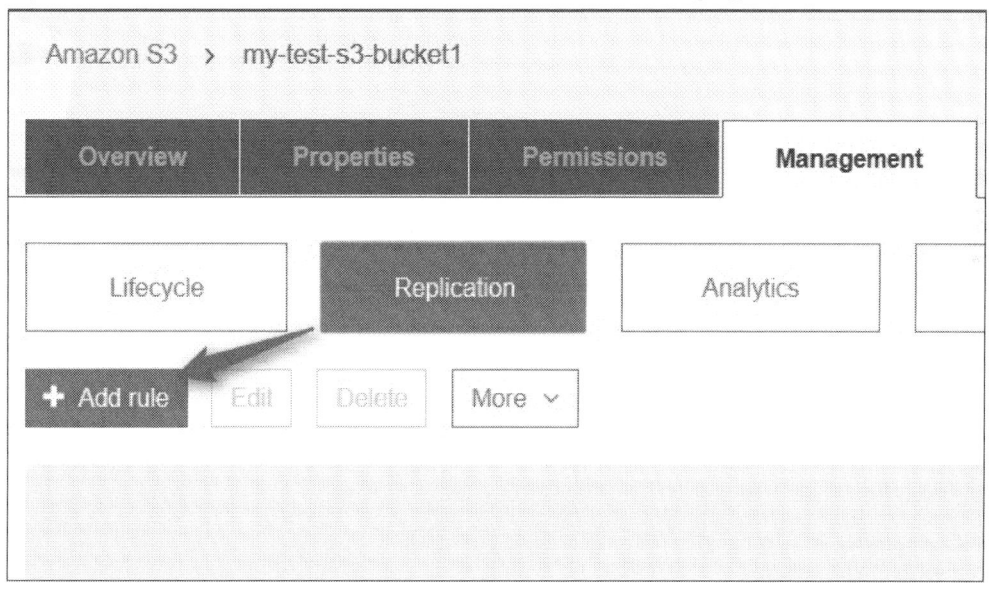

3. On the source page of the **Replication rule** page, enable version if not already and then click **Next**.
4. On the **Destination** page, select the destination bucket name, in this case **my-dest-s3-bucket1**.
5. Enable the versioning, if not enabled already, and then click **Next** and shown in the following figure.

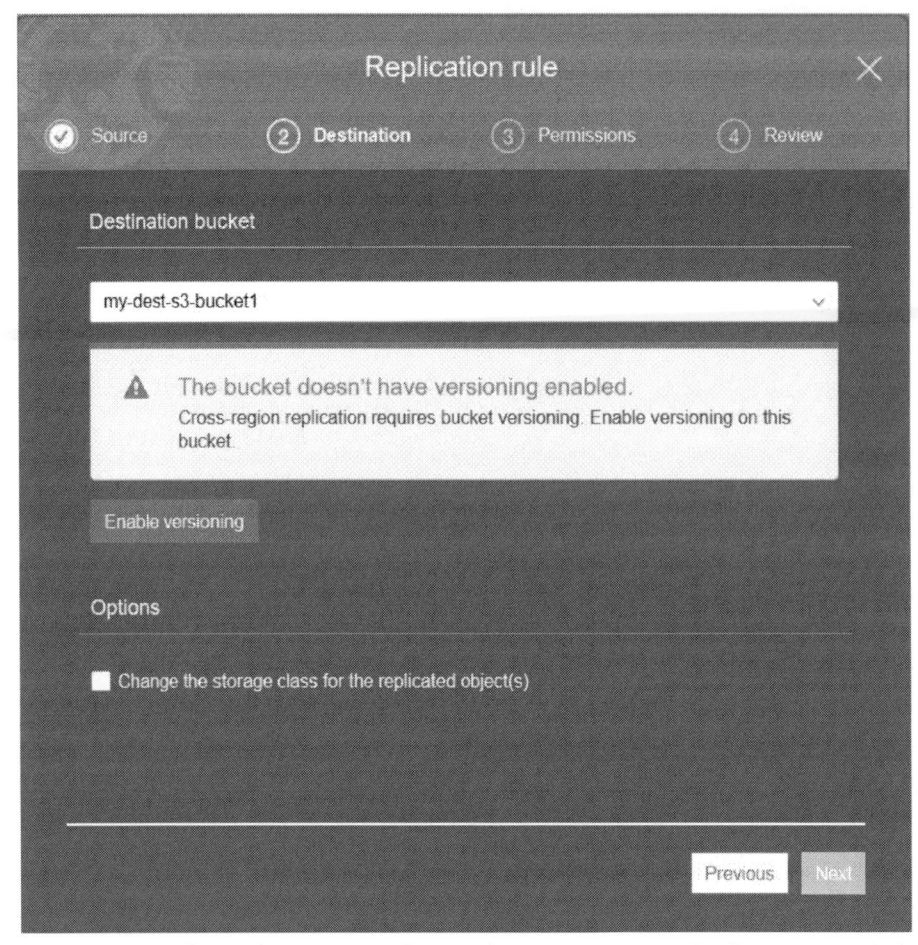

![Replication rule dialog showing Destination step with bucket "my-dest-s3-bucket1" selected and a warning that the bucket doesn't have versioning enabled]

6. On the **Permissions** page, select **Create new role** or select an existing role if you created already.

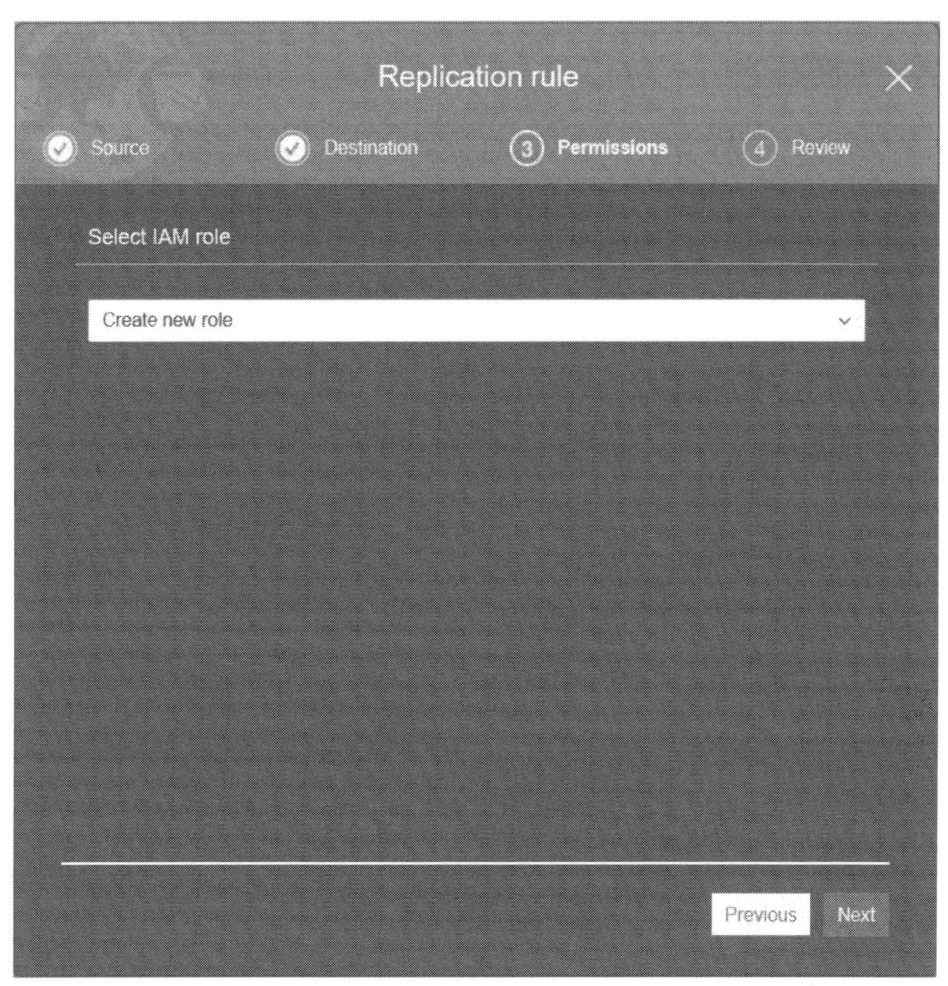

7. On the **Review** page, review the settings and click **Save** to finish the wizard. You will see that a new replication rule in the **replication rule section** is created for your source S3 bucket.

Verifying Cross-region S3 Bucket Replication

To test whether the cross-region S3 replication is configured and working properly, upload a test file in the source S3 bucket and check the destination S3 bucket objects, the uploaded object in the source S3 bucket should be displayed in the destination S3 bucket.

> Note: With the S3 CRR, only new objects (after configuring the CRR) will be replicated from the source bucket to the destination bucket. For the existing objects, lying before configuring CRR, you need to manually copy them from the source bucket to the destination bucket.

Troubleshooting S3 Cross-region Replication

If you face any issue or replication does not happen, refer the following article for the common issues with the cross-region S3 bucket replication.

- Common issues with cross-region S3 bucket replication.

https://docs.aws.amazon.com/AmazonS3/latest/dev/crr-troubleshoot.html

41. Enabling and Configuring AWS CloudTrail

Typically, multiple IAM users perform various activities to work with the AWS cloud services. As an AWS Administrator, you should have a method that you can use to view what actions have been performed by which IAM users. Additionally, you may also wish to know what API calls doing what with the AWS services of your AWS account and its resources. Here, comes AWS CloudTrail as a possible solution for this.

Recommended links:
- Overview of AWS CloudTrail
  http://docs.aws.amazon.com/awscloudtrail/latest/userguide/cloudtrail-user-guide.html
- CloudTrail Pricing
  https://aws.amazon.com/cloudtrail/pricing/

The AWS CloudTrail is an AWS service. It helps you to control, compliance, functioning and risk inspecting of your AWS account. AWS API calls or activities performed by a user, role, or an AWS service are recorded as events in CloudTrail. These events include actions taken in the AWS Management Console, AWS CLI tool, and AWS SDKs, and APIs. The AWS CloudTrail events could be used for the tracking and audit purposes.

Enabling CloudTrail

CloudTrail is limited to a specific region. You need to choose regions for which you want to enable and configure AWS CloudTrail. CloudTrail is enabled by default for your AWS Account. However, you still need to create and configure CloudTrail settings.

Creating a CloudTrail

To create a CloudTrail, navigate to the CloudTrail console.

1. Select **Trails** in the left pane and click the **Create trail** button.
2. On the **Create Trail** page, specify the **Cloud Trail** name and select regions for which you want to collect trail logs.
3. On the **Management Event** section, select **All** as **Read/Write Events** radio button as shown in the following figure.

> **Create Trail**
>
> Trail name* MyDemoCloudTrail
>
> Apply trail to all regions   ● Yes   ○ No
>
> Management events
>
> Management events provide insights into the management operations that are performed on resour[ces]
>
> Read/Write events   ● All   ○ Read-only   ○ Write-only   ○ None

4. On the **Data events** section, select either S3 or Lambda services to record APIs logs. You can also select a specific lambda function or an S3 bucket, depending on your choice.

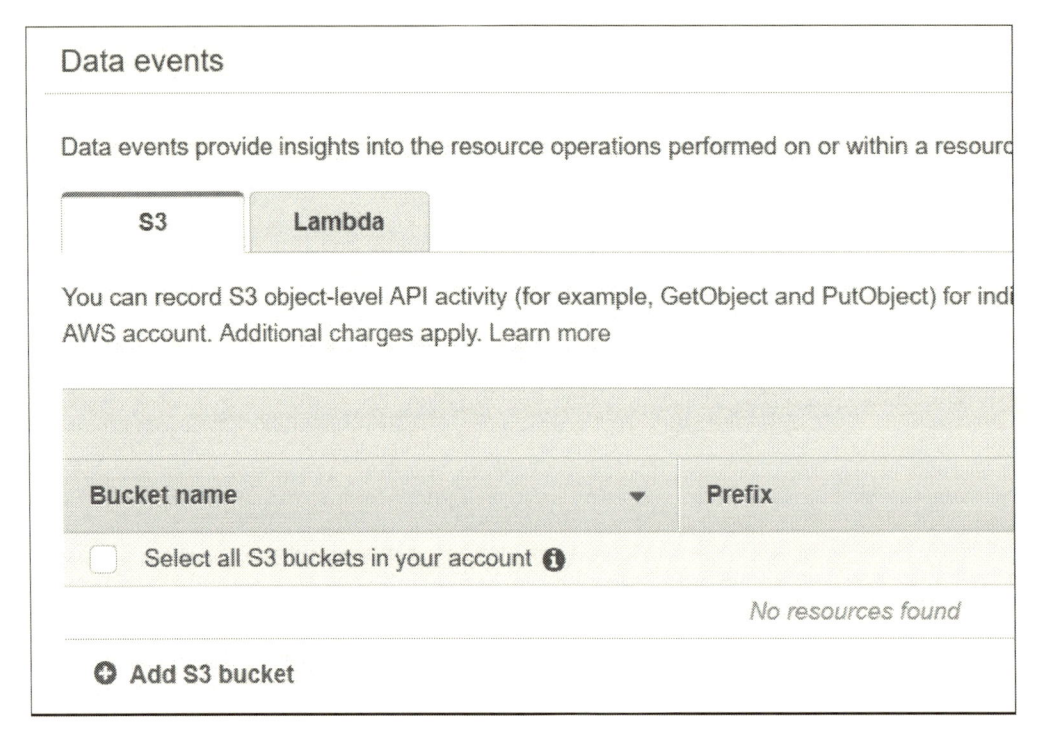

> **Data events**
>
> Data events provide insights into the resource operations performed on or within a resour[ce]
>
> | S3 | Lambda |
>
> You can record S3 object-level API activity (for example, GetObject and PutObject) for indi[vidual] AWS account. Additional charges apply. Learn more
>
> | Bucket name | Prefix |
> | --- | --- |
> | ☐ Select all S3 buckets in your account | |
>
> *No resources found*
>
> ⊕ Add S3 bucket

5. On the **Storage location** section, select **Yes** to create a new S3 bucket where your CloudTrail logs will be stored.
6. I the **Advanced** section, you can specify a prefix to limit the trail logs, you can encrypt the logs in S3 bucket, or you can also select an SNS topic to receive notifications. For the demo purpose, default options are enough.

Storage location

Create a new S3 bucket	● Yes ○ No
S3 bucket*	[_____] ⓘ
▼ Advanced	
Log file prefix	[_____] ⓘ
Encrypt log files	○ Yes ● No ⓘ
Enable log file validation	● Yes ○ No ⓘ
Send SNS notification for every log file delivery	○ Yes ● No ⓘ

Now your logs will be recorded and stored in the specified S3 bucket. The following is the location and format of the CloudTrail Logs.

bucket_name/prefix_name/AWSLogs/Account ID/CloudTrail/region/YYYY/MM/DD/file_name.json.gz

*Note: The recent logs are also visible through the **Event history** section of the CloudTrail console.*

42. Working with Auto Scaling Group

Auto Scaling Group is one of the highly demandable cloud services in nowadays. Almost every organization wants to design and implement a solution that is auto scalable as per the business or application need. This can be done using the AWS Auto Scaling Group and Launch Configuration template.

Recommended links:

- Overview of Auto Scaling Group
  https://docs.aws.amazon.com/autoscaling/latest/userguide/WhatIsAutoScaling.html

Creating a Launch Configuration Group

A launch configuration specifies the pre-defined settings that will be used by your Auto Scaling group. A launch configuration includes information such as the AMI ID to use for launching the EC2 instances, instance type, key pairs, security groups, volumes, and few other configuration settings.

To create a Launch Configuration, you need to perform the following steps:

1. Select **Launch Configuration** in the **EC2 dashboard** under the **Auto Scaling** section.
2. Click **Create Auto Scaling Group** to proceed as shown in the following figure.

3. On the **Create Auto Scaling Group** page, click **Create Launch Configuration** to proceed next.
4. On the next page, select the **AMI ID** that will be served as the base EC2 instance for your Auto Scaling Group. For the demo purpose, select **Amazon Linux AMI** and proceed to the next page.
5. On the **Choose Instance Type** page, select **T2.Micro** and proceed to the next page.
6. On the **Configure Details** page, specify the launch configuration name, and accept the other settings as default.

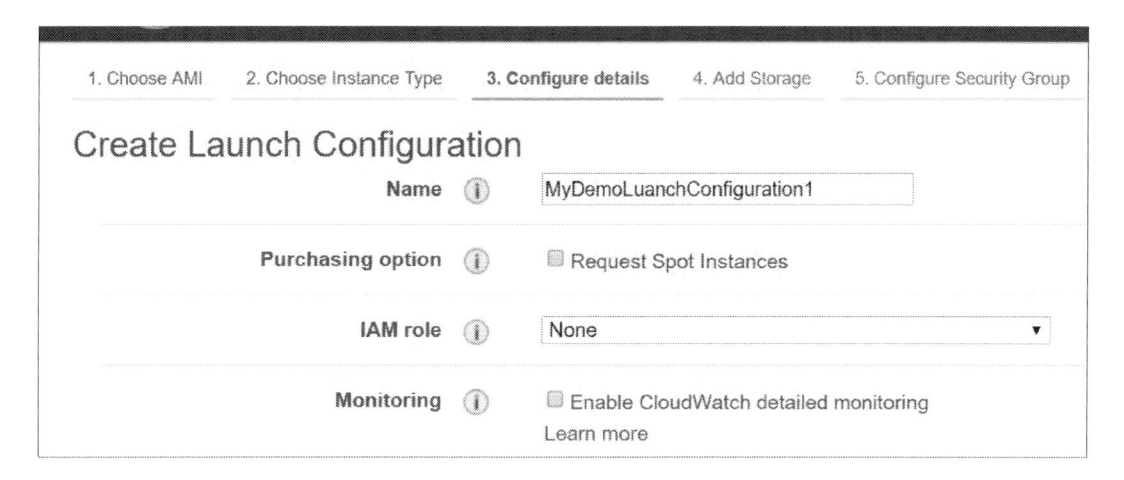

1. Choose AMI	2. Choose Instance Type	**3. Configure details**	4. Add Storage	5. Configure Security Group

Create Launch Configuration

Name	MyDemoLuanchConfiguration1
Purchasing option	☐ Request Spot Instances
IAM role	None ▼
Monitoring	☐ Enable CloudWatch detailed monitoring Learn more

7. On the **Add Storage** page, specify the storage size and additional volumes, if required, and proceed to the next page.
8. On the **Configure Security Group** page, select **Create a new security group**, specify the security group name and description, allow SSH port for your public IP, and proceed to the next page.

1. Choose AMI	2. Choose Instance Type	3. Configure details	4. Add Storage	**5. Configure Security Group**	6. Review

Create Launch Configuration

A security group is a set of firewall rules that control the traffic for your instance. On this page, you can add rules to allow specific traffic to reach your server and allow Internet traffic to reach your instance, add rules that allow unrestricted access to the HTTP and HTTPS ports. You can create a new Learn more about Amazon EC2 security groups.

Assign a security group:	● Create a **new** security group
	○ Select an **existing** security group
Security group name:	AutoScaling-Security-Group-1
Description:	AutoScaling-Security-Group-1 (2017-12-10 12:13:05.342+05:30)

Type	Protocol	Port Range	
SSH ▼	TCP	22	

Add Rule

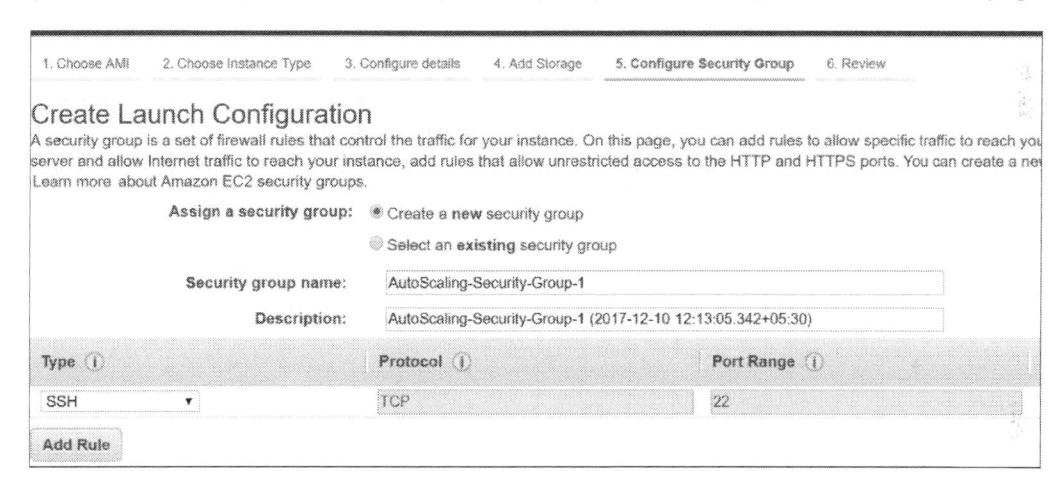

9. On the **Review** page, click **Create Launch Configuration** and review your settings. Modify the settings if you wish, else click **Review** to proceed to the next page.
10. On the **Select key pair** page, select **Create a new key pair** or select an **existing key pair** that you want to use to connect your Auto Scaling instances later.
11. Finally, click **Create Launch Configuration** to create it. You will be redirected to the Create Auto Scaling Group page.

Creating Auto Scaling Group

We assume that you are on the **Create Auto Scaling Group** page from the previous step.

To create an Auto Scaling Group, you need to perform the following steps:

1. On the **Create Auto Scaling Group** page, Specify the Group name, Group size, Network, and subnet as shown in the following figure.

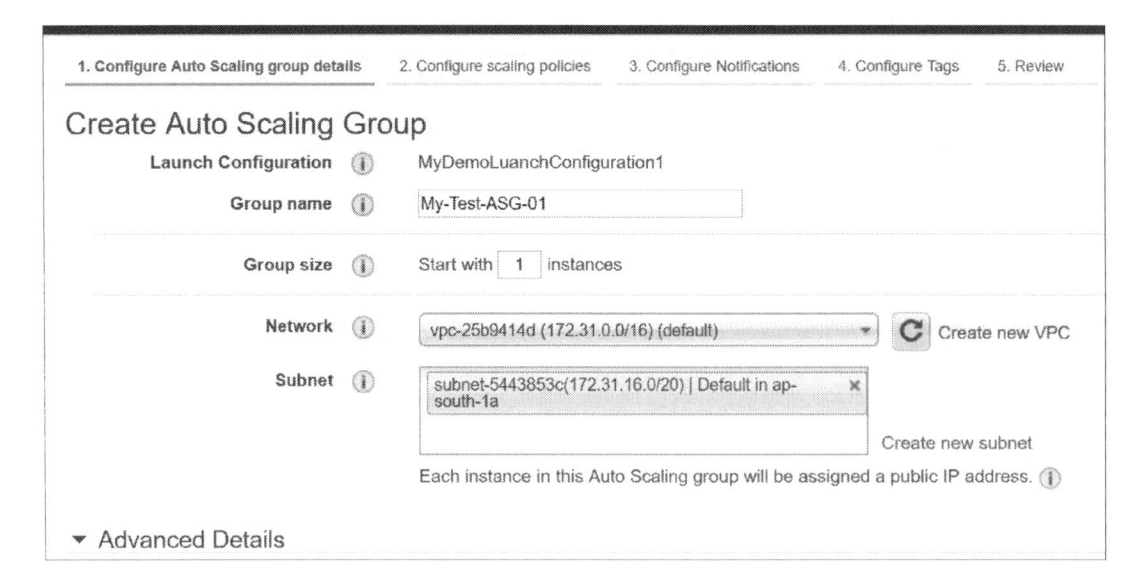

2. Click **Configure Scaling Policies** to configure it.

Note: Scaling policies define when your Auto Scaling group takes the decision to increase and decrease the size of the Auto Scaling group or number of instances.

3. For example, let's assume: - we want to add one more instance to my auto scaling group (My-Test-ASG-01) if the CPU utilization of the first instance crosses more than 80 % for 5 minutes. We also want that the maximum number of instances should not increase more than 2 instances. The policy settings will be as follows for the above requirements.

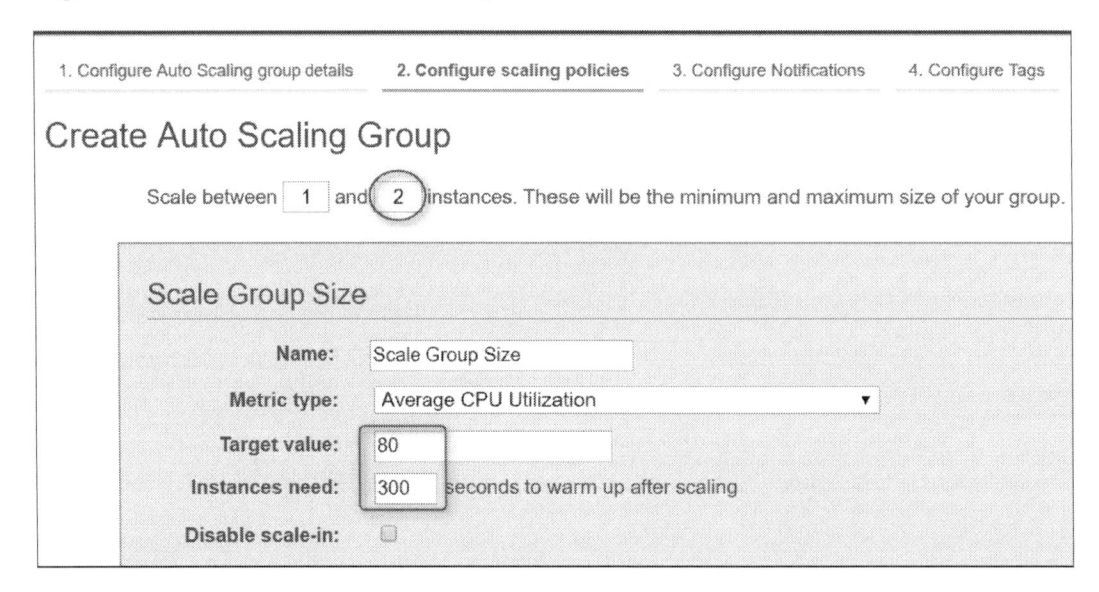

4. On the **Configure Notifications** page, you can specify an SNS topic with your email list where the mail notifications will be sent whenever a change happens in the Auto Scaling Group such as adding/removing instances (or increasing/decreasing the size of your Auto Scaling Group).

> **Create Auto Scaling Group**
>
> Configure your Auto Scaling group to send notifications to a specified endpoint, such as an email address, whenever instance launch, instance termination, and failed instance termination.
>
> If you created a new topic, check your email for a confirmation message and click the included link to confirm you[r subscription]
>
> Send a notification to: [Manually enter a topic name...] use existing topic
> With these recipients: [awsAccount@domain.com]
> Whenever instances:
> ☑ launch
> ☑ terminate
> ☑ fail to launch
> ☑ fail to terminate

5. On the **Configure Tags** page, specify the name of your ASG such as **My-Test-ASG-01** and proceed to the **Review** page.
6. Finally, click **Create Auto Scaling Group** to complete the wizard. Once you ASG is created, you will get the successful creation message as shown in the following figure.

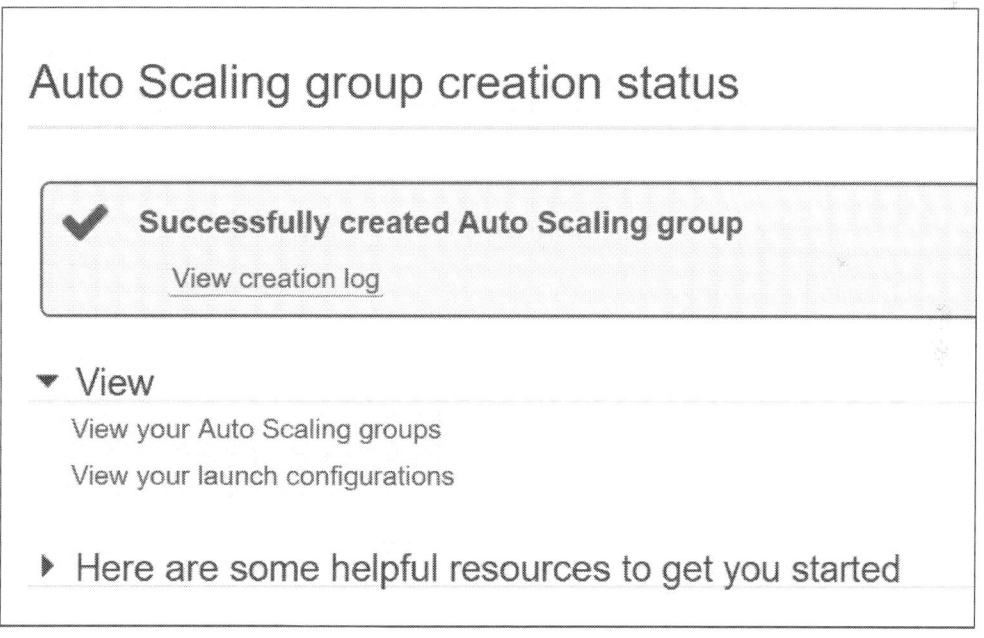

> **Auto Scaling group creation status**
>
> ✓ **Successfully created Auto Scaling group**
>   View creation log
>
> ▼ View
>   View your Auto Scaling groups
>   View your launch configurations
>
> ▶ Here are some helpful resources to get you started

Verifying Auto Scaling Group Configuration

1. Now, you have configured your ASG, go to the instance list and verify that your instance is running as shown in the following figure.

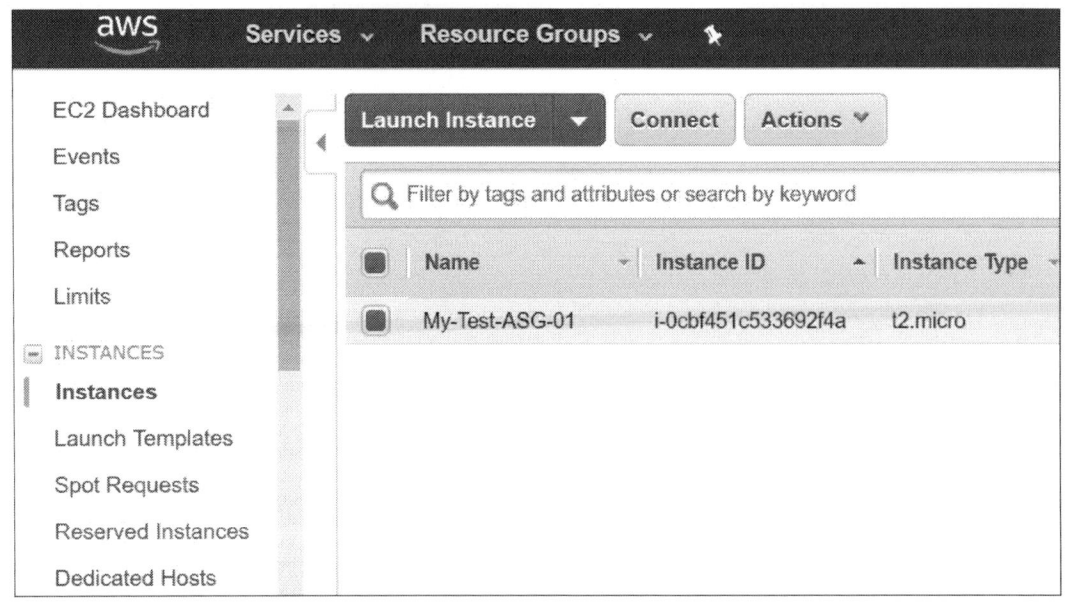

2. Now, navigate to the Auto Scaling Group option and review the settings as shown in the following figure.

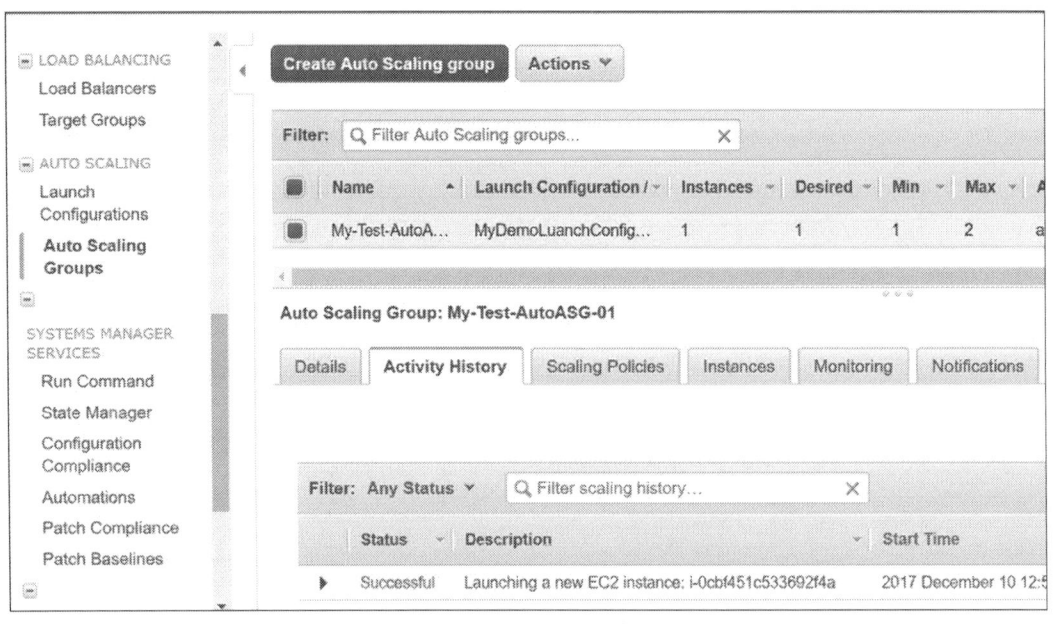

3. We recommend you to spend some time to review each of the auto scaling group tabs and try to understand what information these tabs provide.

Modifying Auto Scaling Group Settings

Now, let's do some fun with our Auto Scaling Group.
1. Click **Actions** and select **Edit** to edit the settings.
   - The **Launch Configuration** option allows you to change launch configuration.
   - The **Load Balancer** and **Target group** options allow you to attach this ASG to your desired load balancer.
   - The **Desired** and **Minimum** options allow you to set the desired and minimum number of instances that you want for this ASG.

2. Here, let's change the Desired and Minimum values as 0 as shown in the following figure and save the configuration.

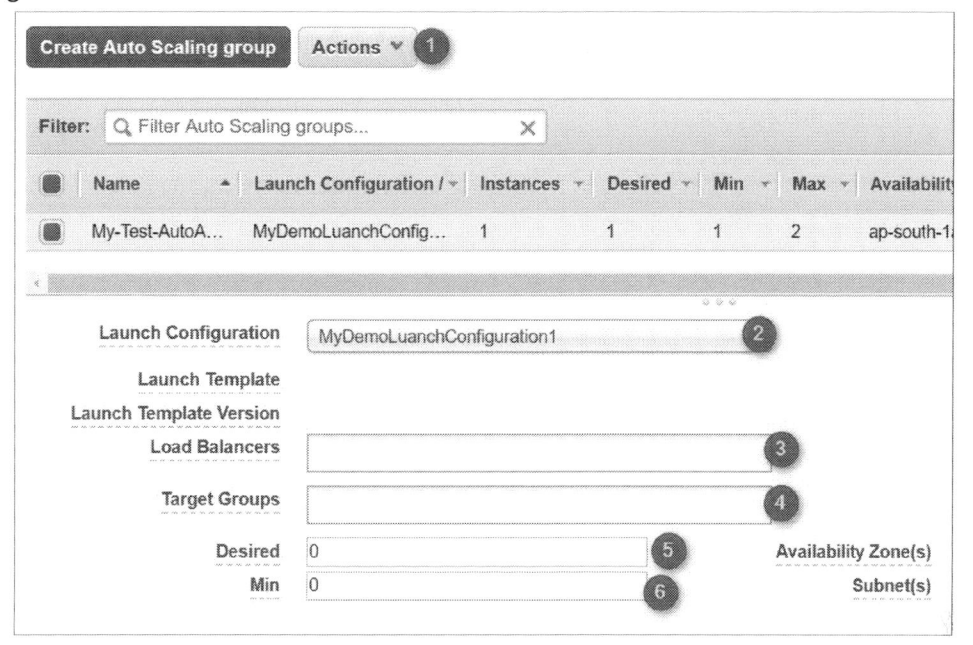

3. Now, go back to the instance list and wait for the few minutes. You will see that your instance will be terminated automatically to meet with the configuration of your Auto Scaling Group.
4. Now, again edit the Auto Scaling Group setting and set the minimum and desired number of EC2 instances value as 1. After a few minutes, you will see a new instance is launched in the Auto Scaling Group and it will be listed in the instance list. Hope, you have understood the power of the AWS Auto Scaling Group.

That's all you need to create and configure the Auto Scaling Group. Optionally, you can integrate this Auto Scaling Group with your Load Balancer.

43. Configuring Amazon Route 53

Typically, one misconception about the Amazon Route 53 is that most people think Amazon Route 53 as just a DNS name resolution service. However, Amazon Route 53 is more than this.

Recommended links:
- Overview of Amazon Route 53
  http://docs.aws.amazon.com/Route53/latest/DeveloperGuide/Welcome.html

Amazon Route 53 helps you to achieve the following major functions:

- Allows you to register and host your domain names such as www.example.com.
- Allows you to route internet traffic to the resources of your domain.
- Check the health of your resources.
- Helps you perform load balancing.

Although, here we will not go into the deep theory of Route 53. We will just walk through the high-level steps to help you to understand the concept and usage of Amazon Route 53.

> Note: Amazon Route 53 does not allow you to register a domain name as a free tier. You have to purchase the domain name of your own choice. If you don't want to spend unnecessary charges. Just follow the steps and try to understand what steps are necessary to work with Amazon Route 53.

Registering a domain name

To register a Domain Name using Amazon Route 53, you need to perform the following steps:

1. Visit the **Route 53 console** page using the following link.
   https://console.aws.amazon.com/route53/home
2. Click **Get Started Now** under the **Domain registration** section.
3. On the **Register Domain** page, either you can register a new Domain name or you can transfer an existing domain name if you own it already.
4. For this demo, let's click **Register new domain**. On the **Choose a domain name** page, select your top level domain such as .com and type your domain name you want to register as shown in the following figure.

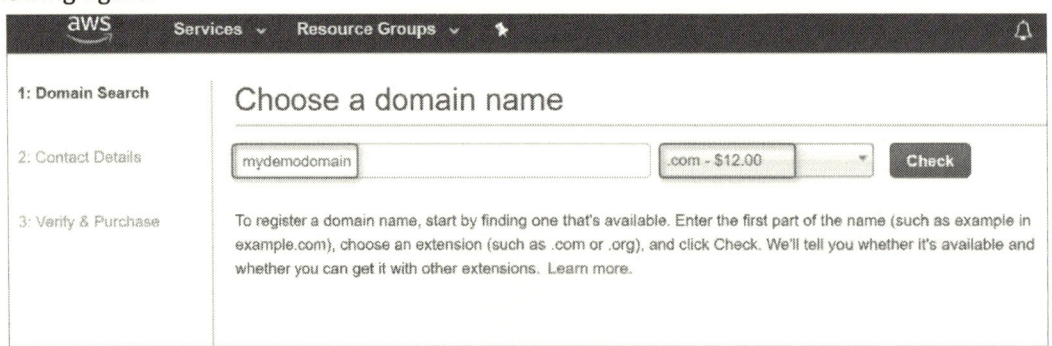

5. Click **Check** to check whether this domain name is available to register or not.

6. It may or may not be available, once you find your suitable available domain name, click **Add to card** and click **Continue** proceed to the next page.
7. On the **Contact details** page, fill the accurate contact details for registering the domain name and proceed to the next page.

![Registrant Contact form with fields for Contact Type (Person), First Name, Last Name, Organization (Not applicable), Email, Phone (+1 3115550188), Address 1, Address 2 (Optional)]

8. On the **Verify and purchase** page, review your settings and click **Complete Purchase** to purchase it or cancel it to avoid getting charged if you are doing this just for the learning purpose.
9. You will get a verification email that you specified in the contact details. Once you verify the email, your domain registration is almost done. However, sometimes it may take up to 3 days to change the status of your registering domain from pending to confirm in the Route 53 Dashboard.

44. Working with Amazon WorkDocs

Amazon WorkDocs is a fully Amazon managed, highly-secure, enterprise-level storage and sharing service. Unlike S3 based stored files, you can also share your files with other members of your organization for the collaboration or review.

Before proceeding for the Amazon WorkDocs, let's have a look at what Amazon says about its pricing:

*"With Amazon WorkDocs, there are no upfront fees or commitments. You pay only for active user accounts, and the storage you use. In most regions, WorkDocs costs $5 per user per month and includes 1 TB of storage for each user. WorkDocs provides a **30-day free trial** with 1 TB of storage per user for up to 50 users. You can invite guest users to log in and view files shared with them at no additional charge."*

As per the above statement, you have 30 days free trial for up to 1 TB of storage that should be more than enough for the learning purpose.

Recommended link:

- https://aws.amazon.com/workdocs

Creating an AWS WorkDocs Site

To setup Amazon WorkDocs, you need to perform the following steps:

1. Navigate to the **Amazon WorkDocs** home page for the supported region (not every region supports this feature).
2. Click the **Get Started Now** button to proceed to the next page.
3. Here, you will see the **Quick and Standard** setup options as shown in the following figure. For the learning purpose, the **Quick Start** setup guide should be enough. So proceed with this.

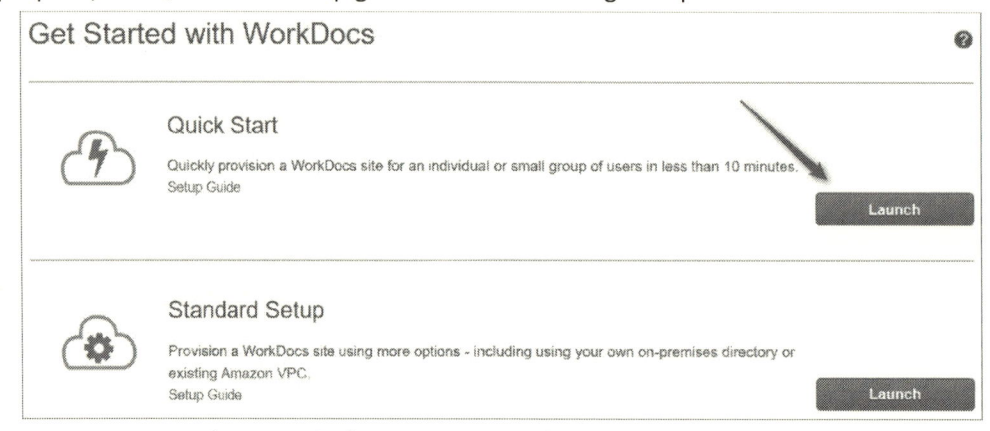

4. On the next page, you need to specify the site URL, email, and name details as shown in the following figure.

Access Point

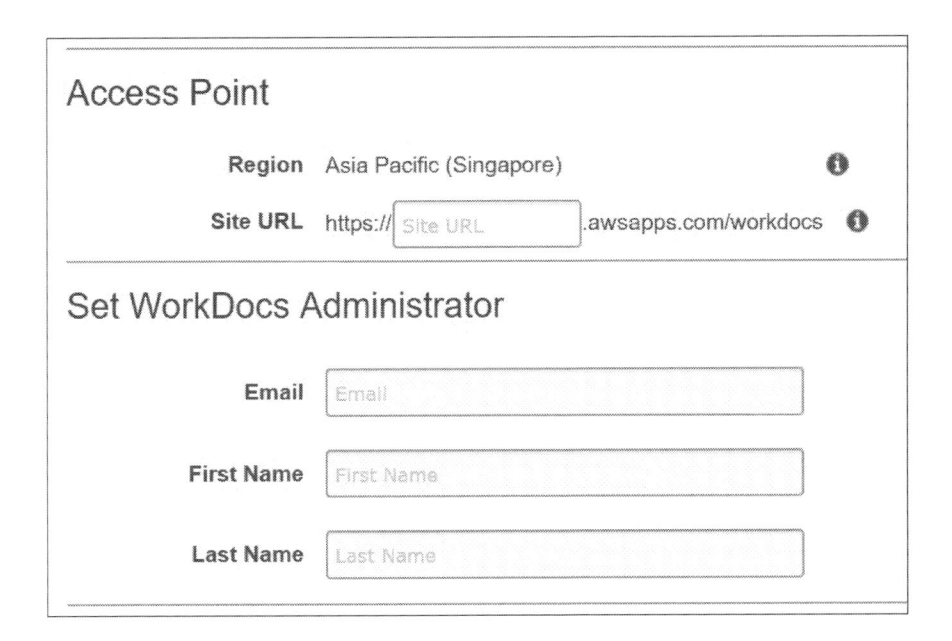

Region Asia Pacific (Singapore)

Site URL https://[Site URL].awsapps.com/workdocs

Set WorkDocs Administrator

Email

First Name

Last Name

5. Finally, click **Complete Setup** to complete the wizard. Your WorkDocs site will be started to initialize and should be available after some time. In fact, you will get an email once your WorkDocs site is ready.
6. Now, click the invite link you receive in your email box and set the desired password on the next page.
7. If you didn't get an invite mail yet, select your created WorkDocs site, click **Actions**, and select **Resend invite e-mail** as shown in the following figure.

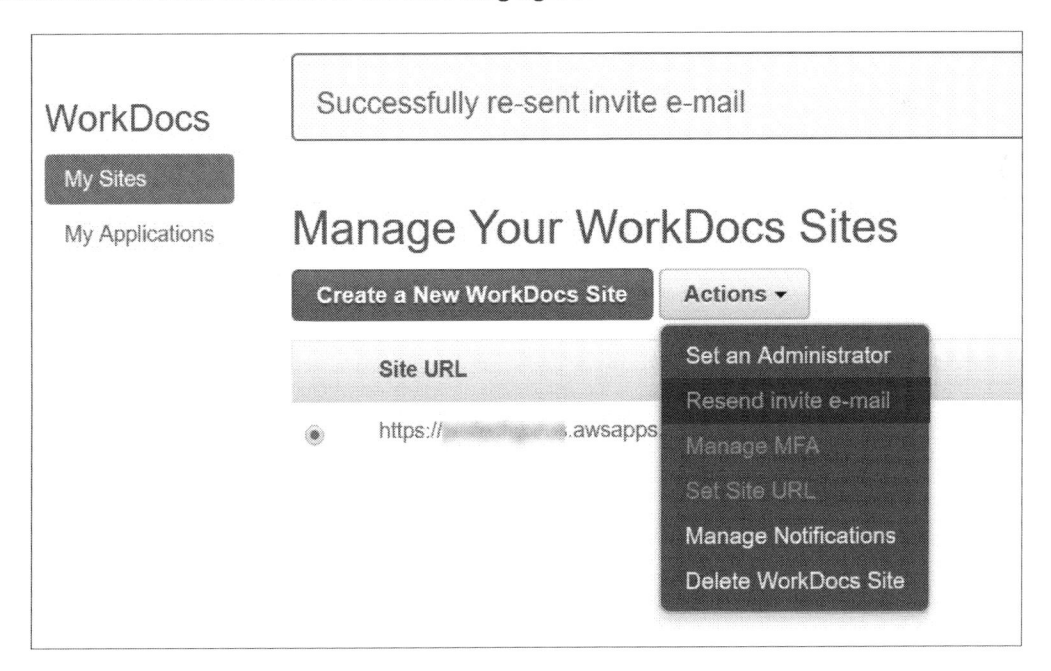

WorkDocs

Successfully re-sent invite e-mail

My Sites
My Applications

Manage Your WorkDocs Sites

Create a New WorkDocs Site | Actions ▼

Site URL

https://[...].awsapps

Actions menu:
- Set an Administrator
- Resend invite e-mail
- Manage MFA
- Set Site URL
- Manage Notifications
- Delete WorkDocs Site

8. Now, click your **WorkDocs site link**, type your registered email ID and login to WorkDocs console. You will see the WorkDocs console similar to as shown in the following figure.

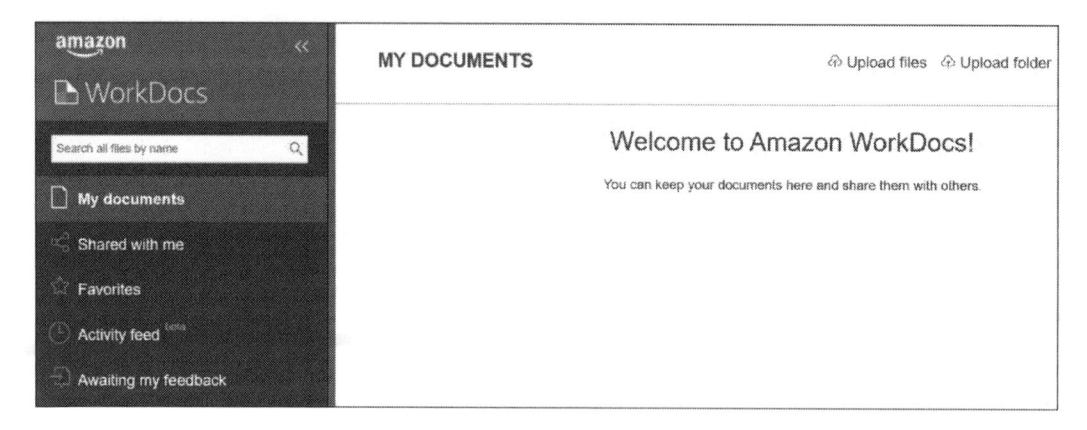

9. In the right pane, you have various options to upload files and folders or create a new folder structure as shown in the following figure.

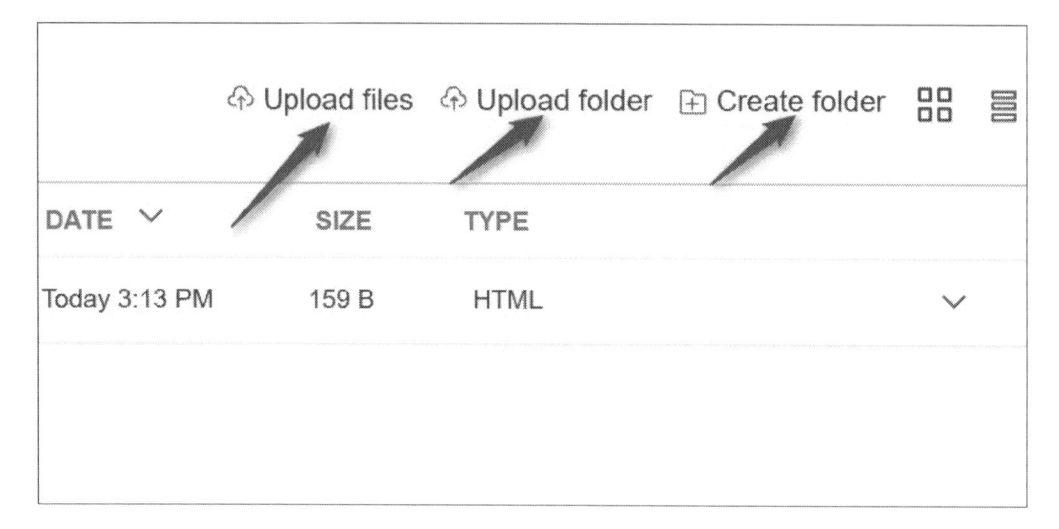

10. In the left navigation pane, there are various options to work with Amazon WorkDocs as shown in the following figure. We recommend you try to explore each one of them for a few minutes to understand and get familiarized with them.

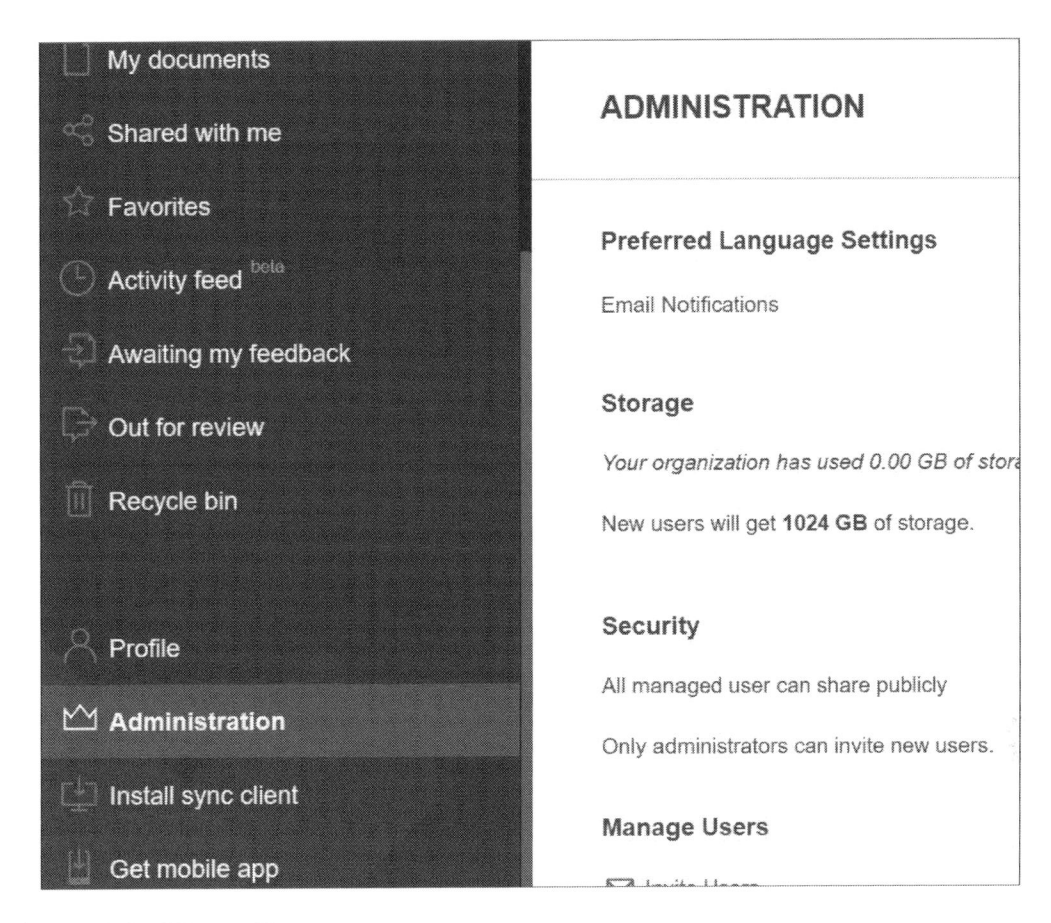

Deleting WorkDocs Site

Once your activity is done, please delete your WorkDocs site to avoid any unnecessary charges. For this, select your WorkDocs site, click **Actions**, and select **Delete WorkDocs sites**.

Follow the on-screen instructions as shown in the following figure and complete the deletion process.

Delete Selected WorkDocs Site

Deleting this WorkDocs site will make all documents for all users in this WorkDocs site inaccessible.

This action will immediately prevent your users from logging on via the web application, mobile applications, and sync clients.

This action cannot be undone.

☑ I also want to delete the user directory

Note: if you do not delete the Simple AD directory or AD Connector, you will be billed accordingly.

Please type "DELETE" below to confirm this action.

`DELETE`

Cancel   **Delete WorkDocs Site**

45. Working with AWS Trusted advisor

AWS Trusted Advisor is one of my favorite tools to optimize cost, enhance security, and improve the performance of AWS services. Trusted Advisor provides real-time guidance to help you provision your resources that meet with the AWS best practices. However, full features of AWS Trust Advisor are only available for those who have the Business Support plan. As a free tier account with the Basic support plan, you are not eligible to use the full features of AWS trust advisor.

Recommended links:
- AWS Trusted Advisor Overview
  https://aws.amazon.com/premiumsupport/trustedadvisor/

Let's have a quick example, how Trust Advisor can help you: Let's assume you have 20 security groups and each security group has 10 inbound rules for different services. You can't remember or check every time that what ports I have allowed to whom. Suppose you have allowed SSH port to open world as 0.0.0.0/0 for the testing purpose and later forget to fix it. Trust Advisor will tell about that security group risk.

Let's assume you have created an RDS instance for the learning purpose and forget to delete it. Since it's in an idle state, when you will visit the Trust Advisor console it will tell you that you can stop this idle instance, RDS, volume etc. to save the cost.

The following is the sample Trust Advisor's report that tells what's good and bad about a particular AWS Account.

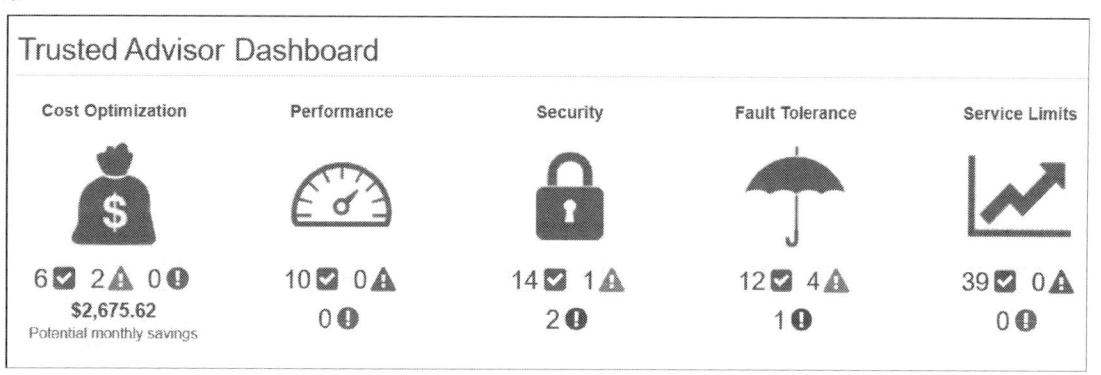

Select and open a specific dashboard option to know more in detail. For example, the following figure shows the details of Security issues. As you can see, as I click on the warning icon it shows me the issue with warning severity.

Security

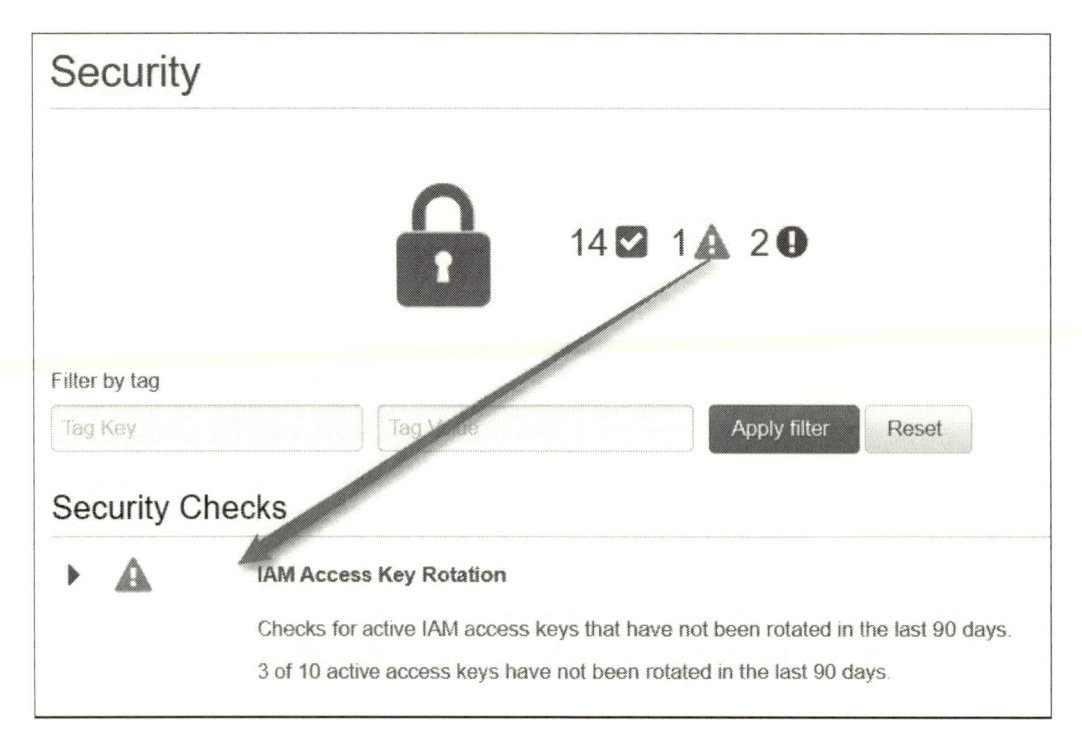

14 ☑ 1 ⚠ 2 ⓘ

Filter by tag

[Tag Key]   [Tag Value]   **Apply filter**   Reset

Security Checks

▶ ⚠ **IAM Access Key Rotation**

Checks for active IAM access keys that have not been rotated in the last 90 days.

3 of 10 active access keys have not been rotated in the last 90 days.

Sometimes AWS Trust Advisor may show you the idle instances that may be occasionally in use. Or you might have a security group rule open to the world as it might be the requirement of your application. But AWS Trust advisor may show you these requirements as issues. So you need to take the decision very carefully while working on the real world productions infrastructures.

Questions and Answers

1. **Question 01:** Which type of AWS Access type you should use while creating an IAM user?

   Answer 01: There is no straightforward answer to this question. It depends on your need, if you want to access AWS services using the AWS console, you should select the Console access type. If you want to access AWS services using CLI/API method, you should select the CLI access type.

2. **Question 02:** What are the two types of methods you can use to configure the authenticator app on your mobile device?

   Answer 02: You can configure MFA either using the bar code scanning or you can directly enter the authentication key.

3. **Question 03:** You can create a VPC with the 192.168.1.0/30 netmask.
   A.   True
   B.   False

   Answer 03: It's a wrong answer, because the allowed netmask limit for an AWS VPC is /16 to /28 CIDR range.

4. **Question 04:** What is the use of the Subnet Associations tab in a VPC Route Table?

   Answer 04: You can use the Subnet Association tab to associate or disassociate subnets to the selected AWS Route Table.

5. **Question 05:** Why do you need to assign an EIP when AWS allows an EC2 instance to get a dynamically assigned Public IP address?

   Answer 05: If don't assign an EIP to your EC2 instance, then a dynamic Public IP will be assigned each time to your EC2 instance when it stops and starts. It means, you need to use each time a different public IP to connect your EC2 instance for SSH access.

6. **Question 06:** If your EC2 instance belongs to availability zone A and your EBS volume belongs to availability zone B, then you cannot attach your EBS volume to any of the EC2 instances belonging to the availability zone A. Why?

   Answer 06: EBS volumes are availability zone specific, means EBS volumes belong to a specific AZ. If you want to attach an EBS volume to an EC2 instance that belong to a different AZ, first you need to copy the EBS volume to target AZ or create and attach a new EBS volume in the target AZ.

Thank You

Thanks for reading this guide with patience. Hope, this book helped you to gain some really nice and useful hands-on skills in major AWS Cloud Services. We would really like to hear your feedback on the content quality, good and bad things. Your feedback will help us to improve the quality. If you think this book was useful for you, please give us an appropriate rating on this and be connected with us to the other books as well. We will be adding more and more lab exercises in the upcoming editions of this book as we know technology never stops inventing new things, specially AWS Cloud.

If you are planning for the AWS Solutions Architect Global Exam, we would highly recommend you to read the following Exam Practice Book before appearing in the exam.

https://getbook.at/aws-questions

Other Helpful IT Books

You may also be interested in the following eBooks:

1. AWS Solutions Architect Associate - Exam Practice Questions
2. Step By Step Windows Server 2016 Lab Manual/Practical Guide
3. Step By Step Azure Cloud Lab Manual/Practical Guide for Ultimate Beginners
4. Step By Step CCNA Lab Manual/Practical Guide for Ultimate Beginners
5. Step By Step Windows Server 2012 R2 Lab Manual/Practical Guide
6. Step By Step VMware Workstation Player Lab Manual/Practical Guide

For more step by step tutorials, please visit our blog tutorials (https://protechgurus.com).

Made in the USA
Monee, IL
16 June 2021